News Discourse

CONTINUUM DISCOURSE SERIES

Series Editor:

Professor Ken Hyland, University of Hong Kong

Discourse is one of the most significant concepts of contemporary thinking in the humanities and social sciences as it concerns the ways language mediates and shapes our interactions with each other and with the social, political and cultural formations of our society. The *Continuum Discourse* Series aims to capture the fast-developing interest in discourse to provide students, new and experienced teachers and researchers in applied linguistics, ELT and English language with an essential bookshelf. Each book deals with a core topic in discourse studies to give an in-depth, structured and readable introduction to an aspect of the way language is used in real life.

Other titles in the series:

Academic Discourse, Ken Hyland
Discourse Analysis, Brian Paltridge
The Discourse of Blogs and Wikis, Greg Myers
The Discourse of Text Messaging, Caroline Tagg
The Discourse of Twitter and Social Media, Michele Zappavigna
Historical Discourse, Caroline Coffin
Metadiscourse, Ken Hyland
Professional Discourse, Britt-Louise Gunnarsson
School Discourse, Frances Christie
Using Corpora in Discourse Analysis, Paul Baker
Workplace Discourse, Almut Koester

CONTINUUM DISCOURSE

News Discourse

MONIKA BEDNAREK
AND
HELEN CAPLE

continuum

Continuum International Publishing Group

The Tower Building	80 Maiden Lane
11 York Road	Suite 704
London	New York
SE1 7NX	NY 10038

www.continuumbooks.com

British Library Cataloguing-in-Publication Data
A catalogue record for this book is available from the British Library.

ISBN: HB: 978-1-4411-2090-8
PB: 978-1-4411-4799-8

Library of Congress Cataloging-in-Publication Data
Bednarek, Monika.
News discourse / Monika Bednarek and Helen Caple.
p. cm.
Includes bibliographical references and index.
ISBN 978-1-4411-2090-8 (alk. paper) –
ISBN 978-1-4411-4799-8 (pbk. : alk. paper) –
ISBN 978-1-4411-3976-4 (ebook pdf : alk. paper) –
ISBN 978-1-4411-8420-7 (ebook epub : alk. paper)
1. Journalism. I. Caple, Helen. II. Title.
PN4731.B333 2012
070.401'41–dc23
2011047843

Typeset by Newgen Imaging Systems Pvt Ltd, Chennai, India
Printed and bound in India

*This book is dedicated to newshounds
the world over*

CONTENTS

LIST OF TABLES

LIST OF FIGURES

PREFACE

This book emanates from our desire to analyse *news discourse* for what it is: sometimes text-dominated, sometimes a combination of both words and images and, increasingly, sometimes image-dominated. It combines our expertise in analysing language (Monika Bednarek) and images (Helen Caple), and treats words and pictures as trading partners in the reporting of news events. Based on our own research into news discourse, we offer readers specific frameworks to analyse different aspects of such discourse, ranging from the expression of opinion through language to the composition of press photographs to the way in which *news values* are discursively construed through both language and images.

The data that we analyse with the help of these and other frameworks in this book come from previous research conducted on British and Australian newspapers as well as new data collections specifically undertaken for this book. This includes a 5-month collection (September 2010 to January 2011) of 29 print newspapers across a range of English-language newspapers in the United Kingdom, Ireland, North America and Australasia. We also draw on radio broadcasts/podcasts collected between December 2010 and April 2011 from national public radio broadcasters in Canada (CBS), Ireland (RTÉ), Australia (ABC), New Zealand (Radio New Zealand), the United States (NPR) and the United Kingdom (BBC). Special reporting of significant news events are also used as case studies of online/televisual news discourse and we draw on a range of other data in exemplifying and illustrating specific aspects of news discourse.

This book is aimed at anyone wanting to get a fuller understanding of news discourse and the many ways in which it can be analysed, with a specific focus on the *discursive* construction of what we call 'news'. We hope that it shows readers how to approach such an analysis systematically, using specific frameworks, while also considering the social and historical contexts of news discourse and the general characteristics of language and images in the news. This offers fuller insights into how events are turned into *news* and 'processed, bundled and delivered' (Brenton and Hare 1985: 10) to a global audience.

ACKNOWLEDGEMENTS

In compiling this book we have received tremendous help and advice from colleagues and friends, financial support from employers, as well as copyright permissions from publishers and news organizations around the world and we would like to acknowledge these here. First, thanks to Ken Hyland, series editor, Gurdeep Mattu, commissioning editor, and Colleen Coalter, editorial assistant, at Continuum for supporting the writing and publication of this book. Helen Caple would like to thank the University of New South Wales (UNSW) for financial support through the School of English Media and Performing Arts Research Grant Scheme. Monika Bednarek is likewise grateful to the University of Sydney for funding through the School of Letters, Art and Media Research Support Scheme. We thank our colleagues – Philip Bell, Katherine Brandon, Wolfram Bublitz, Anne Dunn, Gerard Goggin, John Knox, Brian Paltridge, Roberta Piazza, Louise Ravelli and Michele Zappavigna – who read and commented on earlier chapter drafts. We would also like to thank the students who undertook the following subjects in Semester 1, in 2011: *Multiplatform Journalism* at UNSW and *Media Discourse* at the University of Sydney for their useful input on earlier chapter drafts.

For permission to reprint parts of 'Evaluation in the news', we would like to thank Roslyn Petelin and the *Australian Journal of Communication*. We are also very grateful to the news organizations around the world that lent support for this publication by giving us permission to reproduce news stories and images in this book. We are particularly thankful to the following organizations which waived copyright fees: the *Daily Telegraph* (UK), the *Irish Independent* (Ireland) and the *Boston Herald* (US). Copyright for all news stories remains with the organizations. All sources are fully acknowledged throughout the book, and we have clearly identified where each example was first published/broadcast (including outlet and date of publication).While all attempts have been made to secure copyright permissions where relevant, the publishers and the authors would welcome approaches from anyone who sees any significant omissions and knows where the copyright might lie for these so that we can properly acknowledge them.

Finally, we would like to give heartfelt thanks to our friends and colleagues Naomi Knight and Louise Rowan, who took us over that final hurdle to see the manuscript readied for submission. Thank you for casting that final keen and critical eye over our work. Needless to say, all remaining mistakes and omissions are ours.

CHAPTER ONE

Introduction

1 What is this book about?

This book is about news discourse – the kind of discourse we encounter when we turn on the television, when we open the newspaper, when we go online or when we switch on the radio to get our dose of daily happenings. The book offers readers an introduction to some of the main characteristics of news discourse but it also aims to introduce particular ways of analysing this discourse based on our own research into news discourse. It further aims to demonstrate the insights such news analysis can offer researchers. More precisely, this book is written for anyone interested in the meanings made through language and images in the news. Although it does assume some linguistic background knowledge on the part of readers, we believe that researchers in the area of Media/Journalism and Communications Studies will also find many sections useful.

We start this book by outlining a working definition of news discourse and discuss motivations for studying such discourse. We also summarize the main approaches to the analysis of news discourse, pointing out how this book fits within such approaches. Our objectives for this first chapter are to enable readers to understand:

- what news discourse covers and why we should study it

- what the main approaches to news discourse are in Linguistics

- what some of the key theories of news discourse are in Media/ Journalism and Communications Studies

- what this book is about.

Structure

2 What is news discourse?

Before proceeding any further, it may be useful to clarify what we mean by *news discourse*. There are two issues to consider: First, what do we mean by *news discourse*?, and secondly, what do we mean by ***news* discourse**? Both questions are in fact tricky to answer and we will not attempt to discuss them exhaustively here; rather, we provide a working definition that frames the concerns of this book. Definitions both of *discourse* and of *news* are plentiful and have been discussed in different disciplines (see, for example, Baker 2006: 3–5 on discourse and Lamble 2011: 34–5 on news). In this book, we consider *discourse* as multimodal, or multisemiotic,[1] that is, not being restricted to the semiotic system of language alone but, crucially, also incorporating the semiotic system of images.[2] We also look at how such discourse (language and image) is actually put to use and how it contributes to the construction of news. This distinguishes us from other researchers who only include language in the analysis of news discourse, those who define discourse in other ways or those who see discourse as reflecting rather than actively constructing what is news. We will discuss some alternative approaches in Section 4.

Further, news discourse for us is defined 'externally' at this stage, rather than through common discourse features. In other words, saying that this book is about *news* discourse means that it discusses the discourse that audiences encounter in news bulletins, news programmes, on news websites, or in the newspaper – discourse that reports on newsworthy events, happenings and issues. The four stories in Table 1.1 on pp. 3–5 are examples of what we consider news discourse in this book, showing some of the reporting on the 2010 Pike river coal mine accident in New Zealand in online, print, radio and TV news. Story extracts are in the left-hand column, with further information in the right-hand column.

Table 1.1 illustrates some of the kinds of news discourse that we will discuss in this book. Thus, in exploring news discourse we will draw on examples not only from news stories in newspapers but also discuss online news (e.g. online video news summaries in Chapter 9), radio news (e.g. podcasts in Chapter 6) and televisual news (e.g. text–image relations in Chapter 5). To sum up, this book introduces ways to research and analyse the use of language and images that report on newsworthy events, happenings and issues across a range of news outlets.

We recognize of course, that there is a lot of variety within these kinds of news discourse – for example, newspapers include different sections (national/international/business/sports news). On television and radio we encounter news documentaries, news and current affairs programmes (e.g. *Today Tonight* (Seven network, Australia) and *Panorama* (BBC, UK)), news interviews, or investigative journalism programmes (e.g. NPR's *All Things Considered* (US) and *Dateline* (SBS, Australia)). Online we can come across

Table 1.1 Online, print, radio and TV news discourse

ONLINE NEWS DISCOURSE	Beginning of developing story in www.dailytelegraph.com.au (Australia)
Pike River coal mine blast: the latest developments	Headline
[31 images (not displayed here), captioned *NZ's Pike River blast: who are the trapped miners?*]	Picture gallery
 [continues]	Extract from the developing online news story Source: www.dailytelegraph.com.au/ news/world/daniel-rockhouse- and-russell-smiith-tell-of- escape-from-pike-river-mine/ story-e6frev00-1225958213682- accessed 22 November 2010, 4.50 p.m. Australian (EST) time
PRINT NEWS DISCOURSE	Beginning of the front page story in the *Sydney Morning Herald* (Australia)
Agonising wait as a small town rides a roller-coaster of emotions	Headline
John Huxley	Author by-line
(image cropped)	Large picture left of text shows a woman weeping. Smaller picture in the top right-hand corner shows one young woman with her arm around the shoulders of another young woman.
A GROWING feeling of helplessness, even hopelessness, is creeping across Greymouth, New Zealand, as fears rise that time is fast running out for the 29 men trapped in the Pike River coal mine. As tensions rise in the tough, tight-knit, west coast community, police warn that worries about toxic gases, fires and further explosions are preventing them from rescuing the men, including two Australians, who have been missing since Friday afternoon.	Extract from the print news story Source: 'Agonising wait as a small town rides a roller-coaster of emotions', *Sydney Morning Herald*, 22 November 2010, p. 1

RADIO NEWS DISCOURSE

Headline and beginning of story from ABC *NewsRadio* (Australia)

our top stories

[headline 1]

[music]

Newsreader opens bulletin with the headlines and the first story in the bulletin.

New Zealand rescuers continuing their attempts to reach 29 trapped miners. [= headline 2]

[music]

[headline 3]

[music, weather, music]

[story 1]

Rescuers in New Zealand say they're making progress drilling a hole down a coalmine near Greymouth where 29 miners have been trapped since Friday. They hope to send a camera down once the hole is finished to see if the miners are nearby. Police superintendent Gary Knowles says the mine environment is still not safe enough for a rescue operation. He spoke to the media this afternoon and says they're prepared for outcomes including loss of life although they do remain optimistic. 'We're now going into what we consider a major search-rescue planning phase and we're looking at all options and possibilities. We still remain optimistic. We're still keeping an open mind but we are planning for all outcomes and this also . . . part of this process we're planning for the possible loss of life as a result of what's occurred underground. We're keeping an open mind but we are planning for that.'

Extract from the Pike River mining disaster story, which was the second story in the bulletin.

Source:
ABC *NewsRadio*, 22 November 2010

TELEVISUAL NEWS DISCOURSE

Story 'headline' from ABC *News24* (Australia)

[music]
Rescuers continue to

drill towards 29 trapped miners

in New Zealand. Authorities are hoping for the best but preparing for the worst.

'we are planning for the possible loss of life as a result of what's occurred underground'

[music]

Source: ABC *News24*, 22 November 2010

news blogs, Twitter news updates, Google news, news feeds, You Tube news videos, news via digg or news websites. More generally, there is both mainstream news and alternative or specialist news, both community/local, provincial/rural, regional, metropolitan, and national news, both paid news (e.g. newspapers) and 'free' news (e.g. 'freesheets'). Our main focus in this book will be on the 'news' section of national and metropolitan print newspapers because this is where most linguistic research to date has been done. However, as mentioned above, we will also discuss other news media forms (e.g. online, radio). While we will not be able to explore all different types of news discourse to the same extent, it is clearly important to recognize this variety.

Another focus of this book is that we limit our discussion to English-speaking news discourse of the 'Western' world (UK, Ireland, US, Canada, Australia, NZ), as there are too many cross-linguistic and cross-cultural differences to do justice to news discourse in other languages and cultures within the scope of our discussion. This is also where our own research is situated. There is, however, a growing number of cross-cultural or comparative research projects, for instance comparing Britain, the United States and Germany (Lauerbach 2007), Britain, the United States and Italy (Haarman and Lombardo 2009), Britain and Japan (Murata 2007), Britain and Italy (Semino 2002, Pounds 2010) to name but a few. Research on languages other than English and on English-language newspapers outside the above countries also exists.

3 Why study news discourse?

Now that we have introduced our working definition of news discourse and the focus of our book, it is time to talk about the motivations for studying news discourse. Put simply, three reasons for such study are (1) there is a lot of it; (2) it is easy to collect examples of it; and (3) most importantly, since we all spend a lot of our time consuming it, it has great potential to exert considerable influence over us. In the academic literature, it is well documented that the production and distribution of news discourse is immense and that we spend a large portion of our waking hours attending to the news media. Some will even go as far as to suggest that news is an addiction (see Lamble 2011: 3). We listen, watch, read and then share with family, friends and colleagues. Sometimes we may modify our behaviour, ideas and beliefs, based on what we have read or heard and in this way we navigate our paths through our lives as members of a particular social group. This also points to the power of the media: the influence they exert both on our governments and major institutions as well as their ability to shape our ideas and behaviours.

In this book we study news discourse from a linguistic/semiotic perspective, and there are specific reasons behind this approach as well. Linguists and social semioticians would argue that the relationship between the producers of news media, the institutions and key figures that are scrutinized by them and the audiences who consume their end products is a relationship that is enacted principally through semiotic resources – words, sounds and images. The choices made in the use of language and sounds, in the capture and composition of images and in the layout and organization of these on the page or the screen have meanings, and these meanings may have powerful impacts. A linguistic/semiotic analysis of these choices and the ways in which they combine can help us to discover the meaning potential that lies behind the techniques used by news workers in their daily crafting of the news discourse we immerse ourselves in. We will introduce our own research-based linguistic and semiotic frameworks in Chapters 3, 6 and 7 in this book and hope to demonstrate how the application of such frameworks can give us detailed insights into the way meanings are discursively construed in the news. Other chapters (e.g. Chapters 5, 8 and 9) also demonstrate how looking at news discourse through a linguistic and semiotic perspective throws light upon the construction of news.

Another way in which a linguistic/semiotic perspective may be useful is in providing detailed evidence for researchers in other disciplines, for example in Journalism. A special issue of *Journalism Studies* dedicated to language and journalism (Richardson 2008a) explores this in more detail. Indeed, a systematic linguistic/semiotic analysis of news discourse has the potential to provide useful underpinnings for research in Media/Journalism and Communications Studies – whether that concerns the analysis of ideological positioning and power relations or the analysis of news practice and norms (cf. Chapter 3 on news values). Therefore, cross-disciplinary research projects that include detailed linguistic or semiotic analyses can provide rich multiperspectival results that are empirically grounded and frequently testable and replicable, and often make use of sophisticated analytic frameworks. In the following section, we introduce the principle linguistic frameworks that are commonly applied to the analysis of news discourse and position our own work within these approaches.

4 How to study news discourse?

News discourse has a long history of being explored in a variety of disciplines, including Journalism, Sociology, Linguistics and Semiotics, because its study 'has much to offer to the different disciplines on whose territory it touches' (Bell 1991: 5). For any researcher interested in exploring news discourse it is helpful to be familiar with some of the most important approaches and to locate themselves within this landscape of media research. We therefore start this section with an outline of key approaches in Linguistics, and how we position ourselves in relation to these in this book, and will then touch upon major theories in Media/Journalism and Communications Studies. For further details on each approach readers are directed to the references (not exhaustive) included under each heading.

4.1 Key approaches in linguistics

The sociolinguistic approach

Sociolinguistic concerns about news discourse tend to centre on correlations between style and social factors. In other words, to what extent is there a correlation between features of news discourse and the presumed social status of the audience of such discourse? This kind of research is closely connected to Bell's (e.g. 1991) and Jucker's (1992) study of news discourse. They both found that newspapers targeting different groups of audiences also use different types of apposition patterns. For instance, newspapers targeted at the (upper-) middle classes (such as *The Times*, the *Guardian*) deleted fewer determiners than newspapers targeted more at the working classes (such as the *Daily Mirror*, the *Sun*): the latter newspapers had more instances of naming expressions in the form *businessman John Morris* rather than *the businessman John Morris*. In other words, the language of newspapers varies depending on target audience. Bell calls this *audience design*, meaning that 'newscasters are designing their speech for their audience' (1991: 121). In the context of a different media form, Bell (1991: 110–22) investigates linguistic differences between radio stations in New Zealand. Conboy (2010) takes a sociolinguistic approach to the language of journalism across time.

The conversation analytical approach

This approach is located within the tradition of Conversation Analysis (Sidnell 2010), which focuses on the close analysis of spoken interaction. Regarding news discourse, such studies explore spoken interaction in the context of news interviews (e.g. Greatbatch 1998, Clayman and Heritage 2002). For instance, Clayman and Heritage (2002) found that both in the United Kingdom and in the United States, news interviews involve a mixture of adversarialness and objectivity, which becomes apparent through their investigation of a variety of linguistic features including question design. There are also other studies on news interviews that follow different linguistic traditions (e.g. Bell and van Leeuwen 1994).

The systemic functional linguistic approach

Located in the systemic functional model of language (e.g. Halliday and Matthiessen 2004), this research (e.g. White 1997, 2000, 2006, Lukin et al. 2004) approaches news discourse from the perspective of register and genre and describes and discusses the different purposes, linguistic features and structures of various types of news discourse as well as the notion of authorial voice and the expression of subjectivity in news discourse. For example, Feez et al. (2008) distinguish between genres such as the hard news story, media exemplum, media anecdote and media feature. Martin and White (2005) make a distinction between reporter voice, correspondent voice and commentator voice, which are associated with differences in the extent to which opinion is present in news discourse. Inspired by Systemic Functional Linguistics, 'social semiotic' research investigates meaning-making in news images (Economou 2006, 2008, 2010, Caple 2008a, b, 2009b, 2010a) and online news (Knox 2009).

The pragmatic/stylistic approach

This is a rather broad concept used here to refer to work that is not located within a specific linguistic 'school' (such as Conversation Analysis, Systemic Functional Linguistics) but draws on various linguistic concepts to investigate the language of news discourse. This often includes pragmatic analyses, discussions of presentation and perspective, genre status, style and register. We include here research by Crystal and Davy (1969), Verschueren (1985), Carter (1988), Almeida (1992), Ungerer (1997, 2004) and Ljung (2000).

The practice-focused approach

The practice-focused approach tries to provide insights into news discourse and journalistic practices, and is often pursued by researchers who also worked as journalists themselves. We further include here the 'ethnographic' approach, which puts a spotlight on the social processes that lead to the construction of news (called *entextualization* by van Hout and Macgilchrist 2010), for instance exploring how news stories are selected and constructed in journalistic practice (Cotter 2010). Thus, Cotter suggests that news values – which we will discuss in Chapter 3 – 'govern each stage of the reporting and editing process' (2010: 73).

The corpus linguistic approach

The corpus linguistic approach to analysing news texts makes use of large datasets (called *corpora*) and computer software to analyse news discourse, and often draws on the insights of corpus-based discourse analysis (Baker 2006). Studies in this area vary in the extent to which they use corpora and computer software: For example, Bednarek (2006c) explores a 70, 000 word corpus comprising 100 British news stories mainly 'manually', but her analyses are corpus-assisted in that she makes use of computer software and corpora to guide her analysis and is interested in patterns of frequency. In another study (Bednarek 2006b) corpus linguistic methodology plays a bigger part in exploring the expression of opinion in news discourse. Other research focuses on using large corpora (comprising millions of words) to investigate differences between news discourse and other types of discourse (e.g. Biber et al. 1999, Bednarek 2008a, Biber and Conrad 2009). In between, we find research that combines both methods of Corpus Linguistics (e.g. analysing frequent words or patterns) with Discourse Analysis (e.g. Baker and McEnery 2005, Haarman and Lombardo 2009, Morley and Bayley 2009).

The diachronic approach

A growing number of studies of news discourse (e.g. Ungerer 2000, Westin 2002, Cotter 2003, Ben-Aaron 2005, Brownlees 2006, Jucker 2009) concerns changes in news discourse over time or studies of early news discourse. For instance, in her study of 864 editorials in the UK broadsheets the *Daily Telegraph*, the *Guardian* and *The Times* from 1900 to 1993, Westin (2002) finds that the language changed to become more informal, but also more precise and compact, with an increasingly complex noun phrase and fewer markers of vagueness and uncertainty as well as more varied and specific vocabulary. Such studies draw on a number of other approaches to study linguistic change. For instance, the Zurich English Newspaper (ZEN) corpus (Fries and Schneider 2000) includes 1.6 million words of English news discourse between 1661 and 1791, which can be analysed using corpus linguistic methodology.

The critical approach

The 'critical' approach is probably the most prominent and well-known approach in Linguistics to the study of news discourse and is closely associated with the terms *Critical Discourse Analysis* and *Critical Linguistics*. Such research is interested in uncovering power relations and ideologies behind news discourse. It has the goal of looking beyond texts and taking into account institutional and socio-cultural contexts and often involves a search for aspects or dimensions of reality that are obscured (see Fairclough 1995, Richardson 2007). Areas of critical analysis include analysis of the representation of women (Fowler 1991, Clark 1992), refugees (Baker 2006), war reporting (e.g. Lukin et al. 2004, Richardson 2007: 178–219, Scott 2008) and many others, including an exploration of linguistic devices such as vocabulary, metaphor, transitivity and intertextuality (to name but a few). Critical linguists are differentiated in the methodologies they use: while some prefer a 'manual' analysis of individual texts, a small sample of texts or a larger collection of texts, others use corpus linguistic techniques to analyse small and large corpora (e.g. Mautner 2000, Baker et al. 2008, O'Halloran 2010). Book-length treatments of this approach in the context of news and media discourse are provided in van Dijk (1988a, 1988b), Fowler (1991), Fairclough (1995), Richardson (2007) and Conboy (2007). Carvalho (2008) also provides a useful overview.

It must be noted that not all linguistic research on news discourse fits neatly into one of the above-listed categories: For example, Conboy (2010) combines a sociolinguistic with a diachronic approach as well as with Journalism Studies. Research could also be grouped depending on the topic of interest – for example, research on the news interview or research on news headlines, or research focusing respectively on print news, TV news, online news and radio news. We will draw on such research throughout the course of this book when discussing specific aspects of news discourse.

Concerning our own approach in this book, it is probably best classified as a mixture of some of the above. While one of us used to work as a news photographer and can thus draw to some extent on professional practice, the practical experience of the other is limited to a stint of work experience as a journalist at a local newspaper. In terms of our research backgrounds, one of us locates herself within social semiotic research, while the other uses corpus-based and corpus-assisted discourse analysis. But the general aim of this book is to explore news discourse by drawing on the rich tradition of research outlined above as well as to provide specific analytical frameworks for news analysis that we have developed ourselves. Therefore, we would probably identify our approach in this book as 'inclusive' in that it is not primarily aimed at researchers working within a specific linguistic paradigm such as Conversation Analysis or Systemic Functional Linguistics. Further, we also draw on concepts from Journalism Studies, in particular the notion of newsworthiness and news values (see Chapter 3). Finally, we see our approach to news as *discursive,* focusing on how discourse actively constructs what is news.

4.2 Approaches in media/journalism and communications studies

It is clearly of benefit for linguists/semioticians to understand that there are other theoretical approaches through which substantial amounts of research of news discourse is carried out, and it is often useful to draw on such approaches in interpreting findings arising from linguistic/semiotic analysis. Since theoretical approaches to the study of news discourse are numerous, we only point to a selection of the major theories and the scholars who are renowned for the work they do in this area (see Table 1.2 on pp. 12–13). This list is not exhaustive and is meant to serve as a point of reference for linguists/semioticians who wish to read more on other theories of the media.

There are many ways in which we can organize such theoretical approaches to the study of the media. One classic way is to take a diachronic perspective. For example, early research in Media Studies centred on the notion of establishing a quantifiable empirical base to scholarly inquiry. This was known as 'Limited Effects' theory. Then came the dissection of the media into components of study, for example, production, content, reception in what became known as 'Middle Range' theories, and most recent times have been marked by post-modernist theories of the media. Somewhat similar to the middle range theoretical approach, Watson (2008: 3–4) suggests a prism as a means of organizing theories into Content (texts), Response (audience), Output (institutions) and Medium (technology) analysis. In Table 1.2, we have used Watson's categorization of theoretical positions as a starting point and have mapped the theoretical approaches onto these components. Naturally, not all theoretical approaches fit neatly into one section or another and there may be some overlap. What we hope to demonstrate by dividing the theories in this way is the plethora of approaches and their most significant contributions to the study of the media and to perhaps give researchers in Linguistics an opportunity to see whether their study of the media can benefit from using some of the lenses offered here to help focus their research.

Research methodologies available to media researchers are also vast and range from content and frame analysis, through textual analysis to ethnographic surveys including interviews, focus groups, field studies and case studies, all of which can encompass both quantitative and qualitative research. Linguists and semioticians will see greatest overlap between their perspective and that of media researchers in the Content Theory section and in research methodologies such as content, frame and textual analysis (see Weerakkody 2009 for a comprehensive guide to research methods in Media and Communications research).

Table 1.2 A guide to theoretical approaches to the study of news discourse in Media/Journalism and Communications Studies

Theoretical Approaches	Key Theorists	Area of Study
Media and Audiences (Response Theory):		
• Media effects	Harold D. Lasswell, Fredric Wertham, Max Horkheimer and Theodor W. Adorno	Response theory examines the relationship between the media and consumers of the media; the extent to which they may be influenced by the media (effects), or whether they use the media for specific purposes (as active audiences), and the different kinds of responses audiences may produce depending on their values, beliefs, emotional state, and so on.
• Moral panic	Stanley Cohen	
• Uses and gratifications	Jay G. Blumer and Elihu Katz	
• Reception theory		
— Encoding/decoding	Stuart Hall	
— Reading position	Stuart Hall	
• Active audience		
— Subcultures	Dick Hebidge, Sarah Thornton	
— Fan cultures	Henry Jenkins	
— Culture jamming	David Gauntlett, Alison Hearn	
• Media affect	Jonathan Crary, Michael Hardt and Antonio Negri	
Media and Democracy (Output Theory):		
• Public sphere	Jürgen Habermas	This approach focuses principally on the politics of the media: the relationship between the media, governments and other powerful institutions, and how relationships of power and ideology are played out between the two and then influence or are influenced by society.
— Fourth estate	John Keane	
— PR state (spin)	Sharon Beder, Brian McNair	
— Digital public sphere	Brian McNair	
• Ideology/power	Michel Foucault, Louis Althusser	
— Hegemony	Antonio Gramsci	
— Political economy	Edward S. Herman and Noam Chomsky, Raymond Williams, Stuart Hall	
• Agenda setting	Maxwell E. McCombs and Donald L. Shaw	
— News values	Johan Galtung and Mari Holmboe Ruge, Stuart Hall, Geoffrey Craig, Paul Brighton and Dennis Foy	

Theoretical Approaches	Key Theorists	Area of Study
Media and Technology (Medium Theory):		
• Mediation	Raymond Williams, Marshall McLuhan, Jean Baudrillard, Michel de Certeau	A common approach in Media Studies, examining the evolving relationships between technology and audiences; how we incorporate the media into our daily rituals; and how technology shapes our responses to the media.
— Time (e.g. dailiness)	Paddy Scannell, John Hartley	
— Space (e.g. doubling of place)	Paddy Scannell, Shaun Moores	
• Domestication	Roger Silverstone	
• Convergence	Henry Jenkins	
• Network society	Manuel Castells	
• Mobile cultures	Sarah Gibson, Gerard Goggin	
Media and Texts (Content Theory):		
• Signification	Charles S. Peirce, Ferdinand de Saussure, Roland Barthes	Examines the relationship between signs and meanings, often in the service of power and ideological relationships. This is the closest approach to that in Linguistics.
— Semiotics	Robert Hodge and Gunter Kress	
• Intertextuality	Norman Fairclough, Mikhail Bakhtin	
• Genre/narrative/myth	Tzvetan Todorov, Michel de Certeau, Roland Barthes	
• Visual culture	Karin Becker, Gillian Rose, Barbie Zelizer	

5 How to collect news data?

Finally, a matter that is relevant to all research into news discourse concerns the selection of data. No matter what approach is adopted, an early decision that any researcher interested in investigating news discourse must make is how to collect news data. According to Bell (1991: 12) the analysis of media language demands decisions in three areas:

- the genres: news, advertising, opinion, and so on (type of content)
- the outlets: the publications, radio stations, and so on (carriers of content)
- the outputs: specific newscasts, programmes and the time period to be covered (and the days to be sampled within that period).

As Bell (1991) offers a very good discussion of these issues, we will not say much about this here. However, the importance of a well-considered selection of data cannot be overstated. For example, in a corpus linguistic analysis, the design of the corpus (dataset) needs to be planned with regard to issues such as balance and representativeness (e.g. Wynne 2005) to ensure that the findings are not limited to the corpus at hand and that we can draw valid general conclusions about news discourse. Where individual texts are chosen for analysis, researchers must be careful to be aware of the limitations of their findings, and/or ensure that the texts chosen are 'typical' (Martin and Rose 2007: 313). We should also note that there may be variation between individual newspapers (e.g. Westin 2002: 164–5, Bednarek 2006c: 202, Cortina-Borja and Chappas 2006), between local and national newspapers, between weekday and weekend editions, and that newspapers have their own 'house style'. This means that research design needs to consider both the communicative and the socio-historical context (see Chapter 2) as well as the linguistic variation in news discourse (see Chapter 4).

The news data that we draw on in this book are predominantly taken from either our own and others' research into news discourse or from data collection specific to this publication. The latter involved collecting a 'constructed week' of both broadsheet and tabloid newspapers from the United Kingdom, Ireland, United States, Canada, Australia and New Zealand.[3] The data was collected during the second week of the month between September 2010 and January 2011, giving us a representative five-day sample for each newspaper, by rotating the sample set across the week. For example, American newspapers were collected on Monday in September, Tuesday in October, Wednesday in November, Thursday in December and Friday in January. This is a 'constructed week'. For further explanation of how to compile the constructed week and to see studies that have used this methodology see Bell (1984) or Westin (2002). We also make use of data from online, radio and TV news from a variety of English-speaking countries and accessed via the web (websites or podcasts). Where relevant to the discussion, examples of news discourse that we use in this book are accompanied by specific information on where it was taken from (such as news outlet, date of broadcast/publication, etc.). A full list of all news outlets referred to throughout this book is provided in Table A1.3 in Appendix 1 on pp. 226–8, including country of origin and type of publication.

6 Summary and structure of this book

To conclude, for us news discourse includes both language and image, that is, news discourse is multimodal or multisemiotic. While images are not encountered on the radio (other than on their websites), still and moving images are apparent in television, online and print news discourse. Figure 1.1 shows the world section of the *New York Times* to illustrate the integration of language and image in news discourse.

Figure 1.1 The *New York Times*, World section, www.nytimes.com/pages/world/index.html – accessed 28 October 2010, 3.07 p.m. Australian (EST) time

What Figure 1.1 shows is that much news discourse incorporates both news photography and language. Both the photo and the image can be seen to create meanings by themselves, but there is also meaning created through the interaction of image and language. This means that we can investigate both the meanings made by the language as well as the meanings made by image(s) and, importantly, the relations between these meanings as well. We will discuss this in more detail in later chapters. The structure of the rest of this book is as follows:

Chapter 2 – News discourse in context
Chapter 2 provides a general introduction to the communicative and the socio-historical context of news discourse. In examining communicative context we consider both the production and reception of news discourse, while the socio-historical context explores the evolution of news discourse, issues of ownership, and the regulation and financing of news.

Chapter 3 – News values
Chapter 3 introduces the important concept of *news values* (values that make something newsworthy), and illustrates it with authentic examples from news discourse. It also introduces our own discursive approach to news values, which focuses on analysing how news values are construed through discourse (language and image).

Chapter 4 – Language in the news
Chapter 4 looks at the linguistic characteristics of news discourse, in particular the language of contemporary national/metropolitan print news, although radio, online and TV news are also briefly discussed. The chapter further considers the functions of these linguistic characteristics and the variation that exists in newspaper writing. The aim of this chapter is not to provide a particular framework for analysing language in the news, but rather to 'chart the landscape', as it were.

Chapter 5 – Images in the news
Chapter 5 is a companion piece to Chapter 4 and discusses the use of images in the news. It considers the communicative functions of images (as illustration, evidence, sensation, icon, evaluation, aesthetic) and the historical context underpinning their use, the position of images in the news, and the relationships that hold between words and still and moving images (text–image relations).

Chapter 6 – Evaluation in the news
Chapter 6 introduces a specific linguistic framework for analysing evaluation (the expression of speaker/writer opinion or subjectivity) in news discourse. It uses data from online news podcasts by national public radio broadcasters from Australia, Canada, Ireland, New Zealand, the United States and the United Kingdom to illustrate this framework. Functions of evaluation in news discourse are also discussed, especially their contribution to the construal of news values.

Chapter 7 – Balancing act: image composition
Chapter 7 outlines another analytical framework – one for analysing the composition of images. Using examples from print news, this chapter explores the role of balance, composition and aesthetics in news photography and shows how different compositional configurations can be analysed systematically.

Chapter 8 – The big picture: a case study of stand-alones in print news
Chapter 8 is the first of two case studies demonstrating how frameworks introduced in this book can be put to use. It focuses on an interesting type of news story – the *stand-alone* (using a 'big picture' and little accompanying

text) Using both quantitative and qualitative analysis, this chapter discusses the journalistic practice of packaging news stories in this way, drawing in particular on an analysis of composition in the image and evaluations in the text.

Chapter 9 – Killing Osama: a case study of online news
Chapter 9 offers a second case study, aiming to tie together many of the concepts that we introduce in this book and showing how they may be applied. To do this, we compare how the killing of Osama bin Laden was reported in online video news summaries by two national public broadcasters: the ABC (Australia) and the BBC (UK). The chapter also provides a conclusion to the book.

Appendices
Information in the appendices consists of additional tables that may be used for analysis, a list of all of the news outlets mentioned in this book, and, crucially, also includes a model student assignment on news discourse that uses aspects of the framework of evaluation that we introduce in Chapter 6 and illustrates how it can be applied by students. It is annotated with comments on key academic writing conventions and is targeted at students, junior researchers and lecturers.

Directions for further reading

Baker, P. (2006), *Using Corpora in Discourse Analysis*. London/New York: Continuum. While this is not an introduction to news discourse, it introduces the use of corpora in discourse analysis, partially drawing on the analysis of news discourse.

Bell, A. (1991), *The Language of News Media*. Oxford: Blackwell. Even though this book is now 20 years old, it still offers an excellent introduction to news discourse, covering issues ranging from data collection to speaker and audience roles, news story structure and miscommunication.

Durant, A. and Lambrou, M. (2009), *Language and Media: A Resource Book for Students*. Abingdon/New York: Routledge. An introduction to language and media in general, with some sections focusing on news discourse.

Fairclough, N. (1995), *Media Discourse*. London: Hodder. An introduction to the Critical Discourse Analysis of media texts, including the news.

Feez, S., Iedema, R. and White, P. R. R. (2008), *Media Literacy*. Surry Hills, New South Wales: AMES. An introduction to news media from a systemic functional linguistic perspective and within an Australian context.

Lamble, S. (2011), *News As It Happens: An Introduction to Journalism*. Oxford: Oxford University Press. An introduction to news discourse from the perspective of Journalism and Communications Studies.

Notes

1 Strictly speaking, texts that are 'multisemiotic' (combining two or more semiotic systems, for example, image, language, design) should be distinguished from texts that are 'multimodal' (combining two or more modalities, for example, visual, aural – see O'Halloran 2008). However, the literature on multimodality has typically used the term *multimodal* to mean both 'multisemiotic' and 'multimodal'. We will do the same here, unless specified otherwise.

2 News discourse also includes other kinds of visual material, such as typography, cartoons, figures, tables, layout, and the like. We explore layout to some extent in Chapter 5, but focus primarily on still and moving images in this book. Such images are a key contributor to meaning-making in print, online and televisual news discourse. In broadcast news, non-visual multisemiotic features include ambient sound and music (during the opening to news bulletins when the headline stories are introduced), though for reasons of scope we will only touch upon such features where relevant, rather than offering a full exploration.

3 In this book we use the terms *popular/tabloid* and *quality/broadsheet* to refer to different kinds of news outlets and products that are distinguished in terms of target audiences, favoured linguistic style, formatting conventions, and so on. Both terms are however problematic: Strictly speaking, the term *tabloid* refers to the small format of 'popular' newspapers, but several 'quality' newspapers have more recently also adopted the tabloid or other compact formats. The terms *popular* and *quality* are problematic because of the value judgements they imply.

CHAPTER TWO

News discourse in context

1 Introduction

As mentioned in the previous chapter, researching news discourse involves the sampling, collection and analysis of a dataset according to a particular set of criteria. How these criteria are established will impact on the kinds of conclusions and generalizations that are possible from the project. A good place to start with research design is to consider both the communicative and the socio-historical context of the news discourse to be analysed. This is the focus of Chapter 2. In examining communicative context we consider both the production and reception of news discourse, while the socio-historical context explores the evolution of news discourse, issues of ownership and the financing of news. Our objectives for this chapter are to enable readers to understand:

- how news is produced
- how news is consumed
- how news is developing
- how news is regulated
- how news is financed.

In our view, such an understanding is necessary for linguists and semioticians who study news discourse, enabling them to justify their collection of data, and to appropriately contextualize their interpretation of these data, especially concerning the professional context of journalism.

2 Communicative context

When we talk about the 'communicative context' of news discourse, we mean the relation between news discourse, the producer(s) of the news discourse and the audience(s) of news discourse (Figure 2.1),[1] whereas the socio-historical context to be outlined in Section 3 concerns the social (including economic) and historical circumstances in which this communication takes place.

Figure 2.1 shows that producer(s) are involved in the production of news discourse addressing specific audiences. Producer(s) and audience(s) also interact with each other in specific ways and may hold assumptions about each other. As indicated by the double arrows in Figure 2.1, the relations between aspects of the communicative context may be quite complex. From a discursive perspective, relations between producer(s) and audience(s) are mediated by and construed in the discourse. For example, as we shall see, different kinds of audiences are addressed by different kinds of texts. In this section, we will discuss the production of news with specific reference to producer and audience roles and the relationship between them.

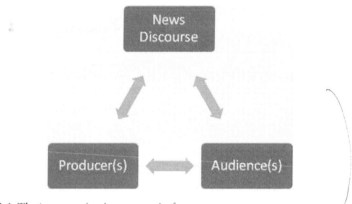

Figure 2.1 The 'communicative context' of news

2.1 Producer roles

Before we turn to discussing **who** produces the news (producer roles), it is important to briefly discuss **how** news is produced and the kinds of material that get turned into 'news' by producers. In fact, the news process is a complex one and one that is influenced by external factors such as news cycles (the time span between the publication/broadcast of a newspaper or news programme and the next edition) and corresponding deadlines as well as practices such as news conferences, newsroom hierarchies or story meetings (where editors meet to discuss stories to appear in the newspaper). Cotter (2010: 54) has the news process starting with news tips and follow-up interviews, writing the story, editing, adding the headline and story placement. It is therefore important to note that much of what appears in the 'news' is 'second-hand', for example, based on interviews, agency copy (copy from news agencies/wire services such as Agence France Press, Thomson Reuters, Associated Press) or press releases (produced by politicians, NGOs, universities, community and special interest groups, etc.). Further, much news copy is syndicated (shared among sister/ participating news organizations). Other input sources of stories include press conferences, interviews, documents, other news stories, social media, WikiLeaks, You Tube, citizen journalism (when ordinary citizens essentially do the job of a professional reporter, usually online), and so on. For example, the *Guardian* has a section on its website called 'community' where citizens can learn how to join in conversations about current issues, submit photographs, contribute their expertise in feature stories and become involved in the production of the site.

In terms of the production of news, the reliance on second-hand input material may at times be problematic. For instance, a University of Technology Sydney/Crikey pilot study (Over half your news is spin 2010), analysing five days in the Australian media, found that almost 55 per cent of the analysed stories were public relations (PR)-driven, with variation between 42 per cent (*Sydney Morning Herald*) to 70 per cent (*Daily Telegraph*). Especially when such stories are used without editing and when they present only the PR point of view, using input material in this way is arguably problematic. This, along with other methods of 'manipulating' the media, such as feeding leaks as exclusives to certain media outlets, restricting access to journalists or burying the release of bad news on a busy news day or on a Friday evening are becoming more common. A classic example of the latter can be seen in a case investigated by Journalism students at Swinburne University of Technology in Australia where more than 200 annual reports of state government departments and statutory authorities were tabled in parliament on the same day (16 September 2010). The convener of Journalism at Swinburne, Dr Margaret Simons, said: 'Tabling so many reports in one go is a technique that ensures no media organisation can possibly get through the lot' (The Brumby Dump 2010). She went on to explain that: 'These are compelling and important issues that any media outlet would want to cover. Some of them are big stories, some of them deserve further investigation. All of them shed light on how Victoria is faring in the eleventh year of Labor Government.' (More information on this project can be found at The Brumpy Dump 2010.)

The processes that lead from turning inputs into the final news story are very complex and involve both multiple producers and complex processes. While there are studies that look at the linguistic differences between input and output (e.g. Bell 1991, Richardson 2007: 106–12), we will focus here on the roles of news workers. Figure 2.2 shows the relation between input material and news room workers in a very simplified way.

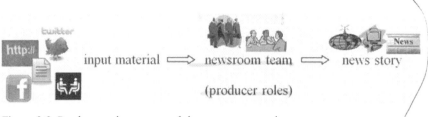

Figure 2.2 Producer roles as part of the news story cycle

As Figure 2.2 illustrates, it is a whole team in the newsroom that puts a story together, from editors-in-chief, editorial managers, to editors (including photographic or video editors), chief-of-staff, subeditors, section heads to senior and junior journalists and photographers. Finally, there are also the newsreaders and correspondents of radio and television. They all have different input into the production of news language and images, and there are many layers of communicative 'creation' and many versions of news stories (Bell 1991, Cotter 2010, Lamble 2011). Accordingly, it is not possible to regard any story as the solo product of a journalist: even a newspaper by-line is 'no guarantee of authorship' (Bell 1991: 42). Bell (1991: 36–44), drawing on Hymes and Goffman, makes a useful distinction between four roles in producing language: the principal, the author, the editor and the animator (see Table 2.1).

Table 2.1 Producer roles

Label	Role
Principals	Originator of position/stance
Authors	Producing an original draft
Editors	Modifying drafts
Animators	Verbalizing the utterance

Principals are the 'originator whose position or stance is expressed'; authors produce an original draft; editors modify the original draft and animators are the ones 'verbalizing the utterance' (Bell 1991: 37), and these days they can even be present as holograms as first seen on CNN (Figure 2.3 on p. 23; CNN Hologram TV First 2008). As Bell suggests, these labels are useful in describing the different roles of staff in the newsroom. For example, journalists/reporters function as 'authors', producing original drafts of stories from inputs, whereas different kinds of editors in the

Figure 2.3 News presenter Jessica Yellin as a hologram on CNN

newsroom modify these drafts, for instance, headlines are usually created by subeditors rather than journalists and journalistic copy can be rewritten by others. In some cases, editors prescribe features of journalistic copy (e.g. in terms of length) – indeed, some editors have been said to 'shape', 'fashion' or 'control' the news to the extent where '[n]ews is whatever the editor says it is' (Neighbour 2011: 21). Further, section heads and the chief-of-staff, who runs the news desk, usually meet to plan and structure developing news (Rau 2010: 69). Finally, newsreaders, correspondents and technicians can be seen as responsible for transmitting the discourse to the audience. Beyond the staff in newsrooms, there is also the influence of the socio-economic context (cf. below). For example, Bell (1991: 38) argues that the position or stance that is expressed in news discourse usually originates with the news media as an institution, such as proprietors, managers, news executives and editors-in-chief with the obvious example here being the levels of influence that are said to be exerted by Rupert Murdoch over his colleagues at News Corporation (US) and by newspaper editors appointed by him (although this is an at times hotly debated issue; see Neighbour 2011: 20). John Hartigan, the chief executive of News Limited (Australia), even suggests that '[w]ith good editors, the newspaper is almost a mirror on their own personality. It reflects their own values' (quoted in Neighbour 2011: 19). For a study on the BBC see Barkho (2008).

While there are some differences between the newsrooms in print, television, online and radio, the roles in news editing are relatively similar (Rau 2010: 68–9) with different names for the equivalent roles (Lamble 2011:

Table 2.2 Producers of language and image, their roles and labels

Label	Role	Producers of Language/Image
Principals	Originator of position/stance	News media as institution (e.g. proprietors, managers, news executives)
Authors	Producing an original draft/ images	Journalists/reporters, photographers, camera people, sound engineers, VJs, . . .
Editors	Modifying drafts/images	Editors, photo editors, producers, . . .
Animators	Verbalizing the utterance/ transmitting the images	Digital software, technicians, newsreaders, correspondents, . . .

69–70). We can also apply Bell's model to still and moving news images: photographers, camera people, sound engineers and video-journalists (VJs) operate as authors, while photo editors and producers select, crop and edit vision in the role of editor, and studio technicians or digital software fulfil the role of animator. Table 2.2 above summarizes producer roles with respect to the production of both language and image.

It is also becoming increasingly common to see members of the public taking on author roles as they use their phones and other mobile devices to provide eyewitness photography and video footage at the scene of major disasters. A more unusual author would be the automated video footage from CCTV security cameras now commonly located at airports, train stations, shopping malls, government buildings, and so on, which also makes it onto the pages of newsprint and into TV news bulletins, especially in criminal cases where audiences may be called upon to help identify the image participants. Finally, it must be noted that the 'multiskilled' journalist is becoming more common and the separation and specialization of roles outlined above may soon be the stuff of legend. Indeed the 'jeder' (digital journalist-editor-producer – see Tickle and Keshvani 2000) who can take pictures, produce videos, capture sound, write the words and the headlines, and then edit them into an electronic news package ready to be published worldwide all in a matter of minutes is very much a reality. Not only are university Journalism degrees starting to offer subjects in such 'multiplatform journalism' but news organizations are retraining their own staff to become multiskilled and are looking to employ graduates who have such skills. To conclude this section on producer roles, it is crucial that our interpretations of news discourse take into account the complex process of news production and the multiple authorship of a single news text or programme including the fact that much news is 'second-hand' text.

2.2 *Audience roles*

Just as the production of news is complex and there are many originators involved, so is the consumption of news. In conceptualizing mass media communication, McQuail (1969) characterizes the audience of such media as large and heterogeneous, with mass media content publicly and simultaneously accessible by fragmented or separated individuals. Further, he says, mass communication is one-directional (from the producers to the audience) and impersonal. In other words, for the most part, there is no direct interaction between the producers of news discourse (absence of direct feedback, anonymity), and their audience or between audience members themselves (separation of the audience). The internet has changed this quite dramatically, allowing readers to see popular stories (most viewed by others), to post comments, to share and discuss stories with other readers, to interact with graphics, to produce mash-ups, and so on. To some extent then, some of the key features of mass media communication have been mitigated by the online revolution (although limited audience participation also exists in the 'old' media, for example, letters to the editor). However, the producers of news language arguably still work with a stereotyped image of their audience, imagining or expecting particular types of viewers/readers. The same can be said for the audience, who usually have no direct face-to-face contact with the producers of the story they are engaging with and may therefore draw on particular perceptions that they have of the news outlet or journalist.

As producer roles can be put into different categories, so can audience roles. Again we can follow Bell (1991: 90–5), who draws on Goffman (1981) in distinguishing audience roles: 'the target audience who is addressed, the auditors who are expected but not targeted, the overhearers who are not expected to be present in the audience, and the eavesdroppers who are expected to be absent from the audience' (Bell 1991: 92) – see Table 2.3. For example, a newspaper like *The Times* does not expect unskilled or semi-skilled professionals as readers – such readers are expected **not** to read *The Times* (eavesdroppers) or they are unexpected overhearers. In

Table 2.3 Audience roles

Label	Role
Target audience	Addressed and expected/targeted
Auditors	Expected but not addressed/targeted
Overhearers	Not expected
Eavesdroppers	Expected to be absent

contrast, readers from higher and intermediate professions, which make up 60 per cent of *The Times*' readership (see further Section 3) are both expected and addressed (target audience). As the dotted lines in Table 2.3 indicate, these roles are not to be seen as clear-cut and clearly separated categories but rather as a continuum, and in TV and radio news the roles become more complex where there is additional interaction between interviewers and interviewees (or others) within the news programme (Figure 2.4).

Figure 2.4 The complexity of audience roles

In general, news discourse is addressed at different kinds of target audience who we can classify according to a number of social factors, such as education, political views, age, gender, and so on. There are two ways in which target audiences can be identified: First, we can consider content, for example, the kinds of stories that are told, the type of advertising in which the stories are embedded, language use – that is, the way in which news discourse *construes* or addresses a particular audience.

Consider the images in Table 2.4 on p. 27 in this respect (partial representation only), comparing the advertisements in the 'popular' *Ottawa Sun* (lottery) with the 'quality' *Globe and Mail* (Tiffany, Bespoke eyewear, etc.). Clearly, these advertisements, together with the kinds of news stories told and the language used in these newspapers, both address and construe different audience groups. We have already seen in Chapter 1 that linguistic research has found that discourse targeted at 'working-class' audiences (usually found in the tabloids) uses different language than that targeted at 'middle-class' audiences (*audience design*). Conboy (2006: 45) suggests that the tabloids employ specific rhetorical features to create a tone that appeals to a particular group of readers. He argues that '[t]he language of the popular tabloid press in Britain is as accurate a prediction of the assumed social class and income of its readership as the advertisements or news content' (Conboy 2006: 14). From a Cultural Studies perspective, Fulton comments as follows:

[F]rom a theoretical perspective, an audience is called into being by a particular discourse, or 'interpellated' by the text, to use Althusser's

Table 2.4 Sample advertisements in the *Ottawa Sun* and the *Globe and Mail*

The *Ottawa Sun*, 11 October 2010, p. 10

The *Globe and Mail*, 14 September 2010, p. A2

term. In other words, an audience doesn't exist until a text addresses it; and by the same token, texts don't simply address a pre-existing and knowable audience. They actually construct a virtual audience . . . As actual individuals who use media products, the extent to which we feel ourselves to be part of an audience depends on whether or not we feel addressed by a media text. Does it speak to us directly? Does it use a language we recognise as ours? Do we feel included in the world view and attitudes articulated by the text? (2005: 5)

To some extent, then, the target audience can be seen in the content of news discourse, whether through the kind of story told, the language used or the advertisements included, which target different kinds of audience. In deciding how they address their target audience, producers may work with information gleaned from market research or base the way they address their target audience on (potentially stereotypical) assumptions they hold about them.

The other way in which target audiences can be looked at is through audience surveys identifying **actual** audiences in terms of audience figures (cf. Section 3). For example, online and freesheet daily readers in Canada are younger (50 per cent under 40 years old) than tabloid (41 per cent) and broadsheet (36 per cent) readers (figures for 2008, from Canadians love their newspapers! 2010). As mentioned above, a newspaper like *The Times* in the United Kingdom pulls 60 per cent of its readers from the social class labelled AB (i.e. higher and intermediate professions), whereas this figure is much lower for the *Sun* which attracts 24 per cent of C1 (more junior professions), 30 per cent of C2 (skilled manual professions) and 30 per cent of DE (semi-skilled and unskilled manual professions) (figures for Oct. 2009–March 2010, Newspaper crib sheets 2010).The two newspapers clearly have very different target audiences. Figures for US, Irish, Australian and New Zealand newspaper audiences are readily available online, also showing this segmentation of audiences.

Section 2 has introduced the complex processes of news production, including its multiple authorship, as well as the ways in which we can look at the audience of news discourse. We must note here that the communicative context of different kinds of news – online, television, radio and print – may differ in various ways and each needs to be considered in its own right. It is further crucial that our interpretations of news discourse take into account the ways in which news texts or programmes target, address and construe different kinds of audiences. However, there are other aspects that we also need to consider when selecting and interpreting news discourse, including social, economic and historical factors. These are the focus of Section 3.

3 Socio-historical context

The socio-historical context of news discourse has been very well documented, especially in the Media/Journalism and Communications Studies literature (e.g. in Barnhurst and Nerone 2001).[2] In this section we briefly touch on some of the most significant developments that have shaped the news media as we know it today. We focus initially on the historical development of the print news media in the United Kingdom, as this form of recorded news has the longest history, before widening the discussion to include electronic news formats. We will also discuss in this section how news is financed and regulated, touching upon economic and legal aspects of the socio-historical context.

3.1 *Development of the print news media*

News in print has transitioned from licensed government mouthpiece (especially during the eighteenth to nineteenth century), through privatization and commodification (during the twentieth century) to what some (e.g. Wilkinson et al. 2009, Craig 2011) describe today as a conversation or partnership between producers and consumers, where the boundaries between the two are becoming increasingly blurred. The early dissemination of printed information came under the control of governments, the Church and absolutist monarchies. This is because they principally had control over the printing presses. However, even when private individuals took over the printing industry, governments still managed to restrict the wide dissemination of information through the imposition of stamp duties and taxes (on paper, for example). This led to the emergence of an underground press, known in the United Kingdom as the *Unstampeds*. Being illegally produced and clandestinely distributed, they placed themselves beyond the reach of the government and their taxes (see Chalaby 1998 and Conboy 2010 for a comprehensive historical account of Unstampeds and the evolution of journalism). Thus, while licensed publications tended to focus primarily on the dissemination of government declarations, new laws and policies, shipping movements, the announcement of births and deaths or to set the latest trade prices for staples like wheat, barley, salt and sugar, the Unstampeds recorded the heroic actions, crimes and deaths of heroes and villains.

The repealing of the taxes (the last one being lifted in the mid-nineteenth century) led to radical changes in newspaper publishing. No longer reliant on government presses or subsidies, newspaper owners began to realize the potential of advertising revenues in offsetting the high costs of production and essentially, news and information became commodities, to be traded just like any other resource in the marketplace. The Unstampeds disappeared and a popular press emerged selling stories of crime and war (mostly focusing on the human angle) to mass audiences. Importantly, news stories became shorter, included headlines to attract attention and were often accompanied by illustrations, first in the form of woodcut engravings and then through the half-tone process that was introduced in the 1880s. By the beginning of the twentieth century, the newspaper industry had cemented its position at the centre of the national psyche in most countries throughout the world, sharing the market among morning, afternoon and evening editions of their publications as well as special weekend editions, packed with more detailed reviews of the week's news, special lift-out section and large photographs and illustrations. Radio and television were introduced during the 1920s and 1950s respectively, and rather than killing each other off, they each found their niches in the dissemination of news, information and entertainment. Having lost the breaking news market first to radio and then to television (and to the online environment in the twenty-first century), newspapers took on a more specialist role, offering in-depth analysis and comment on the news, drawing on the expertise of academics and key political, military, religious and industry figures.

3.2 Digitizing the news

The digital revolution is the latest technological development that is impacting on the creation and dissemination of news discourse in new and very significant ways. Traditionally, audiences have paid for news, either through the price of a newspaper, or through a licensing system (e.g. for the BBC in the United Kingdom). Now they can get the same news for free at point of access via a myriad of online websites, each with varying levels of resourcing and reliability: some are populated by renowned journalists and their long-established news organizations, while others such as blogs and alternative websites reside mainly in the hands of highly motivated ordinary citizens. Newspapers, in particular, have been impacted by the loss of classified advertising revenues to the digital medium. Such revenues underpinned the print industry, heavily subsidizing the huge costs of running and printing a newspaper (see Section 3.3 'Financing the news'). The global financial crisis of the early twenty-first century has also left its mark on the industry, resulting in the closure of newspapers the world over (the media giant News Corp lost US$3.4 billion across the 2009 fiscal year). In the United States, for example, between 2008 and 2010, more than 166 newspapers closed down or stopped publishing a print edition (Lin 2010). Editorial staff numbers have also been decimated (e.g. one regional daily newspaper in the United Kingdom has reduced its editorial staff from 100 in the mid-1990s to 25 in 2011, and in 2011 alone, layoffs and buyout at US newspapers stood at 3,485 in September of that year (Buyouts and layoffs in the newspaper industry 2011)). Many organizations have closed regional and international bureaus (resulting in greater reliance on agency copy) and have also brought editorial decisions for many disparate regions under the control of one centrally located and managed newsroom.

The challenges presented by the digital revolution are significant and news media organizations are reacting to these challenges in many different ways. Some are attempting to put a price on online news, while others are embracing the notion of citizen journalist as content provider. Leading the push towards pay-per-view is Rupert Murdoch and the publications that come under his News Corp umbrella, including *The Times* (UK) and the *Wall Street Journal* (US), although several other news organizations have already been operating very successfully behind a paywall for many years (see, for example, www.crikey.com.au, an exclusively online Australian news website that charges a modest fee for news content and analysis). Furthermore, newspaper organizations are cognizant that many readers who are digitally literate still enjoy the layout, organization and features of the traditional version of the newspaper. Thus they are replicating the formatting of the newspaper through applications for electronic touch-screen tablets, such as the Apple iPad, including the tactile experience of turning the 'page' with the flick of a finger. Again, Murdoch's News Corp is leading the way with the 2011 launch of its iPad-only newspaper called the *Daily*. Charging US 99 cents per week for subscriptions to this paper, this may prove to be another way of underpinning the survival of the newspaper.

Another challenge posed by the digital age is the unprecedented levels of collaboration and sharing of information that have been made possible through Web 2.0 technologies (cf. Section 2.2 'Audience roles'). Some news organizations encourage members of the public to contribute to the conversation by commenting on stories online and offering alternative perspectives on an issue. Amateur photographs and video clips are welcomed by most news organizations, sometimes making it into primetime news bulletins or onto the front pages of newsprint (e.g. amateur video footage of key environmental events such as the 2004 Boxing Day tsunami in the Indian Ocean or the 2011 earthquake and tsunami in Japan). With regard to their contribution to news discourse, however, interesting questions that have yet to be fully explored in the academic literature include the extent to which ordinary citizens will be breaking news stories on their own blogs or on behalf of news media outlets and whether consumer generated content will be seen to set the news agenda. As the managing director of the ABC (Australia), Mark Scott stated at a journalism conference in 2010, knowing the story and telling the story, it seems, are still very much the domain of established news media organizations. But discussing the story has become the conversation that everyone now has the means of contributing to.

News organizations are also engaging with the Web 2.0 phenomenon by encouraging their journalists to set up their own blogs and Twitter accounts where readers can follow their favourite commentators, enter into dialogue with them and feel like they are engaging on a much more intimate level with expert opinion. While tweeting still has to prove itself as a legitimate platform for news reporting, one of the most important stories for 2010 in Australian politics was broken via a tweet from Chris Uhlmann, political editor with the ABC in Australia. With the following 135 characters 'Kevin Rudd's leadership is under siege tonight from some of the Labor Party's most influential factional warlords. Watch ABC News. NOW!' (http://twitter.com/CUhlmann/status/16836890031, 23 June 2010, 9.00 p.m. Australian (EST) time), Uhlmann broke the news of the Labor leadership spill and the handing over of power to Australia's first ever female prime minister in Julia Gillard. Similarly, the death of British singer Amy Winehouse was broken via Twitter where it was talked about 40 minutes before any official news reports (Hart 2011). However, until the BBC confirmed the Twitter story, internet users were still searching for confirmation, with 'Amy Winehouse',

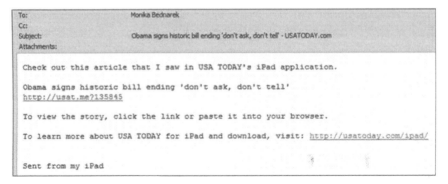

To:	Monika Bednarek
Cc:	
Subject:	Obama signs historic bill ending 'don't ask, don't tell' - USATODAY.com
Attachments:	

Check out this article that I saw in USA TODAY's iPad application.

Obama signs historic bill ending 'don't ask, don't tell'
http://usat.me?135845

To view the story, click the link or paste it into your browser.

To learn more about USA TODAY for iPad and download, visit: http://usatoday.com/ipad/

Sent from my iPad

Figure 2.5 Email alerts – one method of sharing news stories

'Amy Winehouse dead' and 'Amy Winehouse death' the top three google searches (Hart 2011). This shows that news institutions – especially global media players such as the BBC and CNN – have an authority that is not shared by new media sources such as Twitter. They are still regarded as 'authoritative voices' (Paganoni 2008: 337) that confirm and interpret the news for us.

The digital medium has also revolutionized producer roles (cf. Section 2.1 'Producer roles' on holograms and digital software) and where, when and how audiences engage with all forms of the media. In response to this, the news media, including newspapers, radio and TV stations, and online news media organizations now offer a range of news packages in the form of podcasts, vodcasts, online news galleries, and other multimedia such as interactives and graphics (see Chapter 5 for an explanation of these), RSS feeds to mobile devices, specially tailored news packages fed to social networking sites, and email digests to name but a few. Audiences can then share their favourite stories with each other, for example, via email alerts as shown in Figure 2.5 above.

While all of these forms of news dissemination ensure that the general public is still engaging on some level with the news media, it also means that audiences are becoming increasingly fragmented. The implications of audience fragmentation are immense for all news organizations, particularly in relation to funding. This is because it is becoming increasingly difficult to ensure that advertisements are reaching their desired audiences. Newspapers in particular have a long tradition of building community and readership loyalty, which can be easily articulated to advertisers, who can then tailor their advertising to target specific audiences (see also Sections 2.2 'Audience roles' and 3.3 'Financing the news'). This is not so clearly defined in an age where audiences are exerting greater control over the ways in which they engage with the news media. Thus, many news organizations are still developing funding models that will work across these new media, as well as ensure the continued provision of quality investigative journalism.

Awareness of the historical development of print media can be important for the discourse analyst when planning a research project that looks at news discourse, especially over time. Further, the newest technological developments mean that whole areas of new research have been opened up, with barely any linguistic/semiotic research available on newer forms of news discourse.

3.3 *Financing the news*

It has already become apparent from the discussion in previous sections that financial issues impact highly on the production of news, for instance, in terms of targeted audiences. Historically, as mentioned, news organizations have relied heavily on advertising as the principle means of funding the costs of producing news discourse, with circulation, the number of people actually purchasing the news products, making up a very small fraction of this income (especially for 'quality' news products, since 'popular' news products make more money from circulation). Thus news organizations have quite specific types of audiences that they target in order to attract advertisers. We have already talked about this in Section 2 in terms of audience segmentation and above in terms of community-building and readership loyalty. As mentioned, there is a broad distinction between 'quality' and 'popular' news products, which seems to be valid across the countries we deal with in this book (although there are certainly national differences; see Conboy 2002, 2006 on newspapers). This also contributes to the building of a particular audience profile that can be carefully targeted by advertising campaigns. As Richardson (2008b: 155) points out with respect to print news, much research has shown 'the ways that capitalism, and the want for profit in particular, drive newspapers to change their discourses – both linguistic and visual – in order to appeal to affluent target readers'. This is why our interpretations of news discourse need to take into account such financial aspects of the socio-historical context.

But there are further aspects to advertising that need discussing. First, it is ubiquitous, and can be found in most news media, for example, on the radio, on television, in print news and online, and advertisements can and often do dominate the pages of newsprint. Thus, it is very important that we distinguish between advertising and other content – called 'editorial' in a newspaper (Bell 1991: 13). Indeed there are 'firewalls' or boundaries between advertising and other content put in place 'that a reliable news reporter or editor is not supposed to transgress' (Cotter 2010: 60). However, such boundaries are arguably transgressed in cases where advertising is 'disguised' as news – in that it takes on features of news stories, expert interviews or feature articles. Equally, news stories may integrate features of advertising (Ungerer 2004). A good example of the latter was aired on Channel Seven's *Morning News* bulletin on 3 November 2010 (Channel

Figure 2.6 A screen shot of a 'news' bulletin on Channel Seven (Australia, 3 November 2010)

Seven is an Australian free-to-air commercial TV channel). With the rolling news ticker running across the bottom of the screen informing the audience of a suspected arson attack and the background graphics 'SHOCK DEATH' dividing an image of a woman superimposed over another image of a 'family' snap (in Figure 2.6 above), newsreader Ann Sanders began the segment with this: 'More than 2.3 million Australians tuned in to *Packed to the Rafters* last night . . . The shock story line saw Melissa Rafter die unexpectedly in a car crash.' The bulletin then showed footage of the crash – that is, the fictitious crash, involving the fictitious character (pictured in Figure 2.6) on a Channel Seven soap opera *Packed to the Rafters*. No one actually died in this story and it was repeated eight times that day, including on the main six o'clock evening news bulletin. This is a story that looks, reads, and sounds like a tragic news event, but it is not. As Paul Barry (ABC TV *Media Watch* presenter) commented 'News is entertainment and entertainment is news. Sadly, the line between the two has become increasingly blurred. And if TV stations can spruik their shows on the nightly bulletin, they'll jump at the chance.' This is a very clear example of self-promotion disguised as 'news', and one where the 'firewall' arguably has been transgressed. For the linguist/semiotician, this may prove to be a critical area of research, as the battle between TV channels for their share of the viewing public begins to be played out in the discourses traditionally reserved for 'news'.

Another financial consideration concerns maintaining and ideally increasing the number of people paying for news content, which is becoming increasingly difficult to achieve given the amount of information that is now freely available online (see Section 3.2 'Digitizing the news'). For the

Table 2.5 A comparison of daily audience figures for print and online news media in Canada in 2010 (adapted from Overview of results 2010)

Percentage of Adults 18+	Form of News Media Read
47	Daily newspaper on the average weekday
73	Printed daily newspaper in the past week
22	Daily newspaper online in the past week
78	Printed or online edition of a daily newspaper in the past week

researcher, though, it is important to distinguish between circulation and readership figures and to understand the ways in which they are calculated. Circulation refers to the number of copies of a publication that are sold on an average day over a particular period, while readership figures indicate the average number of people reading a publication. For example, *The Times* (UK) had an average daily circulation of 466,311 during November 2010, while its average daily adult readership figures stood at 1,673,000 between October 2009 and March 2010 (see Newspaper crib sheets 2010 for further breakdown of these figures and to access similar calculations for other British newspapers). Compare this to an average daily circulation of 2,898,113 and readership of 7,682,000 for the *Sun* newspaper over the same time period.

Researchers also need to consider whether such figures are increasing or decreasing over time. For example, the circulation and readership figures for the *Sydney Morning Herald*, part of the Fairfax Media stable in Australia, have remained steady all through the economic downturn and it has outperformed all of its rivals in the Australian market. However, even if circulation figures decline, profits may rise at the same time (see Richardson 2007: 229 for examples from the local press in the United Kingdom). There are many ways in which audience figures can be calculated and interpreted and there are numerous websites dedicated to tracking readership trends. Comparisons can also be made across different forms of news media. Table 2.5 above calculates audience figures for online and print newspaper readership in Canada for 2010.

3.4 *The news media and the law*

One final contextual consideration for this chapter is that of media regulation and codes of practice. Every nation has rules and regulations that determine who can own and operate the news media, how much local content they are required to carry and the percentage of audience reach a single news service provider can control, in order to prevent the common ownership of newspapers, TV and radio broadcasting licences that serve the same region. It is said that diverse ownership of the media is important to ensure the expression of points of view antagonistic to the government and the prevailing orthodoxy on any given issue. This helps to ensure 'informed decision-making, cultural pluralism, citizen welfare, and a well-functioning democracy' (Napoli 1999: 9). In order to achieve such diversity, many countries operate on a model of both publicly funded and privately owned news organizations (e.g. in the United Kingdom, United States, Australia, New Zealand, Canada, Ireland). In other countries, the government has complete control over the news media (e.g. in North Korea and Iran). Foreign ownership of the news media is a concern for some countries, as is the concentration of media ownership into the hands of just a few media moguls, for example. Again, Australia is a very good example of both of these points: the Australian media operates with just two major newspaper groups, Fairfax Media and News Limited, which cover more than 90 per cent of all newspaper readership. Further, commercial television is also dominated by foreign ownership with CVC Asia Pacific at the Nine Network, while foreign investor CanWest (a Canadian media company) owned majority shares in Channel Ten until the end of 2009. Such issues are important to consider for linguists/semioticians as they may help us understand why certain content is expressed in certain ways, for instance, with respect to the diversity (or not) of viewpoints represented.

However, the news media are 'not just another business' (Schultz 1994). They are often referred to as the consciousness industry. For this reason, the news media are also regulated by ethics and codes of practice, some of which are legislated for at government level and some are set by the industry themselves as a form of self-regulation. Journalistic endeavour – the investigating and reporting of newsworthy events and issues – requires journalists to 'verify information by drawing on alternative sources and representing rival interpretations' (Wheeler 1997: 7). Thus, the profession is marked by a commitment to public service and the norms of journalistic responsibility, and is built on the values of objectivity, fairness, truthfulness and accuracy. These are the basic tenets of all journalistic codes of practice, even though they can be grossly undermined (as in the *News of the World* phone hacking scandal in the United Kingdom that resurfaced in mid-2011). Other legal constraints that affect the reporting practices of news media professionals include defamation laws, which are put in place as a means of redress to individuals whose reputation has been unjustly tarnished by information published about them. Freedom of Information (FOI) laws allow media organizations access to information held by the government/ state. However, much journalistic investigation attempting to implement FOI laws is thwarted by blanket exemptions or excessive fees that can run into millions of dollars, well beyond the reach of even the major news organizations. Further, the lack of protection for confidential sources has proved to be a considerable obstacle for journalistic endeavour. However, some countries are beginning to introduce shield laws that do offer some protection to journalists and their sources.

Of course, not every country adheres to the same rules and regulations and it is useful for researchers of news discourse to familiarize themselves with the laws and ethical guidelines that operate within a particular context. A good place to start such research would be by examining the Press Freedom indexes that are published on an annual basis by organizations like Reporters sans Frontières (http://en.rsf.org/) or Freedom House (www. freedomhouse.org). For an excellent summary of the ownership and regulation of European media visit the Media Landscape site at www. ejc.net/media_landscape/, organized by the European Journalism Centre. Another more ambitious project investigating ownership and regulation around the world is being conducted by undergraduate media students at the University of New South Wales (Australia) and collated on a wiki. This Global Media Mapping Project aims eventually to map the ownership and regulation of the media in every country in the world. At present, 182 countries have been mapped (see http://arts1091.unsw.wikispaces.net).

Being aware of issues concerning both media law and regulation allows researchers to take into account the (lack of) choices that journalists have in producing news discourse, which may impact on the text that is produced. Being conscious of codes of practice also enables researchers to understand certain choices that have been made in texts.

More generally, we can conclude this chapter by asking the question: what benefit would a linguist or semiotician gain from having a better understanding of the historical and social context of news discourse? In answering this question we can point to at least three benefits: In the same way that Media/Journalism and Communications scholars can draw on the empirical evidence that linguistic and semiotic analyses of news discourse provide, so too are linguists/semioticians able to justify how and why they have compiled their datasets the way they have by drawing on the communicative, historical and social contexts that shape the news media at every level. Further, the subsequent interpretation of data in terms of an appropriate contextualization is often aided by taking into account both the communicative (producer/audience roles) and the socio-historical context of news discourse. This also allows linguists to counter frequent criticism that accuses them of not considering social and historical factors (see Richardson 2008b: 152–3, 158).

Finally, an understanding of both communicative and socio-historical contexts enables researchers to explore in more detail the highly complex relationship between them. Thus, news media speak **to**, **about** and **for** their audience, but they also speak **for** and **about** larger economic and political interests (Phillip Bell, 2011, personal communication). We might conceptualize this complex relationship between news discourse and context as a two-way flow – where aspects of the context shape news discourse and where news discourse itself shapes, or even establishes, aspects of the context. For example, political and social changes influence news discourse, but at the same time news discourse also impacts on social and political developments (Conboy 2010: 1). The professional norms and training of news producers and the roles they perform in the newsroom will impact on the way news discourse is constructed; but at the same time, the way news discourse is repeatedly construed may change professional norms, training and news processes. That news discourse in tabloids is different from that in broadsheets does not merely reflect an aspect of the communicative context, the discourse itself functions to **discursively** construe or 'inscribe a readership' (Conboy 2006: 15). Similarly, technological affordances may give rise to particular ways of presenting news (e.g. online) but these ways in themselves may then constitute a particular variety of news. This may in itself impact on other varieties of news that do not have the same original technological affordances, such as when print news takes on some of the characteristics of online news (see Chapter 4).

In Chapter 3, we take up this discursive perspective more explicitly in our exploration of the journalistic concept of news values, showing how Media Studies approaches can be fruitfully rethought in terms of their implications for news discourse. We believe that this is equally possible with other approaches in Media/Journalism and Communications Studies.

Directions for further reading

Barnhurst, K. G. and Nerone, J. (2001), *The Form of News*. New York: Guilford. US-centric comprehensive discussion of the history of newspaper form.
Bell, A. (1991), *The Language of News Media*. Oxford: Blackwell. Discusses speaker and audience roles in the media.
Conboy, M. (2010), *The Language of Newspapers. Socio-Historical Perspectives*. London/New York: Continuum. Explores the development of the newspaper in England and its relation to social developments.

Notes

1 Other aspects such as genre, which are often included under context, are discussed separately in Chapter 4. We are not using a Hallidayan or Faircloughian conceptualization of context here.

2 For a useful review of the evolution of the news story genre from a linguistic perspective see Feez et al. (2008). Compare also Conboy (2010) for a socio-historical approach to the development of the language of newspapers, and Conboy (2002) for a history of the popular press. For a historical review of the role news photography has played in the media see Caple 2010b (this will be explored further in Chapter 5).

CHAPTER THREE

News values

1 Introduction

In Chapter 1 we mentioned ethnographic research that suggests that news values have a huge impact on the process of reporting and editing news. This chapter provides an introduction to this important concept, illustrating it with manifold authentic examples from English-language news discourse. These examples are taken from Bednarek (2006c), Bednarek and Caple (2010), and our dataset, as well as three additional stories (Weisman and Meckler 2008, Kwek et al. 2011, Sands 2011). Our objectives are to enable readers to understand:

- what news values are and the different ways in which they have been defined
- what different news values we can distinguish
- how news values are construed through discourse (language and image).

We will start by outlining news values as they have been theorized by media researchers and linguists. Then we introduce our own approach, which looks at the construal of news values both linguistically and photographically. Finally, we illustrate this *discursive* approach with authentic examples of news discourse.

2 What are news values?

News values have primarily been described in terms of the factors that take an event into the news. According to Galtung and Ruge (1965) an event has to cross a certain threshold before it will be registered as news. This threshold has been theorized in media studies as 'news values'. In a first definition, news values can thus be described as the 'values by which one "fact" is judged more newsworthy than another' (Bell 1991: 155). However, *news values* have been variously defined as:

- the **criteria** or **rules** that news workers apply to determine what is 'news' (Bell 1991: 155, Richardson 2007: 91, Brighton and Foy 2007: 1)

- 'the (*imagined*) **preferences** of the expected audience' (Richardson 2007: 94, italics in original, bold face ours) about what is newsworthy

- the **values** by which events or facts are judged more newsworthy than others (Galtung and Ruge 1965, Hartley 1982, Fowler 1991, Tunstall 1996), shared both by producers and audiences of news discourse (van Dijk 1988b: 119)

- the **qualities/elements** that are necessary to make a story newsworthy (Cotter 2010: 68).

What these different definitions have in common, however, is that news values are said to determine what makes something newsworthy – worthy of being news. Since the classic study by Galtung and Ruge (1965) on Scandinavian news discourse, varying lists of such values have been suggested by researchers (cf. Bell 1991: 156–60, Brighton and Foy 2007, Richardson 2007: 92, Cotter 2010: 69).[1] However, the kinds of concepts that researchers list as *news values* are clearly not of the same kind (see also Harcup and O'Neill 2001, cited in Richardson 2007: 92) and it is questionable whether or not they should all be covered by the same term. For example, according to Bell's (1991) classification, there are three classes of news values: (1) values in the news text, (2) values in the news process, (3) values in news actors and events. However, these differ quite considerably from each other. For example, Bell's **values in the news text** – brevity, clarity, colour – are more like general characteristics demanded of a news story in order to be included. We will call these three 'values' *news writing objectives* (cf. Chapter 4). Bell's **values in the news process** are factors that impact on the selection of news. These include the following:

- continuity (once a story appears as news it continues as news)

- competition (the competition among news institutions for scoops, the competition among stories for coverage)

- co-option (associating one story with a more newsworthy one)

- composition (the mix of different kinds of stories in the overall news bulletin or newspaper)

- predictability (the scheduling of events, such as press conferences to fit the news cycle)

- prefabrication (the existence of prefabricated input sources – see Chapter 2).

We will call these 'values' *news cycle/market factors*. For example, sometimes photographers may capture a moment in the unfolding of an event that others miss or ignore. Thus, having a photograph or footage that no other news organization has (an exclusive) can get a story into the news. Cotter also notes that factors **other than newsworthiness** that influence the production of news include 'availability of space, the amount of news occurring on a particular day, a balance or mix of types of news . . ., the time to deadline . . ., day of the week . . ., the audience or readership . . . and the focus . . . of the news outlet' (2010: 80).

Table 3.1 Categorizing news 'values'

Bell's (1991) Categories	Our Categories
Values in the news text	News writing objectives
Values in the news process	News cycle/market factors
Values in news actors and events	News values

As we believe that the three different categories that Bell distinguishes are very different in kind (Table 3.1), we only use the term *news values* for Bell's **values in news actors and events**, later offering two perspectives on such values. However, it is important to keep in mind that other researchers often use the term *news values* to include what we call *news writing objectives* and *news cycle/market factors*.

Table 3.2 News values summary

Negativity	Negative aspects of an event
Timeliness	The relevance of the event in terms of time
Proximity	The geographical and/or cultural nearness of the event
Prominence	The high status of the individuals (e.g. celebrities, politicians), organizations or nations involved in the event, including quoted sources
Consonance	The extent to which aspects of a story fit in with stereotypes that people may hold about the events and people portrayed in it
Impact	The effects or consequences of an event
Novelty	The unexpected aspects of an event
Superlativeness	The maximized or intensified aspects of an event
Personalization	The personal or human interest aspects of an event

For us then, news values relate to the events as reported in news stories and to the news actors involved in the events as reported in the news story (see further below on our *discursive perspective*). They are the values that make the story newsworthy. These values include but are not limited to Negativity, Timeliness, Proximity, Prominence, Consonance, Impact, Novelty, Superlativeness, Personalization (Table 3.2 on p. 41). We will now discuss each news value in turn.

Negativity: negative aspects of an event

News stories very frequently concern 'bad' happenings such as conflicts, accidents, damage, injuries, disasters or wars. Negativity is therefore sometimes called 'the basic news value' (Bell 1991: 156), and a common adage by news workers is 'if it bleeds, it leads'. On the other hand, good news also occurs, for example, the downward trend of malaria as detailed in the World malaria report 2010, which featured in news stories throughout the English-speaking world (e.g. Malaria control 'best in decades': WHO 2010). Feez et al. (2008: 72) argue that newsworthiness is in essence about reporting both 'destabilizing' (negative) and 'stabilizing' (positive) events. Conboy also mentions the 'feelgood' stories of the popular press (2002: 174) and we can find 'alternative' newspapers such as *Positive News* (www. positivenews.org.uk, last accessed 21 September 2011) that emphasize the positive over the negative.

Timeliness: the relevance of the event in terms of time

More recent events are often more newsworthy: 'the best news is something which has only just happened' (Bell 1991: 156). But timeliness may also mean that particular seasonal events are newsworthy, such as stories about Christmas in the pre-Christmas period. Given that timeliness in general is about how an event is temporally relevant to the reader (as opposed to, say, culturally relevant, see 'Proximity'), Timeliness can be associated with aspects of an event that only just (e.g. yesterday) happened, that are still ongoing (e.g. breaking news) or that will happen in the (near) future.

Proximity: the geographical and/or cultural nearness of the event

What is newsworthy usually concerns the country, region or city in which the news is published. As Rau puts it in the context of Australian news, in terms of news value 'one person dead in Australia equates to fifty in Britain and 500 in a developing country' (2010: 13). Britain is more newsworthy in Australia than in some other countries because of its history, as well as the similarity of the cultures – what Galtung and Ruge (1965) call meaningfulness (see also Bell 1991: 157). In the United States, the journalistic community 'prioritizes "local" news over international or other types of *cognitively distant* news' (Cotter 2010: 49, italics in original). So Proximity includes both geographical and cultural nearness.

Prominence/eliteness: the high status of the individuals (e.g. celebrities, politicians), organizations or nations involved in the event, including quoted sources

Stories about 'elite' individuals or celebrities are more newsworthy than stories about ordinary people, and sources that are affiliated with an organization or institution or are otherwise officially recognized authorities are preferred over others: 'The more elite the source, the more newsworthy the story' (Bell 1991: 192). Prominence of sources is sometimes given its own news value label, Attribution.

Consonance: the extent to which aspects of a story fit in with stereotypes that people may hold about the events and people portrayed in it

Aspects of a story become newsworthy if they tie in with the stereotypes that people hold (e.g. about a certain news actor such as Paris Hilton and her typical behaviour). This can also relate to people's stereotypes about organizations, institutions or countries: Richardson (2007: 93) mentions a study by the Glasgow Media Group that showed that the coverage of TV news about developing countries focused on negative events such as war, terrorism, disaster and conflict. While this kind of reporting may be in line with the general news value of Negativity (see above), it might also be interpreted more critically as presenting a narrow preconceived view of these countries.

Impact: the effects or consequences of an event

The effects or consequences of an event are aspects of a story that are newsworthy, especially, if they involve serious repercussions or have a more global impact, rather than only minor consequences. Environmental stories frequently feature descriptions of the (negative – see 'Negativity') effects of environmental happenings (Bednarek and Caple 2010). Aspects that can be seen to affect the audience's lives, that are 'relevant' (van Dijk 1988b: 122) to them, are especially newsworthy (Bell 1991: 157–8).

Novelty/deviance/unusuality/rarity/surprise: the unexpected aspects of an event

News stories are frequently about happenings that surprise us, that are unusual or rare. News workers may even specifically label certain content in such a way: for example, a Reuters online news gallery might be titled 'Strange and unusual' (www.reuters.com/news/pictures/slideshow?articleI d=USRTXVSQ1#a=1, last accessed 21 December 2010) and the website of the UK tabloid the *Daily Mirror* features a news subsection called 'Weird

World' (www.mirror.co.uk/news/weird-world/, last accessed 21 December 2010).

Superlativeness: the maximized or intensified aspects of an event

Generally speaking, the news value of Superlativeness says that the bigger, the faster, the more destructive, the more violent, the more famous . . . the more newsworthy something is. Thus, news stories usually focus on maximizing or intensifying particular aspects of an event, say the amount of people it involved, the consequences it has or might have, the numbers mentioned, the size of things, the force of actions, the intensity of behaviour, and so on.

Personalization: the personal or human interest aspects of an event

News stories that are personalized attract audiences more than the portrayal of generalized concepts or processes. For example, a science story can be made more newsworthy if it directly impacts on a news actor who is willing to tell their story. Eyewitness accounts, for example, of survivors, also clearly increase news value. Personalization is thus about the many ways in which a human face is given to the news.

3 News values: cognitive or discursive?

What is the relationship between the above-mentioned news values, the news event, the news workers involved and the news story? In this book, we will make a distinction between a more 'cognitive' view of news values and a more 'discursive' view of news values. From a **cognitive** perspective we can conceptualize news values as beliefs (or criteria), 'intersubjective mental categories' (Fowler 1991: 17) or '*internalized assumptions*' (Cotter 2010: 56, italics in original) that people hold/apply about qualities/aspects that make something newsworthy. For example, a news worker can believe that a news story is newsworthy because it features Prince William, an 'elite' social actor or because the event concerns the deaths of many people from their own country. Such beliefs about newsworthiness may at times vary according to the individuals concerned: '[E]very journalist and every editor will have a different interpretation of what is newsworthy, because it's such a subjective process' (Rau 2010: 14).

From a **discursive** perspective, we can conceptualize news values in terms of how newsworthiness is construed through discourse (both language and image). Newsworthiness is not inherent in events but established through language and image. In the following example for instance,

A family uses a makeshift raft to get about in Ayuttaya province, 80 kilometres north of Thailand's capital, Bangkok, as the **worst** monsoon floods **in more than a decade** sweep through Thailand and Burma.

('Hell on high water', *Sydney Morning Herald*, 12 October 2006, p. 11)

the comparison in bold (*worst . . . in more than a decade*) simultaneously construes the news values of Superlativeness, Negativity and Novelty. From a discursive perspective then, we ask the following question: what is it in the language/image that construes or establishes an event as newsworthy – what aspects of news discourse function to construe/establish the newsworthiness of an event? This question can be asked both when considering the potential of language and image to do so (cf. Sections 4 and 5) and when analysing actual news discourse (cf. Section 6).

In other words, the focus here is not on the 'nature' of news events, but rather on how such events are **mediated** through language and image – how news discourse **makes them newsworthy**. From this perspective, news values are not 'inherent' aspects of events or internalized beliefs, they are values that are established by language and image in use.

Because of these two dimensions of news values (cognitive and discursive),[2] it is possible to establish lists of news values both on the basis of interviewing news workers such as editors or journalists about what they believe is newsworthy as well as by deriving news values from analysing news stories themselves. It is also important to point out that the two perspectives are not separate, nor are they mutually exclusive. For example, when making judgements about newsworthiness, news workers often work with linguistic construals of events such as press releases, and so on (see Chapter 2 for input sources) which may already include a particular discursive construal of how the event is newsworthy. Further, beliefs about and linguistic construals of newsworthiness interact: News workers

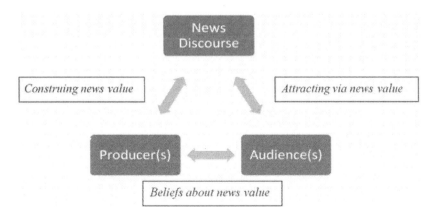

Figure 3.1 News values, the communicative context and the construction of text

have assumptions about what is newsworthy, about what audiences find newsworthy and this may influence (consciously or not) their construction of newsworthiness through discourse. Arguably, the text or news discourse itself is intended to attract an audience through presenting a story to them that is newsworthy (Figure 3.1 on p. 45).

This also explains the variation of news values across media (e.g. popular vs quality press): what is newsworthy to one group of readers is not necessarily newsworthy to another. It is the discursive aspect of news values that we are interested in the most in this book, and that we will discuss in the next two sections of this chapter – first language, then images.

4 News values and language

How, then, does language construe news value, and what are the linguistic devices that may be used? In fact, most editing changes made to input material are 'designed to maximize news value' (Bell 1991: 79). The examples Bell gives include changing the structure of the story to foreground more newsworthy aspects as well as cutting and lexical substitution to make a story more newsworthy, for example, through emphasizing the authority of sources or through the use of stronger vocabulary. So let us first look at some of the main kinds of linguistic devices that can be used to construe news values (as defined above).

Evaluative language
Evaluative language includes linguistic expressions that realize opinion, for example, assessments of positivity or negativity, importance or unimportance, expectedness or unexpectedness (cf. Chapter 6). Negative evaluations of events (*fiasco*), behaviour (*cashes in, made a gaffe*) or news actors (*sexual predator, wannabe*), clearly construe the news value of Negativity. Evaluations of new actors and sources as important (*celebs, famous, superstars, senior, top*) construe Prominence, while the evaluation of events as significant (*key, vital, historic, momentous*) can construe Impact (e.g. *a historic legal case, a potentially momentous day*). Other examples include the use of words like *amazing, astonishing, extraordinarily, curious, unexpectedly, unprecedented, unusually* or contrasts (e.g. *but, although, despite*) to construe Novelty. Meanings of unexpectedness which construe news value can also be encoded in certain expressions used to report information, such as *reveal* or *revelation*, which imply that the reported information is somehow new. In contrast, the use of expressions like *routine, familiar, little wonder* may construe Consonance. Generally, the function of evaluative devices is 'to make the contents of the story sound *as X as possible*, where X is big, recent, important, unusual, new; in a word – newsworthy' (Bell 1991: 152, italics

in original). For extensive discussion of these and other examples see also Bednarek (2006c, 2010a).

Intensification and quantification

Linguistic means of intensification and quantification include devices to intensify number or amount (*thousands of*), size (*huge waves, peanut-size hail*), duration and extent of time (*rapidly rising, continuous rain*), force (*ferocious storm, ravage, blaze*) or degree (*full fury, complete destruction*), including comparative and superlative adjectives (*the most violent type, hardest hit, the largest*). These construe Superlativeness and can be used to maximize any aspect of the reported event. Also common in construing Superlativeness in the news are expressions with the adverbs *only/just/ alone* used to modify time and space: *took only a few seconds, just hours after, just three days before, in the past two months alone, just 10 miles from*.[3] At times, it is specifically the effects or consequences of an event that are maximized – for example, when mentioning that as a result of flooding, *There have been **massive** landslides nearby*. In such cases, we can reasonably argue that both Superlativeness and Impact are established.

Comparison

Happenings in a news story are often compared to similar happenings in the past. This frequently functions to construe Novelty, when the current event is described as, say, the first of its kind or for a long time (e.g. *the first time since 1958*). Figure 3.2 shows all instances of *first* in a news story about the election of Barack Obama as US president in 2008, clearly showing how Novelty is a key news value in this report (this story is discussed in more detail in Appendix 2).

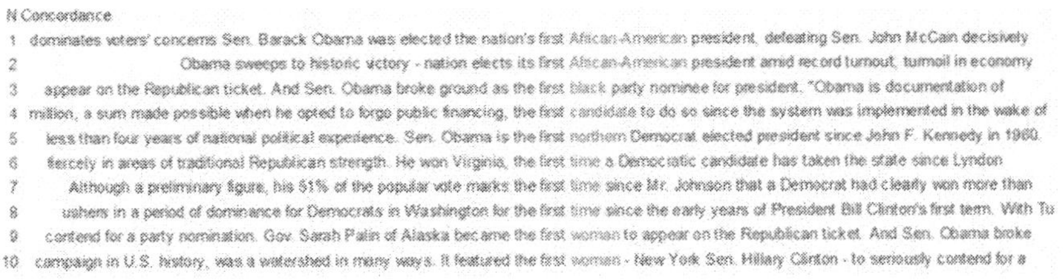

N Concordance

1 dominates voters' concerns Sen. Barack Obama was elected the nation's first African-American president, defeating Sen. John McCain decisively
2 Obama sweeps to historic victory - nation elects its first African-American president amid record turnout, turmoil in economy
3 appear on the Republican ticket. And Sen. Obama broke ground as the first black party nominee for president. "Obama is documentation of
4 million, a sum made possible when he opted to forgo public financing, the first candidate to do so since the system was implemented in the wake of
5 less than four years of national political experience. Sen. Obama is the first northern Democrat elected president since John F. Kennedy in 1960.
6 fiercely in areas of traditional Republican strength. He won Virginia, the first time a Democratic candidate has taken the state since Lyndon
7 Although a preliminary figure, his 51% of the popular vote marks the first time since Mr. Johnson that a Democrat had clearly won more than
8 ushers in a period of dominance for Democrats in Washington for the first time since the early years of President Bill Clinton's first term. With Tu
9 contend for a party nomination. Gov. Sarah Palin of Alaska became the first woman to appear on the Republican ticket. And Sen. Obama broke
10 campaign in U.S. history, was a watershed in many ways. It featured the first woman - New York Sen. Hillary Clinton - to seriously contend for a

Figure 3.2 Concordance lines demonstrating Novelty in a news story on the election of Barack Obama

However, such comparisons can also function to construe Consonance, if an event is said to be very much in line with past events, for example, talking about *yet another personal scandal* for former Italian Prime Minister Silvio Berlusconi. Finally, when aspects of an event are specifically said to be bigger/higher/more forceful . . . than a previous event, this may function to establish both Superlativeness and Novelty (e.g. *this one has just **maxed out** every other flood*).

References to emotion

References to emotion, that is, describing news actors' emotional responses, can take many forms, for example, describing 'emotional' behaviour such as screaming or shouting or labelling emotions (Martin and White 2005, Bednarek 2008a).[4] Examples of such references to emotions are: '*There are others inside' she **screamed**; Deborah **sobbed** to the jury; Di's **terror**; British madam **distraught**; **devastated** Rio; Police chiefs **shocked**; **anxious** Iraqis*. Such references can construe a variety of news values ranging from Negativity (negative emotions) to Personalization (individuals' emotional responses), Impact (when the emotions are caused by an event), Superlativeness ('strong' emotions such as *desperate, panic, terror, . . .*) and Novelty (references to surprise, for example, *note that will **stun** world*). Similar to mentions of surprise, references to expectation (strictly speaking, not an emotional response) also establish Novelty (e.g. *no one was expecting it*).

'Negative' vocabulary

'Negative' vocabulary (e.g. *confusion, damage, deaths, bodies*) refers to the words we use to describe negative events. They have also been described as 'disaster vocabulary' (Ungerer 1997: 315). In contrast to evaluative language, such vocabulary does not automatically and expressly tell us that the writer disapproves of the reported events and is thus not strictly evaluative language. References to the negative effects/impact on individuals, entities, and so on are used to construe both Negativity and Impact (e.g. *flash flood deluged the town*.) The news value that is construed by negative vocabulary is usually Negativity, since we can assume that when a story reports upon the deaths (killings, etc.) of people this is regarded as a 'bad' happening by most. However, consider Figure 3.3, where we would argue that the use of negative vocabulary (*dead, killed, die*) certainly does not construe the event as a negative one from the point of view of these newspapers (and probably many of their readers) – as shown through the use of negative evaluative language (*the bastard, evil, coward*) – and where the event is construed as

Figure 3.3 Front pages on the killing of Osama bin Laden

justice or righteous *vengeance*. Indeed, the Poynter website, which features a collection of 45 bin Laden front pages from around the world, uses the heading 'Newspaper front pages capture **elation, relief** that Osama bin Laden **was killed**' (Moos 2011, bold face ours).

So such negative vocabulary needs to be considered in its context – when negative things happen to 'people like us' or 'people we like', Negativity is construed, but otherwise this may not be the case. We can also include in the category of negative vocabulary the use of labels for socially defined negative behaviour, for instance, *offence* or *crime*. These can be regarded as originating not in the speaker but in 'the institutionalised legal process' (White 1998: 131).

Before we continue with our discussion of resources for construing news values, it may be worth taking a step back to look at an example that illustrates some of the above points:

> The world's best triathletes imposed themselves on Sydney yesterday for all the wrong reasons after mass road closures turned the city into a gridlocked nightmare.
>
> The day began with super fit athletes chasing each other around the Opera House, Harbour Bridge and harbour, and ended with thousands of frustrated motorists cursing the fallout from their efforts.
>
> ('Triathletes reduce city traffic to an Australian crawl', *Sydney Morning Herald*, 11 April 2011, p. 1)

These are the first two sentences of a news story about a triathlon in Sydney, an event that arguably could have been reported in many different ways. In this particular instance, we can see that evaluative language (*wrong, a gridlocked nightmare, imposed themselves on*), references to negative emotions (*frustrated motorists, cursing*) and negative vocabulary (*road closures, fallout*) all emphasize the news value of Negativity. In addition, the use of intensification/quantification (*the world's best, mass road closures, super fit, thousands of*) construes Prominence (of the athletes), Superlativeness and Impact. Thus, this event (the triathlon) has been **made newsworthy** through emphasizing the eliteness of its participants and maximizing negative consequences. There is nothing 'inherently' negative about a triathlon; rather news workers have deployed linguistic resources to make the event more interesting, more newsworthy to their audience (many of whom would commute by car to and from the city). We will now look at further linguistic resources that can be used to this effect.

Word combinations

Certain words are repeatedly combined, or associated with each other to invoke stereotypes or scripts, thus establishing Consonance. For example, Table 3.3 shows the results for a search of words associated with commonly

Table 3.3 Associations with Australia

Search Terms	www.thetimes.co.uk/	www.usatoday.com/
Australia shark	1,869	316
Australia spider	199	317
Australia crocodile	351	56
Australia surfing	358	193
Australia surfer	303	31
Australia drunk	635	69

held beliefs about Australia from two newspaper websites (search results pertain to the whole website, not just news stories).

Most frequent on *The Times* website are associations of Australia with sharks, drinking, surfing and crocodiles, whereas the most frequent associations on the *USA Today* website are with spiders, sharks and surfing. Sharks and surfing seem to be commonly associated with Australia both in the United Kingdom and in the United States, and invoked in mentions of Australia on newspaper websites, arguably drawing on commonly held associations by the audience and construing Consonance. A corpus linguistic investigation of collocations, clusters and concordances (Baker 2006) can help us show the typical associations of words/concepts tied to Consonance.

Metaphor/simile
The terms *metaphor* and *simile* refer to the way one concept is seen in terms of another – either implicitly through metaphor (*a wall of water*) or more explicitly through simile (*like a World War II battle*). News stories can and do make use again and again of common or conventionalized metaphors to construe Consonance. For example, Fairclough (1995) (though not discussing it in terms of news values) notes that a *Sun* article's use of the metaphor of fighting a war in the context of drug trafficking 'links this text *intertextually* to popular media coverage of the drugs issue over a long period, where the representation of the issue as a war . . . is a standard feature of the discourse' (Fairclough 1995: 71, italics in original). Other common practices include the frequent application of 'liquid' (often water) metaphors to the movement of refugees, for example, *the flood of refugees, refugees are streaming home, overflowing refugee camps*, with refugees being 'constructed as a "natural disaster" like a flood, which is difficult to control as it has no sense of its own agency' (Baker 2006: 81). News

texts often address 'an ideal interpreter who is familiar with a particular preconstructed "script" (Montgomery et al. 1989) that is being evoked' (Fairclough 1995: 123). Aside from Consonance, metaphors also function to establish Superlativeness (e.g. describing a flood as *a brown wall of water*), as do certain similes (e.g. *thunderstorms that looked like the apocalypse*).

Story structure

The way a news story is structured, the roles the news actors are construed to play and the events that are said to have happened may fit in with archetypes of stories (e.g. 'hero', 'villain', 'rescue'), thereby construing Consonance: 'When you enjoy a story, you are experiencing an echo, or particular realisation, of other stories you already know (and which give rise to expectations about the one you are experiencing at the time)' (Durant and Lambrou 2009: 34). The structure of news story narratives will be fully discussed in Chapter 4, but again, we can take a step back at this stage to briefly consider another example.

> **Thirsty foreigners soak up scarce water rights**
>
> International investors are circling Australia's water market, looking to snap up hundreds of millions of dollars worth of our most precious national resource, with almost no government limit on how much they can buy.
>
> ('Thirsty foreigners soak up scarce water rights', *Sydney Morning Herald*, 4–5 September 2010, p. 1)

In this extract we can very clearly see how an at first glance 'boring' event concerning water rights has been made newsworthy through a juxtaposition of 'Australians' (*Australia's, our*) with 'foreigners' (*thirsty foreigners, international investors*). These 'foreigners' are associated with a predator metaphor (sharks circle) and represented as the agents of negative actions (*soak up scarce water rights, circling Australia's water market, looking to snap up our most precious national resource*) with Australia and its water rights/market being the victim. A predator–victim construal of the narrative suggests itself here, which is arguably in line with many people's negative assumptions about foreign investment in a country's natural resources and ties in with a commonly used narrative about threats from the outside. Intensification/quantification (*hundreds of millions of dollars, most precious, no government limit*) further heightens the inherent danger in these 'circling thirsty foreigners' but also evaluates the Australian government negatively (because they have set no limit). Thus, news workers have again deployed linguistic resources carefully to make an event interesting and newsworthy through Negativity and Superlativeness. Let us consider resources for other news values now.

References to time and place

References to time and place establish Timeliness and Proximity usually through adverbs (*yesterday*, *currently*), nominal groups/phrases (*this week, this year, last week, last night, the weekend's, Wellington researchers, Canadian soldiers, the wind-swept shores of Lake Ontario, the National Stadium, their home in Washington, a Baltimore county democrat*) or prepositional phrases (*near the Royal Albert Hall in central London; at Eden Park; in London's Leicester Square; in parts of the country; in Connact, Ulster and Leinster; at Arlington National Cemetery*) realizing adverbials/circumstances of time and place. Timeliness can also be construed through verb tense (and aspect) – past, present and future. Regarding the latter, references to future events have been said to fulfil two functions: to increase timeliness and to place something on the news agenda (Jaworski et al. 2003: 64).

References to the nation/community

Related to references to time and place are references that quite explicitly address local or national communities. In this way, the relevance of the event for this community (Proximity) is established. For instance, in the context of reporting a local disaster, a quote may in fact tie this to the national context, thereby establishing a larger community and a higher level of relevance: *The Prime Minister warned **the nation** it must brace for more deaths*. We can also find phrases such as *Local veterans tell us their story* where the adjective *local* construes Proximity for a specific community.

First-person plural pronouns

Using first-person plural pronouns (*we*, *our*, etc.) establishes Proximity both culturally and geographically, but only if the pronoun includes the audience (as in the water rights story above: ***our** most precious national resource*). For example, a quote by an eyewitness that refers to the actions that he and a group of others undertook to save others ('**We** *went into the waters to try to find a safe way to get to them*') does not construe Proximity, but a quote by a politician who refers to the way an event affects not just her but the whole community or even nation ('*It might be breaking **our** hearts at the moment, but it will not break **our** will*') does.

Role labels

Role labels are used to describe the roles, titles or professions of people. The Prominence of news actors and sources, including their professional role, title and affiliation is usually construed through descriptive noun phrases (for their syntactic structures see Bell 1991, Jucker 1992) such as: *England manager Sven Goran Eriksson; the Tory leader; two Premiership footballers; the Sinn Fein president, Commonwealth Bank CEO Ralph*

Norris; ACCC [Australian Competition and Consumer Commission] *chairman Graeme Samuel*; *Carroll County Circuit Judge Michael M. Galloway*; *former Alaska Gov. Sarah Palin*. Sometimes such noun phrases also include evaluative vocabulary or comparison indicating importance (e.g. **top** *psychologist Dr Peter Kindermann*; *Supt Martin Harding*, **the most senior** *black officer in GMP*).

Quotes from 'ordinary' individuals

Quoting what news actors, more specifically, what 'ordinary' as opposed to 'elite' actors say, construes Personalization, rendering an issue personal as we get to hear their view or how it has impacted them, for example: *But one of his victims, who can only be identified as Deborah, sobbed as she said afterwards: 'My sentence has only just begun.'* Hearing from the 'man or woman on the street' (*vox pop*) means we can relate to the quote more than when 'elite' sources (e.g. the prime minister) speaks and it renders the issue personal. However, when elite speakers comment on the experience of individuals this may well contribute to Personalization. An example of this is New Zealand Prime Minister John Key's reported comment on the 2011 earthquake affecting Christchurch: *'"People are just sitting on the side of the road, their heads in their hands. This is a community that is absolutely in agony," Key said.'* Here Key's quote clearly construes Personalization by referring to people's and the community's emotional reactions (see 'References to emotion' above).

References to individuals

References to individuals and their experiences can construe Personalization, framing a bigger issue with a personal slant. For example, a story on airfares and the air industry in the *Miami Herald* starts with references to individuals and their story:

> In the 10 years they have been together, Charissa Benjamin and her Serbian husband have always flown from their home in Washington to spend the winter holidays in her native Antigua. But with the lowest economy-class fare this year advertised at about $1,500 – more than twice the $700 she paid in 2009 – Benjamin is considering ringing in 2011 with her husband's family in decidedly chillier Belgrade. Flights there cost half as much as those to the Caribbean. ('Passengers face sticker shock as airfares soar', *Miami Herald*, International edition, 10 November 2010, p. 1)

Identifying a specific person by name (e.g. *Charissa Benjamin*) is arguably more personalizing than referring to individuals by a more generic label such as *passengers*. There are various ways in which references to 'ordinary' people can be made, including variations in the use of proper names (e.g. first name, last name, full name, use of titles), the inclusion of social categories (such as age, gender, ethnicity, sexual orientation, religion, etc.), reference to roles (teacher, doctor, victim), kinship relations (husband, mother) or physical characteristics (blonde, tall) (van Leeuwen 2008: 40–5). Frequently such information is provided in a 'quasi-title' (Bell 1991: 196) nominal structure such as *estranged husband Captain Mark Phillips*, or *former colleague Colin Wallace* which apes the titles of elite actors and 'embodies the claim of the ordinary person or the newly elite to news fame' (Bell 1991: 196).

* * *

Before we discuss in further detail the relationship between linguistic devices and news values, Table 3.4 on pp. 55–6 provides a summary of the above-listed devices (see also Table A1.1 in Appendix 1).

As has become apparent, there are manifold linguistic devices that can be used to establish newsworthiness. It is important at this stage to point out that there is no one-to-one relationship between these devices and the news values they construe. First, the same linguistic feature can construe more than one news value. For example, the use of a metaphor such as *the flood of refugees* may construe both Superlativeness (because it increases the amount of refugees) and Consonance (because it is a commonly used metaphor). Frequently, references to the impact of an event concern effects/consequences that are **negative**, and thus construe both Impact and Negativity, and when they are furthermore intensified, they also construe Superlativeness. All three news values are clearly construed in the following reference to the effects of the floods in Queensland, Australia, in early 2011 (through use of negative vocabulary and intensification describing their consequences): *Drivers were washed away in their cars, a house was swept off its foundations, a railway line was suspended in midair and a shipping container ripped up roads as the rushing waters savaged Toowoomba, Lockyer Valley, Grantham and Murphys Creek in just one hour.* In fact, there may be a case for arguing that certain linguistic devices feature so frequently in news discourse because they can simultaneously construe more than one news value and hence contribute significantly to rendering the story newsworthy, and to attracting readers. References to emotion are a case in point with their potential to establish Negativity, Personalization, Novelty, Impact and Superlativeness.

Secondly, when we analyse news discourse for linguistic devices that establish newsworthiness, we should proceed carefully and use a functional approach. Rather than, say, identifying all direct quotes and assigning them to the news value of Personalization, we need to take into consideration the likely function of the direct quote – only if it can reasonably be interpreted as functioning to construe Personalization should it be included in the analysis. To give another example, not all references to time within a story

Table 3.4 Summary of linguistic resources that can be used to construe news values

Linguistic Device	News Value	Examples
Evaluative language	Negativity Prominence Impact Novelty Consonance	**terrible** news, a **tragedy** pop **star**, **celebrity** bad boy a potentially **momentous** day a very **different** sort of disaster legendary, notorious
References to emotion	Negativity Impact Novelty Personalization Superlativeness	distraught, worried, breaking our hearts A terror that **took their breath away** **shocked** residents 'It was pretty bloody **scary**' they were **petrified**
Negative vocabulary	Negativity	killed, deaths, bodies
References to time	Timeliness	The Prime Minister **today** warned, **yesterday's** flash flooding
Verb tense and aspect	Timeliness	rescuers **have been trying** to pluck survivors, it**'s** a tragedy, more **to** come, it **is** testing our emergency resources, residents **have described** the horrific moments when they **faced** a brown wall of water
References to place	Proximity	Queensland, Brisbane, Canberra, **Queensland's** residents
References to the nation/community	Proximity	it will test us as a **community** The Prime Minister warned **the nation** it must brace for more deaths
First-person plural pronouns (inclusive)	Proximity	It might be breaking **our** hearts at the moment, but it will not break **our** will
Intensification and quantification	Superlativeness Impact	a **giant** torrent, a tragedy **of epic** **proportions** the . . . storm . . . dumped 100 mm of rain in his gauge **in just 30 minutes** Power has been cut to **thousands** of Queensland's residents the rushing waters **savaged** Toowoomba
Metaphor	Superlativeness Consonance	an **army** of volunteers, a brown **wall** of water a **flood** of immigrants

Contd.

Table 3.4 Contd.

Linguistic Device	News Value	Examples
Simile	Superlativeness	our Queens Park was **like a raging river**, it was **like a World War II battle**
Role labels	Prominence	The Prime Minister, **Queensland Premier** Anna Bligh, **Professor** Roger Stone
References to effects/ impact on individuals, entities, and so on	Impact	overwhelming volumes of water . . . **wrecking families and their fortunes** flash flood **deluged the town** leaving **scenes of destruction**
Comparison	Novelty Consonance Superlativeness	I've lived in Toowoomba for 20 years and **I've never seen anything like that** **yet another** personal scandal this one has just **maxed out every other flood**
Quotes from 'ordinary' people	Personalization	'Myself, I was almost pulled in by the torrent'
References to individuals	Personalization	Panel-beater Colin McNamara
Repeated word combinations	Consonance	Australia – sharks
Story structure	Consonance	N/A

construe Timeliness, some simply establish the temporal flow within the story (e.g. *after, as, meanwhile*).

Thirdly, the various linguistic devices that construe newsworthiness may not occur throughout a news story but may cluster in specific parts – we will look at this further in Chapter 4, and there are also other ways of attracting and engaging with audiences that are less obviously tied to newsworthiness, for instance, the use of word play (e.g. *People smugglers go fishing for a new ploy*), allusions (*George Michael jailed for drug-driving crash as magistrate finally loses the faith*) or direct questions in headlines (e.g. *But can you afford to plug it in?*) or, on a macro-level the undertaking of newspaper campaigns (Richardson 2007). Again, we will look at some of these linguistic characteristics of news discourse in Chapter 4.

Finally, the systematic analysis of the discursive construal of news values is still in its infancy and there may be additional devices that will be identified as key resources for construing newsworthiness. While research has certainly recognized that 'The language of a news story is . . . adapted to *highlight* its newsworthiness' (Durant and Lambrou 2009: 89, italics in original), there have been few attempts to explicitly link specific devices to news values (with only some comments in, for example, Bell 1991, Bednarek 2006c). This is all the more true with regard to news images and news values, as discussed in the following section.

5 News values and image

As indicated above (see n. 1), very little research has been undertaken on news photography and the contribution it makes to the construal of news values, and the most notable of this research comes from Hall (1981). According to Hall (1981: 231), the news value of the photographic sign is the elaboration of the story in terms of the professional ideology of news, which it achieves through the *connotative force* that is carried in the news photograph. What Hall is suggesting here has been theorized by Barthes (1977: 19) in terms of the denotative and connotative aspects of the photographic image. According to Barthes (1977), images exist on two levels: the first of these is the denotative level, or the goings on or happenings in the image. Denotative meanings are articulated through what is presented in the image in terms of the represented participants, the activities they are engaged in and the circumstances or locations where these activities are taking place. The other level, the connotative, is described as the art or treatment of the image. The photograph, as Barthes puts it, is 'an object that has been worked on, chosen, composed, constructed, treated according to professional, aesthetic or ideological norms' (1977: 19). It is this professional treatment of the image that Hall refers to as contributing to its connotative force and news value. We will explore the contributions that both denotative and connotative meanings make to the construal of news values below.

First, however, we will briefly summarize the research on news values in press photography. Hall suggests that news values in the press photograph include the unexpected, dramatic, recent event concerning a person of high status (1981: 231), while other research on news values in press photography by Craig (1994) has identified the following five news values: reference to elite persons, composition, personalization, negativity and conflict/dramatization. Craig also suggests that while press photographs can and do mostly confirm the newsworthiness of the stories they accompany, they may also perform specific functions, often in opposition to the functions of the news stories (e.g. by diverting and entertaining readers with images of people like themselves, rather than depicting the negativity of the hard news) (1994: 198).

Since we are taking a discursive approach to the construal of news values in both words and images, we will outline here some of the key aspects of news images that can construe news value. However, before we continue, it is important to acknowledge the difficulties in providing consistent image analysis. For example, it is not easy to decode the poses, gestures, facial expressions of image participants or whether a close-up, long shot, or wide angle carries the same meaning every time an image makes use of these compositional tools. A smile can signify happiness, cheek or even guilt and can thus construe both Positivity and Negativity, although a person grimacing in agony can generally be construed as Negativity. Further, a head and shoulders shot of a person may be construed as close and intimate to one reader but may be more distant and social to another. So, while the construal of news values in images might appear straightforward on the surface, it is in fact difficult to assess consistently and varies in relation to the social and cultural differences of the reader/viewer.

Following on from the above, and using our discursive approach to the construal of news values, two considerations come into play: the contextualization of the image participants, so where and with whom they are photographed and how much or how little of this is included in the image frame (the denotative aspects); and technical considerations, including shutter speed (how fast), aperture (how much light), focal length (how much in focus), lens (how distorted/natural/condensed the shot) and angle (how high or low the angle) to name but a few of these (connotative aspects). Some of these key photographic devices that can be tied to the construal of news values are described in the following.

Evaluative elements
We can evaluate image participants as important or having high status by photographing them in the middle of a media scrum with microphones and cameras pointing at them, or surrounded by bodyguards, military or a police escort, thus construing the news value of Prominence. A person photographed or filmed walking along a street flanked by lawyers/barristers could also be evaluated as important/high status, but this may be for negative reasons, if they are the defendant in a high-profile court case, so this could also construe Negativity. Uniforms and official regalia worn or carried by image participants can also indicate status and thus construe Prominence. Technical elements that could also contribute to the positive or negative evaluation of image participants include camera angle. When a photograph is taken from a very low angle (looking up towards the image participants), unequal power relations are said to be enacted between the image participants and the viewer, with the image participants said to be in the more powerful position (see Kress and van Leeuwen 2006 for further examples).[5] This technique is commonly used to photograph politicians or military officials and may construe the news value of Prominence in the image participants.

The opposite is true when the camera angle is very high, photographing the image participants from above, and putting the viewer in a dominant position. Such an angle may construe the news value of Negativity, as it is commonly used in photographs of young offenders or prisoners of war.

Intensification

An image that serializes/repeats information in the image frame (e.g. a line of soldiers bearing arms, rather than focusing on one solider) is a device for intensification and as such can construe Superlativeness. Similarly, photographs depicting the aftermath of natural disasters can be intensified by including many, repeated participants (e.g. several cars piled on top of each other, rather than one damaged car). Such images not only construe Impact, but also Superlativeness.

Comparison

Comparisons are also easily depicted in images by placing elements of differing sizes next to each other, again construing Superlativeness and possibly Novelty (e.g. the tallest (a basketballer) and the shortest (a gymnast) member of the Australian Commonwealth Games team photographed side-by-side). The effect of such comparisons can be further intensified and even exaggerated by manipulating technical elements in the camera: a wide-angle lens combined with a low angle perspective can exaggerate the size difference between two elements, just as a long lens combined with horizontal or high angle can condense and therefore reduce size differences.

References to emotion

Showing news actors' emotional responses in an image can construe a variety of news values, ranging from Negativity (depicting negative emotions) to Personalization (an individual's emotional response especially when combined with the use of a close-up shot), Novelty (depictions of surprise/shock in facial expressions/gestures), Impact (in terms of caused emotions) and Superlativeness (depicting strong emotional responses – very clearly seen in the desperate images of the victims of the Haiti earthquake in 2010).

An image that appears to construe several of the news values mentioned here can be seen in Figure 3.4 on p. 60. This is achieved both in the content (who has been photographed) and compositionally (how they have been captured in the frame). Superlativeness is construed by juxtaposing a single protester in the bottom right-hand corner of the frame against a whole army of riot police which fills the rest of the frame. Negativity is construed not only in this mass of riot police, but is also very clearly construed in the facial expression of the protester. Personalization is also construed in the singling out of this protestor as a representative of South Korean farmers in this protest.

Figure 3.4 An image construing the news values of Superlativeness, Negativity and Personalization ('Going against the grain', *Sydney Morning Herald*, 20 November 2004, p. 16, Fairfax Syndication)

Negative elements

The depiction of negative events (e.g. car accidents, injuries) and their effects (traffic congestion, the detritus of natural/man-made disasters) construes the news value of Negativity and/or Impact. These are, indeed, the most common of depictions in hard news photography, as photographers typically attend the scene of a disaster after it has occurred. Thus, while construing Negativity, this is commonly combined with Impact.

References to time and place

Precise references to place and, in particular, time are less easily depicted in images. Easily recognizable geographical landmarks and architecture (e.g the White House in Washington, the Houses of Parliament in London, the Sydney Opera House) included in a shot may be used to construe Proximity (as may be cultural symbols like flags). Seasons can be depicted through the inclusion of certain typical weather conditions (snow = winter) or flora/fauna (Jacaranda blossom = spring) as well as cultural artefacts (Christmas trees) and may thus construe Timeliness, Proximity and even Consonance.

Role labels

The mere depiction of well-known (and easily recognizable) celebrities and politicians construes Prominence. However, other elites, like academics or police officers may not be so easily recognizable. Thus, the depiction of such actors/sources may be enhanced by photographing them in a particular context, for example, academics are often photographed with bookshelves around them, or a police officer may be photographed in uniform, or with the police station signage in the background.

References to individuals

In a way just including a picture of an individual construes Personalization by rendering an abstract issue more personal, especially when that individual comes to represent an entire event. However, we must be cautious in assessing every picture containing an individual as construing Personalization. As noted above, the professional elite are often quoted in the media, but this does not in itself construe Personalization. In the same way, photographing the elite acting in professional roles does not construe Personalization because it is their professional status (hence Prominence) that is emphasized in such images.

Aesthetic elements

How participants are arranged in the image frame can impact on the balance and aesthetic quality of the image (cf. Chapter 7). A 'balanced' and hence aesthetically pleasing image can construe the event as newsworthy because of its beauty. Aesthetics may thus be considered as an additional news value, at least for images. We will discuss this further in Chapter 7 but also illustrate it with an example in Section 6.

In addition to the devices mentioned above, **moving** images can also exploit other methods of construing news value. Camera shake (that causes images to blur) is rarely tolerated in still images; however, excessive movement and blurring in moving images, combined with camera people moving around, running, ducking to avoid missiles, bullets, debris with the cameras still rolling can certainly convey Negativity and Superlativeness (the extreme danger faced by the camera people). Also, the time-based nature of moving images allows the cameras to capture image sequences that may be able to convey both cause and effect, which can emphasize the consequences of an event and thereby construe Impact.

In all of these ways, then, we can see that images do, in themselves, construe newsworthiness. However, news images never appear in print alone, or without voice-over in television. In newspapers, they are always, at the very least, accompanied by a caption, and there may also be a headline and a full story associated with them. Thus, an image is influenced by the caption and other associated linguistic text and it is important to also examine how the words and images combine (see Chapter 5 for further discussion). For

Figure 3.5 'Bloody end to chase', *Daily Telegraph* (Australia), 15 March 2010, p. 13, image © Newspix/Lindsay Moller

example, while an image may depict a news actor who is not culturally prominent (and so not immediately recognized as 'elite'), the caption can bring out his/her Prominence through language, that is, by naming/ identifying the news actor. Or a voice-over can add further information, for instance as to the exact speed of a rising river while showing footage of the river, how far things (or bodies) were carried by it, and so on.

Sometimes the image may be so newsworthy that it impacts on the language choices made in the text. This can be seen in Figure 3.5, where the image depicts a handcuffed bloodied man surrounded by police officers and being restrained by one of them. The blood is emphasized in the image because it was published in colour, and the profusion of blood on the man's head and face is clearly visible. The caption to the image and the headlines are all typical in identifying the news actor and his current condition as *Hurt: The alleged offender, Bloody, arrested*, his crime (*Alleged thief*), and his capture (*chase, head-on with police car*) with the image caption also locating this incident in space and time (*in Zetland yesterday morning*). The first paragraph of the main story text reads *Bleeding profusely from a head wound, this is the dramatic moment an alleged car thief was arrested after ramming a police car in a desperate bid to get away*. The specific reference here to the main image through the use of *this is the dramatic moment* is unusual, and demonstrates the importance of the image for construing this event as newsworthy. Linguistic resources are also usefully deployed to make this event more interesting and newsworthy (contrast the first paragraph as is with an alternative description such as *An alleged car thief tried to get away from police yesterday but had an accident and was arrested*).

6 Construing news values in discourse

In this section we will draw on the general comments that we have made above on how language and image can potentially construe news values (see also Table A1.1 in Appendix 1 for a summary table of devices in both language and image that have the potential to construe particular news values),[6] and illustrate our discursive approach to news values by commenting on authentic examples from print news discourse. For reasons of scope, we will not discuss each news story exhaustively but rather limit our discussion to a few key points concerning the construal of newsworthiness. This means that we do not discuss all relevant news values in each news story, even though most of them include features that construe more than just one news value. Where we comment only on extracts of the story we have included them in tables (with different layout than in the original) rather than reproducing the story in full.

6.1 Timeliness

> **TIMELINESS – THE RELEVANCE OF THE EVENT IN TERMS OF TIME**
>
> Often construed in news discourse through: references to time, verb tense and aspect; visually through seasonal indicators (e.g. flora, environmental conditions), cultural artefacts (e.g. Easter eggs).

What the story in Table 3.5 on p. 64 clearly shows is how the verbs (*O'Donnell to address D.C. parley, Values Voter Summit hosting Delaware candidate for Senate, Christine O'Donnell will make her Washington debut*) and the reference to the near future through a premodifying nominal phrase/group (*this weekend's*) establish the Timeliness of the reported event. This is also reflected in the caption to the image (*Delaware Republican Senate nominee Christine O'Donnell will address social conservatives in Washington this weekend*), since the image itself does not construe Timeliness. The fact that

Table 3.5 'O'Donnell to address D.C. parley', *Washington Times*, 17 September 2010, p. A3

Headlines and First Paragraph	Image and Caption
O' Donnell to address D.C. parley **Values Voter Summit hosting** **Delaware candidate for Senate** BY RALPH Z. HALLOW THE WASHINGTON TIMES In a surprise move, Christine O'Donnell will make her Washington debut as the new Republican Senate candidate from Delaware at this weekend's Values Voter Summit, the nation's biggest annual gathering of religious and social conservatives.	 Delaware Republican Senate nominee Christine O'Donnell will address social conservatives in Washington this weekend.

O'Donnell is photographed looking at something outside the image frame (and therefore not directly engaging with the viewer) may suggest that she is focused on some other place or time, thus linking it to the Timeliness that dominates the verbal text. This naturally requires analysing the image and verbal text together.

6.2 Proximity

> **PROXIMITY – THE GEOGRAPHICAL AND/OR**
> **CULTURAL NEARNESS OF THE EVENT**
>
> Often construed in news discourse through: references to place, references to the nation/community, first-person plural pronouns; visually in well-known or iconic landmarks, natural features or cultural symbols.

In the text in Figure 3.6 on p. 65, there are geographical references to Mexico via adjectives and proper names (*Mexican, Mexico, Tijuana,* etc.) – a country that is closer to the United States and has more relevance to it than for other countries. At the same time, the real newsworthiness in terms of Proximity is established through reference to the local community and the events in Chicago using adjectives and prepositional phrases (*local community, in Chicago* (2x), *at Pritzker Pavilion, the*

A fiesta for history, the future

As Mexico marks its bicentennial, local community is set to make its mark

By Oscar Avila
TRIBUNE REPORTER

Surely the Mexican government views the news coverage as better when it revolves around a cellist from Monterrey rather than a drug lord from Tijuana.

"It isn't just better. It is fair," argued Manuel Rodriguez Arriaga, Mexico's consul general in Chicago. "Often, the bad news dominates the information and the good realities, the good news, are not the main story."

Mexico is trying to burnish a somewhat tarnished national brand with a bicentennial celebration in Chicago stretching over several months that will peak in a massive bash Wednesday at Pritzker Pavilion featuring ballerinas, mariachis and classi-

cal music.

Community leaders in Chicago are embracing the festivities amid serious challenges facing a population that has become a demographic force through a wave of immigration and, now, a

swelling population of Mexican-Americans younger than 18.

The Mexican community in Illinois appears to be buying homes and becoming U.S. citizens

Please turn to **Page 10**

Dancers perform Sunday in the Mexican Independence Day Parade. A bicentennial party is set for Wednesday. NANCY STONE/TRIBUNE PHOTO

Figure 3.6 'A fiesta for history, the future', *Chicago Tribune*, 13 September 2010, p. 1

Mexican community in Illinois). The story is also interesting because of the reference made to news reporting of Mexico, often revolving around a 'drug lord from Tijuana' – which could be discussed in terms of Consonance. The image of the street parade may also be perceived as construing Proximity since the setting – the buildings in the background – may be recognizable to a resident of Chicago, or at least to a resident of Mexican heritage who may frequent the Authentic Mexican food market in the background.

6.3 Prominence

> **PROMINENCE – THE HIGH STATUS OF THE INDIVIDUALS, ORGANIZATIONS OR NATIONS IN THE EVENT (INCLUDING SOURCES)**
>
> Often construed in news discourse through: evaluative language indicating importance, role labels; visually recognizable key figures, uniforms/officials, regalia, media scrum, professional contexts, low camera angle.

Table 3.6 'George Michael jailed for drug-driving crash', *Guardian*, 15 September 2010, p. 3

Headlines and First Paragraph	Images and Captions	
George Michael jailed for drug-driving crash as magistrate finally loses the faith **Latest brush with the law leads to eight-week term** **Singer took prescription drug and smoked cannabis**		George Michael arrives at court in London before being sentenced after admitting crashing his car while under the influence of drugs. Main image: Leon Neal/ AFP/Getty
Alexandra Topping George Michael, pop star, heart-throb and celebrity bad boy, is no stranger to having his collar felt by police. But yesterday the singer experienced the full weight of the law as he was sentenced to eight weeks in prison after he admitted crashing his car under the influence of cannabis.		George Michael arrives at court yesterday
		Top right, damage caused to the shop by the singer's car

The Prominence of the news actor around whom the story in Table 3.6 revolves (George Michael) is established both by the use of proper names and role labels in the headlines, caption and story (*George Michael, Singer, the singer*) but also by more evaluative noun phrases: *pop star, heart-throb and celebrity bad boy*. Two images of George Michael (one mid-length shot on the front page and one with an escort on page 3) naturally construe Prominence as the singer is recognizable in both images. However, the prominent news value in all of the images in this story is Negativity. This is expressed through body language and facial expression (Michael does not appear to be posing for the camera, waving or smiling, as one would expect a celebrity to do at a promotional event), and also through the contextualization of Michael. In the first image, a police officer wearing protective armour is visible (though not in focus) in the background, and in the second image, Michael is closely flanked by a man in a suit (possibly a police officer or a solicitor) with a stern face, while construction workers (not fans) look on in the background. The third image of a damaged wall also construes Negativity.

6.4 Consonance

> **CONSONANCE – THE STEREOTYPICAL ASPECTS OF AN EVENT**
>
> Often construed in news discourse through: evaluative language indicating expectedness, repeated word combinations, conventionalized metaphors, story structure, comparison; visual representations that fit with the stereotypical imagery of an event/person.

ITALY

Berlusconi's pep talk to the gold diggers of the world

BY VICTOR SIMPSON ROME

Italian Premier Silvio Berlusconi says young women should follow the money when looking for a partner, noting that women seem to like him and "I'm loaded."

Mr. Berlusconi, who was embroiled in a sex scandal last year and is known for his gaffes, also raised eyebrows with a joke about Hitler's followers urging him to return to power.

The billionaire businessman appeared at a convention Sunday of the youth wing of his People of Freedom party. When questioned by one of his Cabinet ministers – a woman – he joked about marriages of convenience, saying women were lining up for him because "I'm a nice guy" and "I'm loaded."

He also recalled a much-criticized TV interview he once gave, when "I said to a girl to look for a wealthy boyfriend. This suggestion is not unrealistic."

He also said women favor older men, thinking that 'he's old. He dies and I inherit."

The 73-year-old Mr. Berlusconi was engulfed in a sex scandal last year centering on his purported dalliances with young women, including an escort. Mr. Berlusconi's wife, Veronica Lario, said last year she was seeking a divorce. They are now separated.

The media baron has said he is "no saint" but denied ever paying for sex.

In Italy, a divorce can only be sought after three years of separation. Media reports this summer suggested that Mr. Berlusconi's wife has rejected his early proposals for a financial settlement.

Mr. Berlusconi, who says prosecutors have led corruption investigations against him because they are left-wing, also appeared to be poking fun at himself when commenting on the loss of his AC Milan soccer team on Saturday.

He contended the referee robbed the team of three goals and that Milan often gets "leftist referees."

Associated Press

Figure 3.7 'Berlusconi's pep talk to the gold diggers of the world', *Globe and Mail*, 14 September 2010, p. A2. Used with permission of the Associated Press

The story in Figure 3.7 centres on Berlusconi, arguably construing Consonance by focusing on his quotes about women (e.g. *Berlusconi's pep talk to the gold diggers of the world; Italian Premier Silvio Berulsconi says young women should follow the money when looking for a partner noting that women seem to like him* and *'I'm loaded'*), while at the same time including references to and comparisons with past behaviour that make clear that this is very much in line with expectations and with what others think (*was embroiled in a sex scandal last year and is known for his gaffes; a much-criticized TV interview he once gave; was engulfed in a sex scandal last year centring on his purported dalliances with young women*). It is interesting to compare this story with extracts from a background or feature story on Berlusconi in the *Sydney Morning Herald* where evaluations of expectedness (*legendary, notorious, of course*) and comparisons (*once again, yet another, this time/in this case, always a twist to such stories*) similarly construe Consonance in terms of Berlusconi and women (bold face ours):

> The Prime Minister [Berlusconi] himself accuses his opponents of exploiting uncertainty and deliberately pushing the nation to an early election at a time of austerity – rhetoric that sounds particularly hollow from a man whose love of luxury and lavish parties is **legendary**.
>
> AS IF Berlusconi did not have enough on this plate just days before this defining movement for his leadership and legacy, WikiLeaks – and **yet another** personal scandal – erupted, catapulting him and his **notorious** wandering gaze **once again** on to domestic and world front pages.
>   . . .
> However, attractive young women feature **once again** this week, landing Berlusconi in the sights of the national court of auditors, **this time** amid allegations that he allowed the use of nearly €400,000 in state funds to fly a Bulgarian director-actress and a large entourage to the Venice Film Festival.
>
> **Of course as veteran Berlusconi watchers have come to realise, there is always a twist to such stories, and in this case** claims have emerged that Berlusconi also personally ordered that an award be created for the pretty 39-year-old director, Michelle Bonev, who was reported to have received an "action for women" prize for her film, *Goodbye Mama*.
> ('Embattled Berlusconi faces his nemesis', *Sydney Morning Herald*, *News Review*, 11–12 December 2010, pp. 20–1)

It seems clear that there are associations (negative ones, we would argue) of Berlusconi's behaviour, specifically with regard to (young) women, that are played to and at the same time construed or built up in such news discourse.

While the news story in the *Globe and Mail* does not include an image, images can clearly construe Consonance. A good example can be found in the reporting of seasonal events or cultural festivals and, in particular,

Figure 3.8 Online news gallery image sequence, depicting typical scenes at the *Oktoberfest* in Munich, Germany ('Oktoberfest starts in Munich', www.guardian. co.uk, 21 September 2009)

in the reporting of cultural events occurring in other countries, as the typical, indeed stereotypical, is often what is emphasized in such reporting. Figure 3.8 above is an extract from an online news gallery from www. guardian.co.uk and concerns the festivities at the *Oktoberfest* in Munich, Germany. As can be seen in Figure 3.8, beer, breasts and traditional costumes are the focus of attention and a not at all surprising selection from a British news organization (see Chapter 5 for further discussion of this gallery in terms of text–image relations).

6.5 *Negativity*

> **NEGATIVITY – THE NEGATIVE ASPECTS OF AN EVENT**
>
> Often construed in news discourse through: negative evaluative language, references to negative emotions, negative vocabulary; visual representations of negative events and their effects, showing people's negative emotions, high camera angle, camera movement/blurring.

In Figure 3.9 on pp. 70–1 there are actually three articles grouped together under a common heading (*Gang wars*) and headline ('Dissident quizzed over murder of criminal') but we will only comment on one of them ('10 suspects arrested hours after cold-blooded shooting'). In this story, we can easily find many examples of both evaluative language (some attributed to sources) and negative vocabulary that build up a lexical field of criminals, violent crime and victims, and thereby construe Negativity, for instance:

> *Gang wars, murder, murder victim, criminal, cold-blooded shooting, victim, shooting, offences, illegal, gangland criminals, extortion racket, critically injured, crime gang, shot in the head, attacker, injured, attacks, killer, gunman, grim task, dead, cold-blooded assassination, depressing reality, tough anti-gang legislation . . .*

4 NEWS Irish Independent

Gang wars

Dissident quizzed over

10 suspects arrested hours after cold-blooded shooting

Tom Brady and Louise Hogan

Garda forensic investigators at the scene of the shooting in Portmarnock, Co Dublin, yesterday. Right: the burnt-out car found in Temple View Close, Coolock.

Victim a member of crime gang

DUBLIN'S latest murder victim was a member of a notorious crime gang operating on the northside.

Sean Winters did not have a long string of previous convictions but he was described as a significant player. Associates regarded Winters as a "fixer", with a wide range of contacts on the streets.

A key member of the gang up to two years ago was David Lindsay, of Seacliff Drive, Baldoyle. Lindsay had been heavily involved in drug trafficking since the 1990s.

In 1994, he was arrested when he was a passenger in a car being used to ferry cannabis worth almost £500,000 (€635,000).

He faced trial in Dublin's Circuit Criminal Court in 1996 but the charges were dropped. The driver of the car pleaded guilty and was sentenced to 12 years.

He became a key gangland figure but in July 2008 Lindsay (38) and another gang member, Alan Napper (39), also from Baldoyle, disappeared. They were on their way across the border to collect money owed by criminals in the North but were believed to have been set up by an associate.

An investigation indicated the two were murdered in a house in Rathfriland, Co Down. Bloodstains were matched to Lindsay.

The gang began to split after their disappearance but several members were involved in violent incidents in the following year.

One man was shot in the leg in north Co Dublin in January last year, while in March 2009 David 'Fred' Lynch was shot dead in Coolock, followed by a 'hit' on John 'BJ' Clarke in Artane the following July.

Last December, five men with links to the gang were arrested during a house raid. Gardai seized a Glock handgun and believed their action foiled another shooting. But they were released without charge.

Since then, the area where the gang was based has been quiet. But the shooting of Winters suggests the gang has become embroiled in a new row.

TOM BRADY

Figure 3.9 'Dissident quizzed over murder of criminal', *Irish Independent*, 14 September 2010, pp. 4–5

R

Gang wars

murder of criminal

THE 15 GANG DEATHS THIS YEAR

Stab victim in intensive care after frenzied city attack

Olivia Kelleher

A MAN who suffered stab wounds to his head, back, stomach and legs was in a critical but stable condition at a hospital last night after undergoing emergency surgery.

The 24-year-old victim received multiple knife wounds to his body in the frenzied attack.

He was found face down and unconscious by gardaí who received a call to go to an apartment in the Heritage House complex in Cathedral Road, Cork city, at 3.30pm on Sunday.

The victim, who has not been named, was rushed by ambulance to Cork University Hospital (CUH), where the emergency medical team worked through the early hours of Monday to stabilise his condition.

He received multiple blood transfusions and remained in intensive care at CUH last night.

It is thought the stabbing occurred when an argument between the victim and another man spiralled out of control. Gardaí arrested a 25-year-old man at the scene. He was taken to Gurranabraher garda station for questioning, and later released without charge. A file is being prepared for the Director of Public Prosecutions.

Rare

Locals have expressed shock at the brutality of the incident.

Sinn Féin councillor Thomas Gould, who lives near the apartment complex, said he was taken aback by the severity of the attack. "People are shocked. This would be a rare occurrence, if ever, up here. Cathedral Road is a beautiful place and it is a sign of the times when something like this is happening here," he said.

"Hopefully, he will recover. It was a horrific attack on a young man. There needs to be urgent action taken on crime."

The area where the stabbing occurred was cordoned off and garda technical experts forensically examined the scene yesterday morning.

The incident occurred at an old school, which had been converted into apartments over the past few years.

The injured person and the man in custody are both from the north side of Cork city. The motive for the attack was unknown last night.

The apartment is located at the front of the complex, close to the road, so gardaí believe members of the public out walking between 3pm and 3.30pm on Sunday may have heard the disturbance.

Gardaí have appealed to locals who may have heard a disturbance or noise in or around the apartments to contact Gurranabraher garda station on 021-4946200.

'I heard two shots then screeching tyres'

Louise Hogan

A SHOCKED resident yesterday gave a dramatic account of the minutes leading up to the shooting dead of a man in an upmarket area of north Co Dublin.

The peaceful idyll of the commuter suburb of Portmarnock was shattered at precisely 10.06pm on Sunday night when the man was shot and killed.

The incident took place near a security gate leading into the well-kept complex 'The Links' near Portmarnock village.

It was raised voices that first alerted one resident that something untoward was happening only yards from the door of his apartment just a couple of hundred yards from Portmarnock DART Station.

In such a quiet neighbourhood, the raised voices were enough to attract attention. The young man looked out the window and spotted a silver car parked in the driveway of the complex.

The resident described hearing a sound "like a car backfiring, a small pop".

"One guy was shouting something, it sounded like he shouted something at the guy in the car. I heard the word shot so I kind of got a bag of a shock," he said.

"There was one shot and he shouted something involving the word shot, then there was a ...ond shot."

He said there were more raised voices, before the car doors slammed and the tyres screeched as the silver-coloured saloon took off in the direction of Portmarnock village.

"It was 10.06pm, I sent a message at that time on the internet so I have a log of the time," he said.

Body

A car driving along the road at the time pulled in, while a passing cyclist also stopped.

"I couldn't see until I went out and saw there was a body on the ground," he said.

He said the man was leaning against the wall and appeared to have struggled a short distance up the footpath from where the shooting took place.

"I heard he was shot in the head from when the doctor showed up," he said. "I didn't see it happen but I heard it."

Another resident in an adjacent development described hearing a number of shots wailing at around 10.30pm as different emergency services raced to the scene.

"We heard three or four different sirens wailing which shattered the silence," he said.

Just a few miles away in Teignmouth View Close, Coolock, the burnt-out wreck of a silver 98 Opel-registered Volkswagen Passat was attracting attention.

One man, who lived around 15 yards from the shell of the car, said he heard an "explosion" at around midnight on Sunday. He had noticed the car parked near his home two or three days earlier.

A woman, who lives in the estate in Clarehall, said she drove in at around 10.30pm on Sunday night and the silver Passat was not in the place where it had been parked for the previous few days.

Then she looked out at around 10.45pm and spotted two men in a small white van slowing down and checking out the vehicles on the street.

She said a while later they heard an explosion and they spotted the car was engulfed in flames.

"There were five or six explosions, every neighbour rang the gardaí," she said, describing havoc in the housing estate as neighbours screamed in panic.

Figure 3.9 *Continued*

Focusing on the main picture on page 4, Negativity is construed in the tape used to cordon off the area (restricting access) and the blue covering (shielding onlookers from the scene). This is also a very long shot, taken with a powerful zoom lens, suggesting that the event is so serious/grave that even the media cannot get access. The white suited figures of the forensic team are commonly seen at crime scenes, adding to the construal of Negativity.

6.6 Impact

IMPACT – THE EFFECTS OR CONSEQUENCES OF AN EVENT

Often construed in news discourse through: evaluative language and intensification/quantification relating to the impact of an event, references to emotions caused by an event, references to effects/impact on individuals, entities, and so on; visually showing the after-effects of events, sequences of images conveying cause–effect relations.

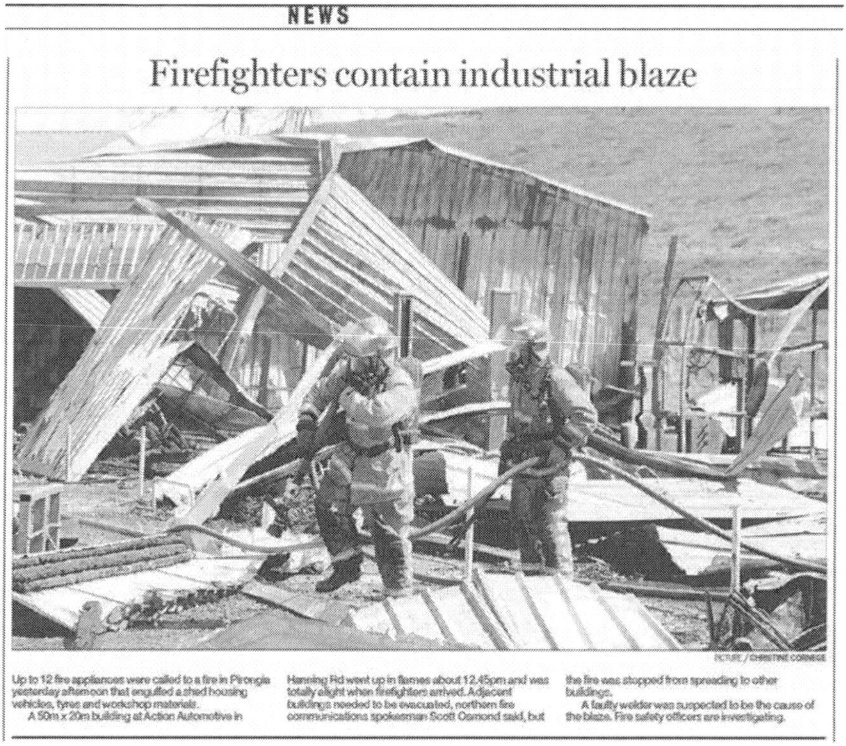

NEWS

Firefighters contain industrial blaze

PICTURE / CHRISTINE CORNEGE

Up to 12 fire appliances were called to a fire in Pirongia yesterday afternoon that engulfed a shed housing vehicles, tyres and workshop materials.
A 50m x 20m building at Action Automotive in

Hanning Rd went up in flames about 12.45pm and was totally alight when firefighters arrived. Adjacent buildings needed to be evacuated, northern fire communications spokesman Scott Osmond said, but

the fire was stopped from spreading to other buildings.
A faulty welder was suspected to be the cause of the blaze. Fire safety officers are investigating.

Figure 3.10 'Firefighters contain industrial blaze', *New Zealand Herald*, 13 October 2010, p. A6

News stories frequently focus on the impact of events. In the story represented in Figure 3.10 on p. 72 this is construed through intensification/ quantification as well as references focusing on the effects of the fire: for example, *industrial blaze, up to 12 fire appliances, engulfed, totally alight, adjacent buildings needed to be evacuated*. The photograph of the damaged shed is typical of aftermath images and clearly construes the news value of Impact. Professional photographers are rarely in a position to photograph the causes of accidents, explosions, disasters, but do frequently capture the consequences. This is transitioning though, with more and more people carrying mobile devices that can capture images of sufficient quality. News organizations do publish such images of the unfolding of major incidents, both natural and man-made, which are captured by eyewitnesses, or even by the victims themselves.

An example of how environmental stories are frequently construed in terms of Impact (cf. also Bednarek and Caple 2010) comes from the front page of the popular newspaper *New York Post* (Figure 3.11).

Figure 3.11 'Wild', *New York Post*, 17 September 2010, p. 1

Here again intensifications of force and evaluative language (*savage,
hammers, wild, killer storm, tore, 100-mph winds, jungle*) as well as more
descriptive references to the storm's negative effects (*toppled trees*) focus on
the impact of the environmental event. The typography and exclamation
mark reinforces the intensification of the **wild** storm and its impact. News
values of Impact (and Superlativeness) are thus construed through the
language. Damage to property (cars) is clearly depicted in the image in
Figure 3.11 thus construing Impact, and similar to the verbal text, the image
also construes Superlativeness, as this is not only damage to one car but
three (and possibly more beyond the frame). This is enhanced technically
through the use of a wide angle lens that fills the frame with branches and
leaves. In fact, the story from the *New York Post* suggests that the use of
devices that establish the news value of Superlativeness may be especially
significant in the popular press. Conboy (2006: 16) notes the frequent use
of extremes, exaggeration and hyperbole in such newspapers, all of which
may be used to construe Superlativeness.

6.7 Novelty/deviance/unusuality/rarity/surprise

NOVELTY – THE UNEXPECTED ASPECTS OF AN EVENT

Often construed in news discourse through: evaluative language indicating
unexpectedness, comparison, references to surprise/expectations; visually
in the juxtaposition of elements within the frame to create stark contrast,
the depiction of shock/surprise in the facial expression of participants.

The story in Table 3.7 (on p. 75) construes Novelty in a variety of ways: the
headline simply describes what audiences would view as an unusual event,
without explicitly evaluating it as such (but construing Personalization by
using what seems to be a direct quote). Negations, evaluative adjectives
and intensification also construe this unexpectedness, including: *doesn't
speak French. It **just** sounds as if she does; has **only** ever been to France
twice and hasn't spoken the language since taking her O-levels, **rare**
condition, **strange**, so **rare that** there are **just** 60 recorded cases.* However,
the portrait image of the news actor in this story does not construe Novelty.
Indeed, it is difficult to match this image with any news values other than
Personalization.

But in the example in Figure 3.12 (on p. 75), the news value of Novelty is
clearly construed through the depiction of a naked (save his trilby) farmer at
the wheel of a tractor and a naked vet posing with a turkey – all in a good
cause!

Table 3.7 'I went to bed with a migraine and woke up with a French accent', *Daily Mail*, 15 September 2010, p. 19

Headline and First Paragraphs	Image and Caption
I went to bed with a migraine and woke up with a French accent *By Luke Salkeld* [email provided] KAY Russell doesn't speak French. It just sounds as if she does. As soon as she opens her mouth the 49-year-old grandmother gives the impression she grew up on the other side of the Channel. She has foreign accent syndrome, a rare condition thought to have been caused by damage to her brain after a series of migraines.	 Kay Russell: 'You lose your identity' [cartoon omitted]

Mrs Russell, who lives in Gloucestershire, went to bed one day with a particularly painful headache and woke to find her speech was 'strange and slurred'.

An MRI scan ordered by a hospital neurologist indicated the headache had inflicted a mild form of brain damage. She was then diagnosed with FAS – a condition so rare that there are just 60 recorded cases worldwide.

Yesterday Mrs Russell, who has only ever been to France twice and hasn't spoken the language since taking her O-levels, said having no control over speaking so differently had destroyed her self-confidence.

Figure 3.12 'Calendar boys Businessmen bare all for charity', *Irish Independent*, 11 October 2010, p. 14

6.8 Superlativeness

SUPERLATIVENESS – THE MAXIMIZED OR INTENSIFIED ASPECTS OF AN EVENT

Often construed in news discourse through: intensification/quantification, comparison, references to strong emotions, metaphor, simile; visually construed through the repetition of elements in the frame, or extreme emotions in participants, use of wide-angle lens.

Consider this extract from a story in *USA Today*:

Record rise in U.S. uninsured: 50.7 M
Numbers reignite debate over health care law
By Richard Wolf USA TODAY

[direct quote preceding main story text omitted]

A record rise in the number of people without health insurance across the nation is fuelling renewed debate over a health care law that could to [*sic*] work better at boosting coverage than controlling costs.

More than 50 million people were uninsured last year, almost one in six U.S. residents, the Census Bureau reported Thursday. The percentage with private insurance was the lowest since the government began keeping data in 1987.

The reasons for the rise to 50.7 million, or 16.7%, from 46.3 million uninsured, or 15.4%, were many: . . .

('Record rise in U.S. uninsured: 50.7 M', *USA Today*, 17 September 2010, p. A8)

This extract features a variety of expressions that construe Superlativeness at the beginning of the article, mainly intensification/quantification and comparison: *record rise*; *more than 50 million people*; *almost one in six U.S. residents*; *the lowest since the government began keeping data*; *the rise to 50.7 million*.

Images can construe Superlativeness through the depiction of excessive emotion. In the example in Figure 3.13, the image participant is completely overwhelmed at the news of the imminent release of loved ones from the Chilean mine disaster in October 2010. The sense of movement and use of a wide-angle lens contribute to the intensification of this emotional reaction.

world**news**

Irish Independent
Monday 11 October 2010

R

Miners vie to be last man out as rescue tests begin

Frank Bajak
in San Jose

AFTER more than two months trapped deep in a Chilean mine, 33 miners were tantalisingly close to rescue last night.

Sources at the mine said they were so giddy with confidence of success they were arguing over who would be the last one out.

The first tests of the three rescue capsules built by Chilean naval engineers will likely begin early on Wednesday, with the rescue to begin later that day and last about 48 hours, said Mining Minister Laurence Golborne.

A day after drillers broke through to where the miners have been abiding, officials began detailed monitoring of their health and sweating every detail of the half-mile ascent that is expected to last about 20 minutes for each man.

"Today we sent down special equipment to measure their heart rate, their respiration rate and skin temperature," said Jaime Manalich, Chile's health minister.

He said officials were concerned about hypertension because of the speed with which the miners will ascend the nearly half mile to the surface.

Another concern is blood clotting. To counteract it, the miners began taking 100 milligrams each of aspirin yesterday and will do so until the rescue, he said. They'll also put on compression socks and will be on a special high-calorie liquid prepared and donated by the US National Aeronautics and Space Administration for the final six hours before being removed.

That's to prevent them from becoming nauseous as the rescue capsule is expected to rotate 360 degrees when it makes 10-12 times through curves in the 96-inch-diameter escape hole on its way up.

And officials' biggest worry? "Panic attacks," said Mr Manalich.

A relative of one of the 33 miners trapped underground since August 5 reacts to the good news of their imminent escape at San Jose mine near Copiapo city. REUTERS/IVAN ALVARADO

"This is the first time in many weeks that the miners are going to be completely alone," he added.

A small video camera will be placed in the escape capsule so each miner's face can be watched as he ascends. Each will also have a mask attached to an oxygen tank affixed to their face and two-way voice communication.

A list has been drawn up suggesting the order in which the 33 miners should be rescued, and Mr Manalich said the otherwise co-operative miners were squabbling about it. "They were fighting with us yesterday because everyone wanted to be at the end of the line, not the beginning," he said. "It's a question of solidarity."

"I think they're more excited than scared or nervous," said Brandon Fisher, president of Center Rock Inc, the Pennsylvania company whose hammer-style drill heads created the hole. "That first guy up might be a little nervous, though."

The completion of the escape shaft on Saturday morning caused bedlam in the tent city known as 'Camp Hope', where the miners' relatives had held vigil for an agonising 66 days since a cave-in sealed off the gold and copper mine on August 5.

The drill that punctured through worked constantly for 28 days with a few breaks when some of its hammers fractured.

When it broke through on Saturday, the rescuers chanted, danced and sprayed champagne so excitedly that some of their hard hats tumbled off.

The escape capsules, equipped with spring-loaded wheels that will press against the hole's walls, will be lowered into the hole via a winch and the trapped miners will be brought up one by one. The completion of the escape shaft thrilled Chileans, who have come to see the rescue drama as a test of the nation's character and pride.

"What began as a potential tragedy is becoming a verified blessing," President Sebastian Pinera said in Santiago. "When we Chileans set aside our legitimate differences and unify in a grand and noble cause, we are capable of great things."

Group ensures equal share in story goldmine

THE 33 trapped Chilean miners have moved to stop any individual from profiting at the expense of the group, drawing up a contract to share the proceeds from the story of their ordeal.

The men have called in a lawyer to draw up the contract, ensuring they will equally profit from the lucrative media deals they expect for their two-month survival – in the hope that they never have to work again.

"We have received offers to be filmed and interviewed by national television," miner Yonni Barrios (50) wrote in a letter sent up to the surface.

"But we didn't accept because we are going to form a foundation, and all our daily experiences during our time down here will go into a book and other projects." (© Daily Telegraph, London)

FIONA GOVIN

Figure 3.13 'Miners vie to be last man out as rescue tests begin', *Irish Independent*, 11 October 2010, p. 28

6.9 *Personalization*

PERSONALIZATION – THE PERSONAL OR HUMAN INTEREST
ASPECTS OF AN EVENT

Often construed in news discourse through: references to emotion, quotes
from 'ordinary' people, references to individuals; visually by singling out one
participant in the frame, depicting emotions, close-up shot.

The construal of Personalization is strong in Figure 3.14 on p. 79 from the
Ottawa Sun. This is clearly visible in the use of an extreme close-up shot of
the victim on the front page, with the black background bleeding into both
the image and the words. The headline points to Personalization in that
Tragic Case of Elder Abuse together with the subheadline (*EXCLUSIVE:
Dorothy Linklater, 92, lost her life savings, her home and her dignity*)
and the image construe this news story as one about a particular case and
person. The story continues on page 3 with the heading *Nieces Save Aunt
from Fraudster* and the subheading *92-year-old's life savings frittered away
by 'caregiver'*, continuing the construal in terms of personal relationships
(*Nieces, Aunt*) and the focus on the *92-year-old* and her exploitation by the
fraudster, with the story starting with an attribution of Dorothy Linklater's
wishes and plans and how they were thwarted:

> Dorothy Linklater never wanted to be a burden on her family. And at 92
> she hadn't planned to come back to Ottawa. She left her hometown in
> the 1950s for southern Ontario, and after her husband died 30 years ago
> that's where she intended to live out her final days. The pair never had
> children of their own. But those plans have been dashed at the hands of
> a live-in caregiver who fleeced Linklater of her entire life savings, home
> and dignity.

The news actor is also identified both through proper names (*Dorothy
Linklater, Linklater*), reference to age (*92, 92-year-old's, at 92*), and
reference to kinship relations (*aunt, the pair*). This is reinforced in the
image, where the intimate moment of one person holding and kissing
the other is captured. Fowler notes that '[t]he concreteness of individual
reference is heightened, especially in the tabloids, by supplying personal
details such as age, residence, job and personal appearance – with a liberal
use of photographs' (Fowler 1991: 92). The story also includes direct
quotes from one of the nieces and the aunt herself as well as references to
their emotions (*shocking, tears welled up in her eyes, it crushed my heart*).
In fact, this is an example where Personalization is not about showing

Figure 3.14 'Tragic case of elder abuse', *Ottawa Sun*, 12 November 2010, pp. 1, 3

how an abstract issue affects individuals, but rather a news story about one person's negative experience (with a strong construal of Negativity as well as Personalization). Indeed, Personalization has been said to be 'most striking in the popular press', working 'to promote straightforward feelings of identification, empathy or disapproval' (Fowler 1991: 15) and from a critical perspective to avoid a discussion of more complex underlying socio-economic factors (Fowler 1991: 16).

6.10 Aesthetics

Sometimes, an event is construed as beautiful or aesthetically noteworthy and therefore newsworthy, as in the story on 'Deer' in Figure 3.15 on p. 81 – an example of a stand-alone (also theorized as an image-nuclear news story (Caple 2008a, 2008b, 2009b)). The aesthetic quality of the image, along with the ability to make a pun between the headline and the image (see Chapter 4 on headlinese) make this event newsworthy and the story worthy of a position on the front page. In fact the 'news story' is not essentially about the deer pictured, rather it is about the cold snap gripping Britain at that time, which is alluded to in the caption and then reported on in full on page 4. Thus, we argue that an event can be construed as newsworthy by construing it as aesthetically significant (e.g. beautiful) and therefore of news value. This is in contrast to language, where aesthetic aspects of language as they occur in poems, for instance, are not in line with the conventions of the hard news story – compare Chapter 4. (This may be different with more 'narrative', 'feature' or 'soft' news, where there is more freedom in terms of linguistic style (Bell 1991: 14) and where we might find some 'aesthetic' uses of language.)

In this chapter, we have taken a discursive approach to news values and have introduced a framework that allows for analysis of how these are construed in both words and images. From this perspective, news values are not aspects of events or internalized beliefs; they are values that are established by language and image in use. Such a discursive perspective allows researchers to systematically examine how particular events are construed as newsworthy, what values are emphasized in news stories, and how language and image establish events as more or less newsworthy. There is great potential here for comparative studies. It is only through a systematic analysis of both modalities – language and image – and how they contribute to the construction of news discourse that we can gain a fuller understanding of how events are retold and made 'newsworthy'. Then we may begin to also understand the motivations behind maximizing news value, which can include the journalist's (and photographer's) desire for a front page story, or commercial functions such as selling more copies (increasing circulation) or attracting particular kinds of audience that can be sold to advertisers (cf. Chapter 2).

Free tomorrow
Luxury biscuits at Waitrose
Plus
80-page two-week Christmas TV guide
The Daily Telegraph
NEWSPAPER OF THE YEAR
Winter fuel rationing on way
Oh deer, it's turned out cold again
7m home owners at risk from rate rises, says Bank of England
Billions spent on extra NHS wages but productivity falls
Blake Edwards dies, aged 88
English pay £6,000 to study in Scotland
MIKIMOTO
PETER OBORNE
TREMLETT LEADS CHARGE

Figure 3.15 'Oh deer, it's turned out cold again', *Daily Telegraph* (UK), 17 December 2010, p. 1

Directions for further reading

Bednarek, M. (2006), *Evaluation in Media Discourse: Analysis of a Newspaper Corpus*. London/New York: Continuum. A book-length investigation of evaluative language and its functions (including news values) in the British popular and quality press.

Bell, A. (1991), *The Language of News Media*. Oxford: Blackwell. Includes a discussion of copy editing and linguistic characteristics of news stories in terms of news values.

Brighton, P. and Foy, D. (2007), *News Values*. London: Sage. Applies the concept of news values to the online environment.

Craig, G. (1994), 'Press photographs and news values', *Australian Studies in Journalism*, 3, 182–200. Applies news values to press photography.

Galtung, J. and Ruge, M. H. (1965), 'The structure of foreign news', *Journal of Peace Research*, 2 (1) 64–91. The classic study of news values, focusing on Scandinavian news.

Hall, S. (1981), 'The determinations of news photographs', in S. Cohen and J. Young (eds), *The Manufacture of News. Deviance, Social Problems and the Mass Media*. London: Sage, pp. 226–43. The classic study of news values in press photography.

Niblock, S. and Machin, D. (2007), 'News values for consumer groups: the case of Independent Radio News, London, UK', *Journalism*, 8 (2), 184–204. Addresses the relation between news values, market segmentation and the packaging of commercial radio news bulletins.

Notes

1   Not only do lists of news values differ in the number and kinds of news values recognized, news values have also been grouped differently, for example, depending on whether or not they are culture-free or culture-bound (Galtung and Ruge 1965) and how important or 'core' they are (Conley 1997). More recently, Brighton and Foy (2007) have proposed a new set of news values that reflect recent changes in the news media landscape. However, most of this research does not address press photography (for exceptions see Hall 1981, Craig 1994 and Caple 2009b).

2   Researchers who work with a more 'cognitive' definition of news values also emphasize the role language plays, with news values being said to be 'embedded' in text or shaping text (e.g. Cotter 2010: 67), especially news story structure. Cotter (2010: 95–7) also gives some examples of how news values are construed in story meeting exchanges. Language is also relevant to some of the *news cycle/market factors*. For instance, composition can be signalled through the use of common headings where there are spreads on specific topics such as WikiLeaks and stories grouped under such common headings will also share some common vocabulary, from the same semantic field. In fact, there may even be a case for including composition under our category of news values (rather than a news cycle/market factor) because it can be discursively construed.

3 *Just* has a range of different meanings and can express both intensification (e.g. *just hours after*) and concession (e.g. *He's just a student*). It would not construe Superlativeness in the latter meaning. There are various linguistic classifications for intensification and quantification that provide further detail on relevant linguistic devices (e.g. Hood and Martin 2007).

4 Comparison, intensification and references to emotion could also be included as part of evaluative language or appraisal (Martin and White 2005). Also note that evaluative language has many additional functions apart from construing news value (cf. Hunston and Thompson 2000, Martin and White 2005, Bednarek 2006c). The distinction between evaluative and non-evaluative language is sometimes hard to draw, although there are grammatical tests, for instance, for evaluative adjectives (Halliday and Matthiessen 2004: 319). Compare also the discussion of evaluation in Chapter 6.

5 Other research that has examined evaluative meaning in images includes Economou (2006) and Martin and Rose (2007), although this has not been in relation to the construal of news values.

6 Table A1.1 in Appendix 1 takes as its starting point news values and how they may potentially be construed through language and image; Table 3.4 in this chapter summarizes the potential of linguistic resources only. Depending on research question and focus either one or both can be drawn on.

CHAPTER FOUR

Language in the news

1 Introduction

Chapter 3 has already shown the significance of language in construing newsworthiness, but in fact language is involved in all stages of the news process: from the input materials that are gathered, used and incorporated (Chapter 2) to the conceptualization, construction and subsequent assessment of the news story. Language is also involved in the skills that the producers of news must possess (interviewing, news writing, copy editing) and in valued objectives for news writing, which include balance, objectivity, brevity, clarity, colour, precision and accuracy (Bell 1991, Richardson 2007, Cotter 2010). Such news writing objectives or rules 'are operating factors behind the production of all stories' (Cotter 2010: 171), and should be kept in mind when reading this chapter.

However, our focus here is not so much on these objectives or other factors influencing news writing, but rather on language in the **output** of the news process – the linguistic characteristics of newspaper writing.[1] Our aim is not to provide a particular framework for analysing language in the news, but rather to 'chart the landscape', so to speak. In this endeavour we focus on contemporary national/metropolitan print news, although we also briefly comment on radio, online and TV news (this is why we group these together in Section 5, rather than say, grouping online with print). Hence, our objectives for this chapter are to enable readers to understand:

- what linguistic features are typical of newspaper writing
- what the functions are of linguistic features in news discourse
- what variation exists in newspaper writing.

We start the chapter by looking at newspaper writing as a type of language, which is different from other types of language such as conversation or academic writing. We then go on to describe the structure of print news stories as well as what print news headlines look like, before commenting on online, radio and TV news.

2 News discourse as a type of language

The focus of Section 2 is on outlining key lexical and syntactic features, as well as other linguistic characteristics that distinguish news discourse from other varieties or types of language.

2.1 Lexical and syntactic features

Corpus linguistic analysis (cf. Chapter 1) has found a number of lexical and syntactic features characteristic of 'newspaper writing', distinguishing it from academic writing and conversation (Biber and Conrad 2009: 116–17). A study by Bednarek (2008a), comparing a corpus comprising more than 2.5 million words of British tabloid and broadsheet news reports against the British National Corpus (a 100 million word corpus of spoken and written British English) also found particular key words. The syntactic and lexical features that Biber and Conrad (2009) and Bednarek (2008a) found can be related to the communicative context or situational characteristics of news discourse. Drawing on their research, we will in turn discuss nouns and noun phrases, verbs, and adverbials.

Nouns and noun phrases

Regarding nouns, the above-mentioned research (and see further Bell 1991, Jucker 1992) suggests that they are very common in newspaper writing, and that they frequently act as premodifiers of other nouns (e.g. *earthquake cost*). Nominalizations (e.g. *moves toward closer military cooperation*), attributive adjectives that premodify nouns (e.g. *wealthy supporters*) and prepositional phrases following nouns (e.g. *his surrender **to British police over a Swedish sex-crimes warrant***) are also common. The key nouns and adjectives that dominate UK news discourse refer to cities, countries and people, and are part of commercial, sports or entertainment discourse (see Table 4.1) reflecting the different sections of newspapers as well as the different preoccupations of the tabloid and broadsheet press. In contrast, personal pronouns are uncommon, although they occur slightly more often in newspaper writing than in academic writing.

Table 4.1 Key nouns and adjectives in UK news discourse

Key Nouns and Adjectives	Examples
'cities, countries, people'	*Britain, Germany, American, Europe, west, east, David, John, London, Hong Kong*
'commercial discourse'	*pound, cent, million, market, shares, sales*
'sports discourse'	*season, team, league, players, club, game, champion*
'entertainment discourse'	*TV, star*

To illustrate, let us examine the first two paragraphs from a news story in the *Baltimore Sun*:

No bidders for slots license at Rocky Gap

Second attempt to attract developer for casino in W. Md. comes up empty

By Nicole Fuller

The Baltimore Sun

Tuesday's deadline for bids on a license to operate a slots parlor at the state-financed Rocky Gap Lodge in Western Maryland came and went without a single submission – the second time that gambling at the struggling resort has failed to draw a qualified proposal.

Donald C. Fry, chairman of the state Video Lottery Facility Location Commission, which is tasked with choosing proposals and awarding licenses for the state's five approved slots sites, said about four companies expressed interest when the bidding process on the Rocky Gap site began late this summer, but by the afternoon deadline, no one had submitted a proposal or the required $100,000 deposit.

('No bidders for slots license at Rocky Gap', *Baltimore Sun*, 10 November 2010, p. 3)

This extract demonstrates the preponderance of noun phrases in newspaper writing, with a multitude present in the headline and beginning of the story. We can see that such noun phrases:

- are used to indicate time (e.g. *Tuesday's deadline*; *this summer*; *the afternoon deadline*; *the second time*) and place (e.g. *the state-financed Rock Gap Lodge in Western Maryland*; *at the struggling resort*; *the state's five approved slots sites*; *the Rocky Gap site*)

- function to label news actors and sources (e.g. *no bidders*; *four companies*; *chairman of the state Video Lottery Facility Location Commission*)

- include intensification (e.g. *without a single submission*), evaluation (e.g. *the struggling resort*) and descriptive or background information (e.g. *the state-financed Rocky Gap Lodge*, *the state's five approved slots sites*).

The extract also has several proper nouns referring to relevant places and people (e.g. *Rocky Gap*; *W. Md.*; *Rocky Gap Lodge*; *Western Maryland*; *Donald C. Fry*), but hardly any pronouns (*no one*). As can be seen, the noun phrase, with its possibility of pre- and postmodification allows an adherence to brevity at the same time as allowing the incorporation of various kinds of information. It thereby permits the construal of news values such as Timeliness, Proximity, Negativity, Superlativeness and Prominence (cf. Chapter 3), for example, attracting readers' attention through references to prominent news actors. The noun phrase is also a source for evaluating and labelling news actors and sources. It allows a maximum packaging of meaning in minimum space, which is not just important for the news story as a whole but in particular for headlines (see Section 4). Proper nouns are used to identify the relevant places and news actors/sources participating in the reported events.

Verbs

Turning to verbs, according to Biber and Conrad (2009), modal verbs (*may, can, will, should*, etc.) are uncommon in newspaper writing (slightly less common than in academic prose),[2] but if they do occur, *will/would* are most common. In fact, *will* (along with *has*, *win*) was found by Bednarek (2008a) to be a key verb in UK news discourse. Further, about 15 per cent of all finite verbs occur in the passive (vs 25 per cent in academic prose and only rare occurrences in conversation). Verbs tend to occur in present tense slightly more often than in past tense, although verbs in the past tense are much more frequent than in academic writing and slightly more common than in conversation. Again, let us consider an example from a newspaper, this time from the *Boston Herald*.

Mom claims bagel defense

New Castle, Pa. – The American Civil Liberties Union **is representing** a western Pennsylvania woman who **says** her newborn baby **was seized** by county welfare workers after she **failed** a drug test because she **ate** a poppy seed bagel.

ACLU attorney Sara Rose **said** authorities from Lawrence County Children and Youth Services **came** to Elizabeth Mort's home three days after she **gave** birth at Jameson Hospital in New Castle last month.

A state law **allows** hospitals to give blood tests to protect new-borns from mothers who **may** be abusing drugs.

Rose **said** the hospital and welfare workers **rushed** to judgment without thoroughly investigating.

Heroin **is made** from poppies and eating the seeds **has been known** to cause false positive drug results.

The hospital **says** it **is comparing** its procedures to other hospitals.

The baby **has** since **been returned**.

(AP)

('Mom claims bagel defense', *Boston Herald*, 15 October 2010, p. 3; used with permission of the Associated Press Copyright © 2010. All rights reserved)

Excluding the headline, this story features 16 tensed lexical verbs and one modal verb (*may*) which we have marked in **bold** (non-finite verbs excluded). The lexical verbs are used to introduce reported speech (e.g. *says*) or to report events (*ate*). Of the tensed lexical verbs,

- six are in the present tense (*is representing*; *says*; *allows*; *is made*; *says*; *is comparing*)

- two in the present perfect (*has been known to*; *has been returned*)

- eight in the past tense (*was seized*; *failed*; *ate*; *said*; *came*; *gave*; *said*; *rushed*).

Both present, past and present perfect are used to provide bases of information, for example, as hearsay (*says*; *said*) or knowledge (*has been known to*). The present tense is also used to refer to ongoing relevant processes (*is comparing*), laws (*allows*) and timeless truths (*Heroin is made from poppies*). In contrast, the past tense provides mainly information on events that happened. The present tense emphasizes the recency and relevance of the event, construing newsworthiness. Both past and present tense can be connected to the focus of news stories on reporting events in the recent past or currently happening.

Concerning voice, four verbs are in the passive (*was seized*; *is made*; *has been known*; *has been returned*), with one providing an agent (*by county welfare workers*) and three not doing so, perhaps because the agent is not relevant or unknown. The passive can in general be used to structure and foreground/background certain information, treating some of it as known and other parts as new – compare the different effects of *her newborn baby was seized by county welfare workers* and *county welfare workers seized her newborn baby*. In fact, 'critical' approaches to news discourse (see Chapter 1) have pointed out that this can be used to obscure agency (for further discussion of this point see Richardson 2007: 55–9).

Adverbials

Turning now to adverbials, here specification of time is most common but place adverbials are also frequent in newspaper writing, whereas linking adverbials (e.g. *however, so*) are rare (Biber and Conrad 2009). For instance, *yesterday* and *after* are key words in UK news discourse (Bednarek 2008a).

Looking at adverbials in a specific example, we can describe references to time and place in a story from the UK tabloid the *Daily Star* ('Jordan set to divorce in new year', 17 December 2010, pp. 1, 6, 7). In this story, references to time include: *in new year; in the new year; these days; over Christmas; in recent weeks; early next year; until January; in the new year; at the moment*. Such references can be connected to placing the news event in time, whether or not the story focuses on reporting past and current events or hypothesizes about/predicts future events. Temporal references can also clarify the sequence in which events happened, and allow a comparison of events in the past and present in terms of similarity and difference.

Three references to place also occur in the 'Jordan' story, two in captions: *they were both out clubbing; in Las Vegas; at a book signing*. While references to place can construe Proximity (cf. Chapter 3), here they seem more concerned with providing background information and identifying the location of a news photo, placing the event in space. The language of captions, just like that of headlines, is quite specific, as the caption interacts with the image (cf. Chapter 5 on text–image relations).

Summary of lexical and syntactic features

The features discussed so far can all be related to the main components of the '*events* of the day' (Leitner 1986: 189, italics in original), as they can be used to refer to actors, times and places and relate to at least some of the basic facts that journalists focus on reporting (who, what, when, where). Other features of newspaper writing mentioned by Biber and Conrad (2009) include a rare occurrence of questions. This is because news reports, even when quoting from interviews and press conferences, tend to focus on the sources' answers without the eliciting questions and even when questions are included they would typically be in indirect forms (e.g. *when asked about*). A further characteristic is a type-token ratio (the number of different words / the number of total words) that is higher than in academic prose or conversation, suggesting that the vocabulary used is varied rather than repetitive. Finally, short sentences are used that frequently make up one paragraph – corresponding to the valued objective of brevity, and standard syntax is employed – suggesting standardization as a feature of newspaper writing (see Cotter 2010: chapter 9 for discussion). In the following sections we draw on further research into news discourse to discuss the use of figures/numbers and evidentiality/intertextuality before turning to a brief discussion of linguistic variation.

2.2 Figures/numbers

Figures/numbers are an important component of news stories, providing 'facts' to journalists that enable the news story to seem objective while at the same time construing newsworthiness (e.g. Superlativeness). Bell (1991: 158) even includes Facticity as a news value. The extent to which numbers are included and what kinds of numbers are mentioned may depend on the type of news story: For instance, in the first 12 sentences of a front page news story on fuel rationing in the UK's *Daily Telegraph* ('Winter fuel rationing on way', 17 December 2010, p. 1) the following numbers were included: *up to two million, up to four weeks, more than 70 p, just over 40 p, around six per cent, 828,000 users in England, 155,000 in Scotland, six out of 10 families, 505,000 homes, reaching –15 C (5F), the freeze of 1962–63.* In other words, the amount and kinds of numbers included in a news story depends to a certain extent on the news event that is reported. As this example also shows, numbers are frequently rounded with expressions such as *up to, at least, more than* at times intensifying the numbers involved.

2.3 Evidentiality/intertextuality

In Chapter 2 we mentioned that there are many types of input material for news stories ranging from press conferences, agency/wire copy, syndicated copy to interviews, documents, other news stories, social media, You Tube, WikiLeaks, blogs, phone hacking, and so on. The producers of the news transform this material into a news story through processes of selection, reproduction, summarization, and so on (Bell 1991: 61–5). It is for these reasons that news can be considered as 'embedded talk' (Bell 1991: 52) and the way in which material is integrated in news stories is an important area of research (Verschueren 1985, Fairclough 1988, Caldas-Coulthard 1994, Semino and Short 2004), often investigated with reference to the concepts of intertextuality or evidentiality (e.g. Bednarek 2006a, Garretson and

Ädel 2008). Such material can be integrated in various ways into the news story:

- it can remain unattributed – when the news story does not mention where a piece of information comes from

- it can be attributed but without mentioning the specific source – when linguistic structures such as *allegedly, is expected to, is said to* are used without mentioning **who** *alleges/expects/says*

- it can be attributed to specific sources (human or not). These can either be named (*Prime Minister Julia Gillard*) or unnamed (*federal prosecutors based in Los Angeles*) and sources can also be institutions, rules, written material, and so on.

In general, named (rather than anonymous or unnamed) sources are valued more highly by editorial policy and reasons for anonymity are sometimes provided when the latter are used (Stenvall 2008). However, unnamed sources do occur frequently in the news (Garretson and Ädel 2008, Stenvall 2008), and vague expressions such as *alleged* may be used to avoid accusations of defamation (cf. Section 3.4 'The news media and the law' in Chapter 2). Below is a list of mentioned sources in all front page stories in the *Los Angeles Times* on 15 October 2010 showing some of the variety in sources and their naming:

- *The Justice Department; government layers; the military; Obama; the president; the pentagon; Col. Dave Lapan; the law*

- *Prosecutors; federal prosecutors based in Los Angeles; CVS Caremark Corp. Chairman Thomas M. Ryan*

- *Angelica Penn, wife of 34-year-old miner Edison Pena*

- *Government records*

Why are such sources used? Journalists want information, evidence and facts, they want to adhere to objectivity (balancing viewpoints from different sources) and they need newsworthy quotes (contributing, for example, to Personalization) and elite speakers that increase newsworthiness and credibility. Quotes can be used to summarize or illustrate a point and they allow news workers to include strong evaluations (in the quote) that might not otherwise be included to allow news to appear objective and impartial (cf. Chapter 6). Frequently, utterances themselves have news value and become the story, when stories are issues- rather than event-based (White 1997: 101).

Another question concerns **how** the attributed material is integrated into the story. For this, the devices of reported speech and thought are generally used with a reporting expression being used to attribute. The sequencing of reporting expression (in **bold**) and reported speech (in *italics*) can vary:

Up to two million homes, schools and hospitals face fuel rationing over Christmas, ministers **said** yesterday [reported speech first]

as households **were warned** *that supplies of heating oil would hit "crisis" point during the latest cold snap.* [reporting expression first]

('Winter fuel rationing on way', *Daily Telegraph* (UK), 12 December 2010, p. 1)

Table 4.2 Types of reported speech

Type of Reported Speech	Example from News Story
Direct quote	"The suggestion that I was racist because of the response to Katrina represented an all-time low," Bush told a surprised Matt Auer on NBC on Monday night. ('The new Bush . . . is a lot like the old one', *Miami Herald*, Int. edition, 10 November 2010, p. 1)
Partial direct/mixed quote, including scare quotes	He [Apari] told reporters that Berenson was "once again trying to adjust, and organizing her things" at the residence in Lima's upscale Miraflores district . . . ('Peru releases imprisoned U.S. activist', *Miami Herald*, Int. edition, 10 November 2010, p. 1) . . . as households were warned that supplies of heating oil would hit "crisis" point during the latest cold snap. ('Winter fuel rationing on way', *Daily Telegraph*, 12 December 2010, p. 1)
Indirect	He said he still felt sickened that no weapons of mass destruction were ever found in Iraq. ('The new Bush . . . is a lot like the old one', *Miami Herald*, Int. edition, 10 November 2010, p. 1)
Free indirect speech (indicated via tense shift, use of pronouns, etc.)	Defence Minister Wayne Mapp said joint exercises were being discussed . . . **It was also possible American soldiers would visit for joint exercises agreed between the two former allies** . . . ('Mapp predicts NZ-US joint exercises as ties strengthen', *Dominion Post*, 9 November 2010, p. A2)
Summary/paraphrase of speech act	U.S. President Barack Obama . . . criticized Israel on Tuesday for its decision to advance the approval of some 1,000 new housing units in East Jerusalem during a sensitive time in the peace negotiations with the Palestinians. ('In Indonesia, Obama criticizes Israeli plans', *Miami Herald*, Int. edition, 10 November 2010, p. 1)
Nested/embedded (reported speech within reported speech)	"We really have to do something about it," Kerry **said**, **according to** a Democratic official. (cited in Garretson and Ädel 2008: 177)

Further, various options are available to integrate reported speech and thought in news stories. Since these are outlined in grammars of the English language, we will not explain them here, but Table 4.2 on p. 92 provides an overview with examples from our dataset.[3]

While the sequencing and type of reported speech/thought may be varied for stylistic or structural reasons, they carry specific meanings. For instance, direct quotes provide authenticity, flavour and colour, and scare quotes ('crisis') can be used to distance oneself from what is quoted. Indirect speech, on the other hand, may appear more neutral and less immediate or vivid. Fairclough (1988) argues that direct speech clearly distinguishes the voice of the newspaper and the voice of the news source, whereas this is not the case in indirect ways of reporting. Some studies have found that indirect speech is used more frequently than direct speech in print news (e.g. Garretson and Ädel 2008: 170), although there may be differences between the popular and the quality press concerning the specific kinds of reported speech/thought used (see Semino and Short 2004).

Another important aspect of reported speech and thought is the kind of reporting expression used. First, there are variations in the grammar of the reporting expression, with verbs (*says, believes*), nouns (*claim, fears that*), adverbs (*allegedly*) and prepositions (*according to*) available. More importantly, reporting expressions vary in the meanings they carry. For instance, Bednarek (2006c, adapting Caldas-Coulthard 1994) makes a distinction between different ways of reporting speech (Table 4.3). There are clear differences in the meanings expressed by the reporting expressions in Table 4.3 – for instance, it is significant whether or not something is referred to as a *threat* or *promise*. Certain types of reporting expressions

Table 4.3 Reporting expressions

Type of Reporting Expression	Definition
Neutral (e.g. *say, tell, according to*)	The reporting expression does not give any additional information other than identifying something as hearsay
Illocutionary (e.g. *demand, promise*)	The reporting expression gives information on the speaker's purpose
Declarative (e.g. *acquit, plead guilty*)	The reporting expression refers to an institutionalized linguistic act
Discourse signalling (e.g. *add, conclude*)	The reporting expression makes explicit the relation to previous or following discourse
Paralinguistic (e.g. *whisper, scream*)	The reporting expression gives information on the quality of the speech

(e.g. *claim*, *allege*) carry less reliability than others (e.g. *reveal*) and others allow an insight into someone's emotional state (e.g. *scream*). Much research investigates such differences between reporting expressions, and some studies have shown that neutral expressions are most frequent in print news discourse (see Bednarek 2006c, Garretson and Ädel 2008 on British and US newspapers). This can be linked to the aim of maintaining objectivity in news discourse. The following examples of reporting expressions used in one story ('Legal aid applicants facing long waits', *Irish Times*, 18 December 2010, p. 4) show the high reliance of news stories on neutral expressions:

- *The chairwoman of the Legal Aid Board says . . .*
- *In the forward [sic] to the board's annual report for 2009, published yesterday, Anne Colley said . . .*
- *The increases were attributed to . . .*
- *Ms Colley said . . .*
- *". . ." Ms Colley said.*
- *She said . . .*
- *". . ." she said*

There are also other ways in which sources' voices can be introduced into the news discourse, for example, in representing what they *fear, hope, think* or *expect*, as in *there were growing **fears** that the government forces would wreak a horrible revenge on Benghazi for weeks of rebellion there* (cf. Chapter 6).

2.4 Variation in newspaper writing

One issue with some of the above studies that is worth commenting on is the type of writing included as newspaper writing or news discourse. For example, Biber and Conrad's (2009) corpus includes both news reports and editorials, although there are clear linguistic differences between them, as Conrad and Biber also note, for instance, in terms of the amount of overt opinion. Opinion genres (editorials/leaders, letters to the editor, reviews, etc.) are therefore located in dedicated sections or labelled as 'opinion' in newspapers. However, what is presented as 'news' rather than 'opinion' may still include subjectivity or bias. Indeed, much linguistic research is targeted towards uncovering such (cf. Chapter 1 on the 'critical' approach).

To give another example, Bednarek's (2008a) corpus comprises discourse from various sections such as sports and business, and is made up of both tabloid and broadsheet newspapers. Again, though, there are linguistic differences between popular/tabloid and quality/broadsheet news outlets (as there are between metro, regional, local, daily or weekly newspapers with their different foci and topics and between newspapers from different countries). For instance, broadsheet newspapers may be richer in vocabulary than tabloids (Cortina-Borja and Chappas 2006).This means that keywords for a particular newspaper such as the *Guardian Weekly* may be different than those for another newspaper (Scott and Tribble 2006) and keywords in the popular press may be different from the quality press. We have already briefly discussed this in terms of the discursive construal of different readerships in Chapter 2. The language of the popular press is further explored by Conboy (2006) and differences between UK broadsheets and tabloids by Bednarek (2006c).

Further, there are also differences in the language of the various news sections such as local, national and international news, business news, sports news.[4] In fact, reporters covering these 'beats', need to learn the specific communicative features that are involved (Cotter 2010: 51–2). Thus, key words for a sports section will look different than keywords for all sections (Scott and Tribble 2006: 164). Other sections of print newspaper content that have specific linguistic characteristics include sections or supplements such as Style and Travel or service information (weather, share prices, TV guide, results, etc.). Indeed, newspapers pride themselves on the different types of content that they provide and use it to attract readers:

> No other Sunday newspaper in the country has more comprehensive news, features and coverage. You are sure to enjoy *The Sun-Herald*'s additional feature sections; and our unrivalled columnists . . . . We've expanded our arts and culture and included more comprehensive, independent sports coverage.
>
> (Advertising letter to subscribers of the *Sydney Morning Herald*, 19 November 2010)

Finally, there are many different kinds of articles in newspapers – many news *genres* or *text types*, that is, articles that share particular linguistic characteristics and functions or purposes. In news sections, we can find stories about immediate events or follow-up stories, human interest stories or political stories, etc. In 'opinion' sections, we can find letters to the editor, regular columns, leader articles/editorials, political cartoons, etc. In sport sections, there are match reports, match previews, player/team profiles, etc. Journalists use different terms to refer to these genres than linguists do,[5] but no doubt both would agree that each genre or text type has its distinct features.

So when researching newspaper writing, it is worth keeping in mind this inherent variation, especially in terms of thinking about data and relating findings to what others have found. It seems worthwhile both to try to identify general characteristics of newspaper writing or news reportage as compared to other kinds of language, as well as to compile more specific data collections that allow an investigation of say, the language of headlines or specific news genres. While this chapter has so far discussed general characteristics, we now move to discussing news story structure and news headlines.

3 The structure of the news story

The linguistic text in most print news genres can structurally be separated into three parts:

- Headline
- Intro/lead
- Body/lead development.

However, how these three parts are realized, especially intro/lead and body/lead development differs according to genre and is described from linguistic and journalistic perspectives in Ungerer (2004), Feez et al. (2008), Cotter (2010: 135–70) and Lamble (2011). Early descriptions of news structures/schemata include van Dijk (1988a, 1988b), Bell (1994) and Caldas-Coulthard (1997).

We will look here at the structure of a (hard) news story – this is the kind of story that we characteristically associate with news discourse. Such news stories usually report on new or recent events that are considered newsworthy. This is in contrast, for example, to articles that report on events that are not new/recent or longer articles that provide background (see further Chapter 8 on hard vs soft news). The contemporary (hard) news story also has a particular structure that has developed over time (Bell 1991: 172–3, Feez et al. 2008: 76–89, Ungerer 2002), and like other news genres this structure includes headline, intro/lead (generally the first paragraph) and body/lead development (see Figure 4.1 on p. 97).

As Figure 4.1 demonstrates, the position of the image (and its caption) within the hard news story structure has not yet been fully explored – theories into the structure of news stories are text-dominant theories. Following previous research, we will therefore discuss news story structure purely with reference to the verbal text here, but in Chapter 5 we will also investigate in detail the relations that hold between images and text in news stories, including the story in Figure 4.1.

Starting with headlines, they function to frame the event, summarize the story and attract readers. They have specific linguistic characteristics which we will explore in more detail in Section 4. Considering the intro/lead, most

Headline

Children OK, jake injured in blaze

By RENEE NADEAU ALGARIN

Intro/lead

A two-alarm fire sent the kids and staff at a Dorchester day care scrambling yesterday morning, but everyone made it out safely.

Body/lead development

The fire broke out at 18 Boyden St. on the Dorchester-Mattapan line at 10:08 a.m. yesterday, said Boston fire department spokesman Steve MacDonald.

The blaze was caused by an electrical short circuit inside the walls of two-story wood-framed house.

"The fire got in the walls and just traveled throughout the house," MacDonald said.

Two adults at the Pride N Joy Day Care center on the building's first floor managed to get all 10 children out safely before the fire engines arrived at the scene, MacDonald said.

Residents of an upstairs apartment were not home at the time of the fire.

One firefighter suffered a hand injury fighting the flames. He was treated and released from Carney Hospital in Dorchester.

Damage was estimated at $350,000, MacDonald said.

— nnadeau@bostonherald.com

HOT AND COLD: Boston firefighters battle a fire at 18 Boyden St. in Caption that caused $350,000 in damage to a day care.

Figure 4.1 The structure of a 'typical' hard news story, reprinted with permission of the *Boston Herald*

linguists in fact see headlines and intro/lead as one unit – called the *abstract* (Bell 1991) or *nucleus* (Feez et al. 2008). Like the headline, the traditional hard news intro/lead frames the event, summarizes the story, construes newsworthiness and attracts readers. It presents the point or newsworthy element(s) of the story and simultaneously works as a beginning of the story. 'Typical' intros/leads are short (20–35 words, 1 to 2 sentences) but informative and include the 'most important news element of the story in addition to the choice of angle or "hook", or approach to the subject' (Cotter 2010: 162). Intro/lead paragraphs thus describe newsworthy aspects of the event (e.g. the who, the what, the where). Therefore, linguistic resources that construe newsworthiness (Chapter 3) occur frequently in the intro/ lead. More specifically, in analysing ten international agency hard news stories, Bell (1991: 177–83) found that the intros/leads:

- mention main event and place (who, what, where)
- construe newsworthiness
- rarely attribute information
- begin with actor (the who)
- often cover more than one event
- embed background (such as events in the past) through a complex discourse structure.

Let us briefly look at the intro/lead paragraph of the story in Figure 4.1 to illustrate its characteristics.

A two-alarm fire sent the kids and staff at a Dorchester day care scrambling yesterday morning, but everyone made it out safely.

('Children OK, jake injured in blaze', *Boston Herald*, 15 December 2010, p. 11)

We can see that this intro/lead paragraph is fairly typical for a (hard) news story. It is very short, consisting of only 1 sentence and made up of 22 words. The paragraph mentions the main event and place, and construes newsworthiness in terms of Proximity (*Dorchester day care*), Personalization (*the kids and staff*), Superlativeness (*two-alarm fire*) and Impact (*sent . . . scrambling*). There is no attribution, and it begins 'at the point of greatest crisis, intensity or human impact' (Feez et al. 2008: 93) or the most newsworthy element.

Turning now to the body/lead development – the paragraphs following the intro/lead paragraph – there is general agreement that this adds different types of information (often background or context) and features attribution of information (including direct quotes). Table 4.4 on p. 99 shows the structure of the *Boston Herald* story, and illustrates the kinds of information that are often included in the lead development of a (hard) news story.

The structure of hard news stories, such as this one in the *Boston Herald*, usually involves the recycling of information at different stages of the story, often adding more detail with each mention. This can impact on the potential for the chronological development of the story events. There is, in fact, general agreement on the structure of hard news stories that the order in which events are reported is non-chronological and does not mirror the order in which events happened in 'real life'. For instance, the rough order of the events reported in the *Boston Herald*'s story is as follows:

electrical short circuit – fire breaks out at 10.08 am – fire gets in the walls, travels throughout the house – adults get children out safely – fire engines arrive – fire fighter suffers hand injury – fire causes damage – fire fighter treated at hospital – fire fighter released

Table 4.4 Structure of the 'fire story' from the *Boston Herald*

Children OK, jake [firefighter] **injured in blaze**	*Headline*	
A two-alarm fire sent the kids and staff at a Dorchester day care scrambling yesterday morning, but everyone made it out safely.	*Lead*	
The fire broke out at 18 Boyden St. on the Dorchester-Mattapan line at 10.08 a.m. yesterday, said Boston fire department spokesman Steve MacDonald.	*Lead development*	Attribution: restating and adding details
The blaze was caused by an electrical short circuit inside the walls of [*sic*] two-story wood-framed house.		Background information/cause
"The fire got in the walls and just traveled throughout the house," MacDonald said.		Attribution: adding details
Two adults at the Pride N Joy Day Care centre on the building's first floor managed to get all 10 children out safely before the fire engines arrived at the scene, MacDonald said.		Attribution: restating part of the event, adding details
Residents of an upstairs apartment were not at home at the time of the fire.		Background information
One firefighter suffered a hand injury fighting the flames.		Consequences
He was treated and released from Carney Hospital in Dorchester.		Consequences
Damage was estimated at $350,000, MacDonald said.		Attribution: consequences

However, if we look again at the structure of this text (Table 4.4), the lead paragraph starts with everyone making it out safely. The first paragraph of the body text then gives specific details about the location of the day care centre and the exact time the fire broke out. This is followed by two paragraphs on the cause of the fire and how it spread, before returning to the occupants of the building who were mentioned in the lead and offering more detail about them (that there were ten kids and two adults). Thus, the way in which events are ordered in news stories does not mirror the real-life temporal progression. Journalists work with the notion of the 'inverted pyramid' to explain that elements of the news story are ordered in decreasing order of importance or newsworthiness. Linguists are more interested in the logical or rhetorical relations between headline/lead and the rest of the story, and have conceptualized this in terms of dependence on episodes and events (Bell 1991: 170) or the links that are made back to the headline/lead nucleus (Feez et al. 2008). Such research is interested in teasing out which parts of the news story provide follow-up, commentary or background to an event or the types of information that are added to the lead/intro in the rest of the article (e.g. restating information, adding information, giving reasons, causes or consequences).

We need to point out here that there are degrees to which a newspaper article contains typical structural components of the hard news story. Different structural approaches can be taken by news workers to reporting various kinds of events. Whether or not an article is a hard news story is often a matter of degree. Finally, the typical news story structure can also be mimicked by other genres (Ungerer 2004).

4 Headlinese

As mentioned in Section 3, headlines are an integral part of news stories. It is interesting to examine their functions and features in more detail, as 'headlinese' is quite a specific type of language. This section summarizes linguists' findings on headlines as described in Bell (1991), Reah (1998), Feez et al. (2008) – more recent research includes Ifantidou (2009) and Brone and Coulson (2010). For detailed grammatical/syntactic analysis see Mardth (1980), Gonzalez Rodriguez (2006) and Piakova (2007).

First, as far as the news process is concerned, headlines are usually not written by the reporter/journalist but by a subeditor (cf. Chapter 2), usually after lead and lead development have been constructed. They should work independently, but are mainly derived from the lead and share many structural correspondences with it (Kniffka 1980). The headline has multiple functions:

- an informative function in terms of summarizing or abstracting the story
- an interpersonal function in terms of attracting the reader
- a news value function in terms of maximizing newsworthiness
- a framing function in terms of providing a lens on, stance towards or angle on the rest of the story.

The characteristics of headlines, which can easily be related to these functions, include the following:

- visual features:
  - visually attractive, foregrounding urgency (font size/layout/typography)
  - several 'decks' of headlines are possible
- linguistic features:
  - strong', 'intense', emotional/evaluative words
  - rhetorical devices and foregrounding techniques, such as word or sound play (punning, intertextuality/allusion (Lennon 2004, Caple 2010a), alliteration, rhyme), metaphor, idioms, proverbs, pseudo-direct quotes (which seem like they are direct quotes but are not)
  - omission of functional/grammatical words (e.g. determiners, auxiliaries/finite verbs, etc.)
  - if verb is present: use of present tense
  - premodified noun phrases (often nouns as premodifiers)
  - rare specification of time, but often specifying the 'how' and sometimes specifying place or a previous action
  - rare use of attribution (unless it is an issues-based story).

Not every headline has to include all of these features, although they are typical of headlinese. For instance, not every headline will feature word or sound play and not every headline will be a pseudo-quote. Let us look again at some examples from print news; Table 4.5 on p. 102 shows the main (most prominent on page) headlines (but not subheadlines) of 29 newspapers on the same day (30 August 2010).

We can see many of the identified linguistic characteristics of headlines here. For instance:

- the use of 'strong', 'intense' or emotional/evaluative lexis to maximize news values (e.g. *pain*; *hundreds*; *love triangle*; *risky*; *scandal engulfs*; *fights for life*; *global drug syndicate*; *sex assault shame*; *thousand*; *wonder drug*; £6 million)
- the use of word or sound play (e.g. *Pump the pain*; *Deval's labor pain*; *Off the Wal*; *Tamil 'tourists'*)
- the use of premodified noun phrases (e.g. *Big Bro love triangle*; *bank plan*; *bet scandal*; *global drug syndicate*; *Canty road crashes*; *sex assault shame*)
- the rare specification of time and place, with place being more frequent than time (e.g. *Chicago*; *Iraqi*; *in Iraq*; *Pakistan*; *Tamil*; *Canty*).

Table 4.5 News headlines from around the world

Newspaper	Headline
Baltimore Sun (US)	Prime the pump
Boston Herald (US)	Deval's labor pain
Chicago Tribune (US)	Chicago is our home now
Los Angeles Times (US)	Newcomers steal the show
New York Post (US)	Off the Wal
San Francisco Chronicle (US)	Meager results in mortgage initiative
The *Philadelphia Inquirer* (US)	A new Iraqi election possible
The *Seattle Times* (US)	Hundreds of refugees adrift in our community
The *Washington Times* (US)	No letup in Iraq for some forces
The *Washington Post*	Human tests set for stem cells
USA Today (US)	Safety net catching more in recession
The *Miami Herald* (Int. edition)	Man of the people
Daily Star (UK)	Chantelle in Big Bro love triangle
The *Daily Telegraph* (UK)	Bank plan to cap risky mortgages
The *Guardian* (UK)	Cricket thrown into crisis as bet scandal engulfs Pakistan
The *Independent* (UK)	'We need to raise taxes for the better-off'
Daily Mail (UK)	£1-a-day heart wonder drug
Daily Express (UK)	Thousands in heart drug boost
Daily Mirror (UK)	Cops quiz stars over £6 million bungs
The *Globe and Mail* (CAN)	Tamil 'tourists' await next boat – and it's not for sightseeing
Ottawa Sun (CAN)	Sens' doc fights for life
Irish Independent (IR)	Michaela was raped, beaten and strangled
The *Irish Times* (IR)	Greens want quicker wind-down of Anglo Irish Bank
The *New Zealand Herald* (NZ)	Drink age: where our MPs stand
The *Dominion Post* (NZ)	Maori claim part of cape
The *Press* (NZ)	Canty road crashes cost $1.4 m a day
The *Age* (AUS)	Police out global drug syndicate
The *Australian* (AUS)	Nats push Abbott for better deal
The *Daily Telegraph* (AUS)	Sex assault shame

We can also see the rare use of attribution, with some possible exceptions where the news story is issues-based (e.g. the use of direct quotes '*We need to raise taxes for the better-off*'; *Chicago is our home now*; compare also the mention of plans, wishes and speech acts in *Bank plan to cap risky mortgages*; *Greens want quicker wind-down of Anglo Irish Bank*; *Nats push Abbott for better deal*; *Cops quiz stars*).

In terms of the presence and tense of verbs, Table 4.6 below shows the distribution in the 29 headlines and confirms that verbs are frequently omitted or occur without tensed auxiliaries, but if they do occur they are usually in the present rather than the past tense.

Note that just as there is linguistic variation concerning other aspects of news discourse (cf. Section 2), there may be variation in 'headlinese', for instance, differences between the headlines of tabloids and those of broadsheets (see Schaffer 1995, Aitchison 2007: 137). To investigate variation in headlinese between national varieties and different news genres, over time, prints versus online, and so on would also be a worthwhile endeavour.

Together with devices that construe newsworthiness (Chapter 3), the above features of newspaper writing in general and news stories in particular enable news discourse both to attract, inform and entertain

Table 4.6 Verbs in the headlines

No verb in headline	*Deval's labour pain*; *Off the Wal*; *Meager results in mortgage initiative*; *A new Iraqi election possible*; *No letup in Iraq for some forces*; *Man of the people*; *Chantelle in Big Bro love triangle*; *Sex assault shame*; *£1-a-day heart wonder drug*; *Thousands in heart drug boost*
No tensed verb in headline	*Prime the pump*; *Hundreds of refugees adrift in our community*; *Human tests set for stem cells*; *Safety net catching more in recession*; *Bank plan to cap risky mortgages*; *Cricket thrown into crisis*
Verb in present tense	*Chicago is our home now*; *New comers steal the show*; . . . *as bet scandals engulfs Pakistan*; *We need to raise taxes for the better off*; *Tamil 'tourists' await next boat – and it's not for sightseeing*; *Sens doc fights for life*; *Greens want quicker wind-down of Anglo Irish bank*; *Drink age: where our MPS stand*; *Maori claim part of cape*; *Canty road crashes cost $1.4 m a day*; *Police out global drug syndicate*; *Nats push Abbot for better deal*; *Cops quiz s1tars over £6 million bungs*
Verb in past tense	*Michaela was raped, beaten and strangled*

readers: 'the best stories from a newspaper company's perspective are those that get to the point, have a strong impact on readers, and provide enough information to succinctly and effectively inform, educate and/or entertain in as small a space as possible' (Lamble 2011: 135). At a conference panel on Journalism Education (JEAA 2010), news workers indeed emphasized the importance of 'engaging', 'accurate' (John Coomber, AAP), or 'short, sharp' stories (Mark Hollands, PANPA). This chapter has shown how **linguistic** features of news discourse contribute to telling such stories in print news (see Chapter 5 on image and visual storytelling).

5 Online, radio and TV news

To what extent the characteristics of print news discourse discussed above are present in online, radio and TV news discourse is a matter of research and there should be no assumption that what is typical of print news is also typical of online, radio and TV news. While some features may occur throughout (e.g. standard language, language that gets readers'/viewers' attention, structural similarities of hard news stories online or in print), others are specific to a particular media form. For example, TV news reports are characterized by the use of present tense, proximate deixis referring to visuals and specific interactions between the verbal and the visual track (see Chapter 5) and may feature typical characteristics of spoken language, for example, in live interviews and exchanges where questions, untypical of newspaper writing, also occur (Haarman 2004, Tolson 2006, Montgomery 2007). In fact, language in TV news discourse may vary quite significantly, as 'practices of news presentation are now diverse, ranging from scripted monologues to experiments with various kinds of verbal performance' (Tolson 2006: 70).

Other examples of differences in media forms include content separation: where print news separates different content spatially and with labels, online news separates it through 'tabs' (see Figure 4.2), whereas radio and television separate such content temporally and through switching to different correspondents.

With respect to headlines, there are also clear differences. Unlike print newspaper headlines, online headlines have to consider the demands of search engines, and while headlines arguably occur in radio and

Figure 4.2 The *Irish Times* (online), www.irishtimes.com – accessed 28 October 2010, 3.24 p.m. Australian (EST) time

TV broadcasts (usually collected at the beginning and/or end of news programmes but also occurring throughout a news programme), their function and form differs to a certain extent (Montgomery 2007: 78). While they feature some of the characteristics of print news headlines (such as deletion of verbs or articles, use of nominalization), they can also be full sentences with only the verbal group omitted or reduced to a non-finite form or even consist of several sentences with full verbal groups. Table 4.7 provides examples from radio and TV news.

Table 4.7 Radio and TV 'headlines'

Sentence with verbal group reduced to a non-finite form	*New Zealand rescuers continuing their attempts to reach 29 trapped miners*
	(radio 'headline' quoted in Chapter 1)
Several sentences with full verbal groups	*Rescuers continue to drill towards 29 trapped miners in New Zealand. Authorities are hoping for the best but preparing for the worst. 'We are planning for the possible loss of life as a result of what's occurred underground'*
	(TV 'headline' quoted in Chapter 1).

Another common pattern for such broadcast news 'headlines' consists of the structure *X does Y as P does Q* (Montgomery 2007: 81). Despite these differences, however, some of the functions of radio and TV headlines appear similar to those of print headlines, for example, to attract audiences.

Other differences between media forms include story length (the typical US radio newscast being 3 minutes or less, Cotter 2010: 203), story structure (see Montgomery 2007 on broadcast news) and differences in the way embedded speech is represented. Television can include the clothes, appearance, facial expression, gesture, voice quality, and so on of a source; it can show people speaking (*grabs/talking heads*), which is not possible in print news. Conventions of recording and editing sound and images apply to TV and radio broadcasts (sound, not images) and are also present in certain online news material (see Chapters 5 and 9). Other differences concerning embedded speech include the sequencing and tense used for reporting speech (Leitner 1986, Bell 1991: 210), although there are also similarities, for instance, in the preference for neutral reporting expressions (Leitner 1986, Lombardo 2004).

There are also techniques (e.g. voice-overs, split screens, thumbnails, hyperlinks) and genres that may be present in one media form but not in another. The news 'ticker' on television at the bottom of the screen is an example (see Figure 2.6 in Chapter 2), as is the online 'newsbite' (Knox 2007) and the 'developing' or 'breaking' news updates that happen online. Table 4.8 shows the online reporting of two important news stories, the Royal Wedding (Kate Middleton and Prince William) and the repeal of the United States 'don't ask, don't tell policy' (preventing gays and lesbians from openly serving in the army), with the stories in the left-hand column illustrating intro/lead paragraphs and the stories in the right-hand column illustrating 'breaking' news updates (videos, images, original typography/ formatting not reproduced).

Table 4.8 Different ways of structuring the news

Lead/Intro Paragraphs	Updates
Obama signs repeal of 'don't ask, don't tell' policy President Barack Obama brought the long political struggle over the military's controversial "don't ask, don't tell" policy to a close Wednesday, signing legislation that will bring an end of the ban on openly gay men and women serving in the armed forces. *CNN* online (www.cnn.com, 22 December 2010)	**Obama signs historic bill ending 'don't ask, don't tell'** **Updated at 9:36:** Obama just signed the bill. **Updated at 9:35**: Obama says he hopes all those who left the service because of "don't ask, don't tell" will seek to re-enlist. To all gays interested in joining the military, he says "Your country needs you, your country wants you, we will be honored to welcome you into the ranks" *USA Today* online (www.usatoday.com, 22 December 2010)
William and Catherine marry in royal wedding at Westminster Abbey **London (CNN)** – Prince William of Wales slipped a gold ring onto the finger of Catherine Middleton Friday, and the couple vowed to love, comfort, honor and to keep each other in London's biggest royal wedding in three decades. *CNN* online (www.cnn.com, 29 April 2011)	**Royal wedding: The play-by-play** -**7:34 a.m.:** Next up, the Duke and Duchess of Cambridge's first kiss from the balcony! -**7:32 a.m.:** Princesses Eugenie and Beatrice – and their wacky fascinators – emerge from the car and head into the Palace with their dad Prince Andrew, the Duke of York. -**7:30 a.m.:** The Queen and Prince Philip leave their carriage as they arrive at home. Kate Middleton's parents are not far behind. *USA Today* online (www.usatoday.com, 29 April 2011)

Note that the same website may feature both ways of reporting simultaneously; for example, CNN also reported the Royal Wedding as a breaking news blog with such updates in their Entertainment section.

More generally, there is an obvious linguistic variation in terms of differences between **written** (print, online) and **spoken** (radio, TV, online) language and there are differences in terms of multimodality, with radio using the aural channel, television/online the visual and the aural, and print the visual channel. However:

> [T]here are seepages of one media form to another, 'modality bleeds' that come about through changes in media technology. This is most evident in daily newspapers' inclusions of video on their websites; radio stations' inclusion of pictures and visual elements on their websites; and television stations including the written word on the screen, as well as the development of multimedia platforms on the Web. (Cotter 2010: 61)

A particularly interesting area for future research in terms of variation across media is the way news is told in the new media, with their preference for short stories (Twitter stories need to be told in 140 characters), and new ways of storytelling (bite size stories, visual storytelling, etc. – see Caple 2008a, 2008b, Knox 2009, Caple and Knox in press). Interestingly, new ways of telling stories may also have 'a flowback effect on the printed versions of newspapers' and may result in the latter presenting the news in more compressed and visual ways (Conboy 2010: 146).

To conclude this chapter, our aim was to give readers an overview of how linguists have described news discourse and to enable them to make a decision as to what area of news discourse their own investigation could target. Our focus in this chapter was on the output of the news process – linguistic characteristics of newspaper writing. But it must be kept in mind that this output may interact with a whole range of factors, of various kinds:

- beliefs and assumptions (about newsworthiness, accepted news practices, the audience, about language standards, about social actors)
- local style guides (e.g. newspaper style guides), editorial policies and codes of practice/ethics
- the media form, including its affordances and technical constraints (online, radio, television, print)
- media laws (e.g. defamation)
- economic factors (e.g. space for news vs advertising)
- practice, expertise and experience
- deadlines and the news cycle.

At the same time, as suggested in Chapter 2, the relationship between such factors and news discourse is more complex than one merely being the outcome or reflection of the other. News discourse is constrained by various situational and cultural factors, but at the same time it actively contributes to the establishment of such factors, even where it just reinforces them – as in the consistent use of linguistic devices to construe what readers accept as 'typical' news discourse or in the consistent use of language and images to establish recurring news values (Chapter 3). Knowing more about these 'typical' or consistent uses of language and images allows researchers to identify whether or not the discursive uses they observe in a particular text are an instantiation of the norm. Knowing about the communicative and socio-historical context and concepts such as news values allows them to hypothesize about potential reasons behind or functions of such discursive uses. This could be enriched through complementary ethnographic research into news production and audience studies into how the discourse is interpreted by readers/viewers/ listeners (cf. Chapters 1, 9). In any case, an analysis of news discourse as comprising just language remains necessarily incomplete, so Chapter 5 now turns again to images in the news.

Directions for further reading

Since the sections above include key references on print news, we have included only references here that focus on TV, radio and online news.

Television and radio

Haarman, L. (2004), '"John, what's going on?" Some features of live exchanges on television news', in A. Partington, J. Morley and L. Haarman (eds), *Corpora and Discourse*. Bern: Peter Lang, pp. 71–87. Combines corpus and discourse analysis to examine 33 live news exchanges between newsreaders and reporters on the BBC's *Nine O' Clock News*.

Lorenzo-Dus, N. (2009), *Television Discourse. Analysing Language in the Media*. Basingstoke, England: Palgrave Macmillan. Includes sections on live news interchanges and news interviews.

Montgomery, M. (2007), *The Discourse of Broadcast News. A Linguistic Approach*. Abingdon/New York: Routledge. Close analyses of broadcast news, including both radio and television, and both news reports and news interviews.

Digital/online

Barkho, L. (2008), 'The BBC's discursive strategy and practices vis-à-vis the Palestinian-Israeli conflict', *Journalism Studies*, 9 (2), 278–94. Explores the BBC's

English and Arabic online reports about the Palestinian-Israeli conflict, also incorporating interviews with BBC editors, BBC guidelines and editors' blogs.

Bucher, H.-J., Büffel, S. and Wollscheid, J. (2005), *Digital Newspaper as E-paper: A Hybrid Medium between Print and Online Newspaper*. Darmstadt: IFRA. Compares the e-paper with online and print versions.

Knox, J. S. (2010), 'Online newspapers: evolving genres, evolving theory', in C. Coffin, T. Lillis and K. L. O'Halloran (eds), *Applied Linguistics Methods: A Reader*. London: Routledge, pp. 33–51. Investigates the challenges posed by new media genres, in particular newsbites in online newspapers, to existing theories of communication and language.

Paganoni, M. C. (2008), 'Local and global identity on news sites: Al Jazeera's English-language website', in M. Solly, M. Conoscenti and S. Campagna (eds), *Verbal/Visual Narrative Texts in Higher Education*. Bern: Peter Lang, pp. 331–49. Draws on Critical Discourse Analysis to analyse Al Jazeera's English-language website from a multimodal perspective.

Notes

1 These may have an impact on newswriting rules or objectives in offering models of the ways in which newswriting is repeatedly done, again demonstrating a two-way flow between news discourse and professional norms (cf. Chapter 2).

2 Looking at variation within newspaper writing and the different kinds of modal meaning, modals are more frequent in editorials than in news reports, with many of these modals being directive (*deontic modality*), for example, telling readers about best or preferred behaviour, but modals that predict future events and consequences (*epistemic modality*) also occur (Biber and Conrad 2009: 125).

3 There are differences between how speech (*she said that …*) and thought (*she thought that …*) are typically reported and how different kinds of speech acts (e.g. commands vs questions) are rendered. Grammars of the English language provide further detail (see also Semino and Short 2004).

4 See Jucker (1992) on variation in noun phrase structure between tabloids and broadsheets and between different sections of newspapers. Crystal and Davy (1969), Bell (1991), Conboy (2001, 2006), Bednarek (2006c) and Richardson (2007: 137–43) also discuss the popular and the quality press. Walsh (2004) and Ho (2009) examine financial news; Wallace (1977), Ferguson (1983), Ghadessy (1988), Crolley and Teso (2007) and O'Shaughnessy and Stadler (2008: 20–1, 42–4, 191–2) discuss sports.

5 Terms that journalists use include *advance, folo* [*sic* – a follow-up story], *brief, rewrite, breaking news, enterprise, investigative, brite, sidebar* and *feature* (Cotter 2010: 143–5). Linguists in the systemic functional tradition talk about genres such as media exemplum, media anecdote, media feature (Feez et al. 2008), image-nuclear news story (Caple 2008a) or online news gallery (Caple and Knox in press). Much linguistic research concerns different subgenres or types of news interviews (Jucker 1986, Bell and van

Leeuwen 1994, Ljung 2000, Clayman and Heritage 2002, O'Connell et al. 2004, O'Keeffe 2006, Tolson 2006, Montgomery 2007, 2008, Thornborrow and Montgomery 2010). Other types of news content classified as 'genres' or 'subgenres' include spot news, features, headlines (Bell 1991: 17) and categories such as weather story, bank holiday travel story (Cotter 2010: 136). Other ways of categorizing news texts include considerations of *journalistic voice*, that is, the extent to which evaluative meanings are made use of (Martin and White 2005).

CHAPTER FIVE

Images in the news

1 Introduction

Chapter 4 showed us some of the key features and functions of language in the news. This chapter now focuses on still and moving images in the news, including the kinds of images that get taken up in the news and their role within news discourse. This means examining the communicative functions of images, which have been largely influenced by the historical contexts underpinning news discourse. Since Chapter 2 has already introduced the socio-historical context of news discourse, we will focus in this chapter on the ways this relates specifically to photography. Historically, print news has been somewhat text-dominated, and where images have been used, little attention has been given to their position or function within news discourse (see also Caple 2010b). However, as can be seen in Figure 5.1, news story structure has shifted and images now tend to dominate the verbal text: indeed, in some cases, it is the image that is propelling a story into the news.

Figure 5.1 Story packaging – the evolution of news print from text-dominance to image-dominance

New ways of telling stories online, such as on news homepages or in multimedia sections, also incorporate both verbal and visual elements. The organization of such verbal–visual texts and the relations between the verbal and the visual thus deserve further attention. In this chapter we examine the ways in which words and images relate to each other within a particular news story, be it in the newspaper, on television or online. Our objectives for this chapter are to enable readers to understand:

- the communicative functions of images in the news
- the historical context underpinning the use of news images
- the position of images in the organization of news
- relationships between words and still and moving images.

2 The communicative functions of news images

While illustrations have appeared in news print since the very beginnings of the mass news media (see Chapter 2), their position and prominence have been somewhat (but not totally) contingent on the development of technologies capable of clearly rendering them on the printed page and on the screen. We will refer to these technological developments throughout this section, but for ease of reference Table 5.1 on pp. 113–14 offers a timeline of major shifts in the technological advancement of photography, film and printing as they relate to and impact on the use of images in the news.

More importantly though, when and how images have been used in the reporting of news events has been very much contingent on the prevailing attitudes towards photography (see Barnhurst and Nerone 2001 for a comprehensive historical review). These attitudes are evident in both the professional rhetoric on the role of images in the news and in academic theorizing. They range from viewing images as mere *illustration* and therefore adjunct to the more important verbal descriptions of news events, to seeing them as reflecting reality (giving them the function of *evidence*), or as *sensation*, as visible in the early tabloid press. Images also have the ability to function as *icons*, symbolic representations of key moments in history;[1] and, more recently, they have been viewed as functioning *evaluatively* (carrying emotional appeal) and *aesthetically* (showing concern for composition). In the following paragraphs we discuss each of these communicative functions and make reference to the role of technological developments (as outlined in Table 5.1) in this process. Given its long history in news discourse, we focus primarily on press photography.

Table 5.1 Timeline of technological advancements in relation to photographic reproduction

1800s	**1839:** Daguerreotype: one of the earliest photographic methods to produce a single positive image exposed directly onto a silver-coated plate.
	1842: *Illustrated London News* (UK), *L'Illustration* (France) relied on the reinterpretation of the daguerreotype using woodcut engravings; reporting on events such as ceremonies, royal visits and even a fire in Hamburg.
	1851: The (wet plate) collodion process is invented and photography becomes mobile: Roger Fenton took 360 photographs of the Crimean War between 1853 and 1856 and Mathew B. Brady similarly photographed the American Civil War.
	1881: The half-tone process is invented: it converts different tones into dots of varying size. This allowed for the simultaneous and more accurate reproduction of photographs in newspapers.
	1888: Kodak camera introduced – reducing the size and weight of camera equipment dramatically.
	1890s: Roll film was introduced, allowing for multiple exposures of an event to be taken in quick succession. Flash powder also allowed for photography in poor light conditions and was used to freeze the action in scenes where there was a lot of movement, such as horse racing.
1900s	**1902:** British Pathé, established in London, is credited with producing the first newsreel – a compilation of moving images depicting news stories that was screened in movie theatres before the main film.
	1920s: Newsreels became 'talkies' from the 1920s on when movie companies like Fox Movietone, Paramount, Universal, Warner-Pathe and Hearst Metrotone in the United States added sound. Newsreels continued to be screened in cinemas until the beginning of the 1970s.
	1925: The Leica 35 mm roll-film camera was introduced. Wide-aperture lenses meant that exposure time was drastically reduced, allowing for more active, narrative type images to emerge; indoor photography using available light became possible.
	1935: Kodachrome perfected the art of colour photography.
	1940s–1950s: Single lens reflex cameras introduced and shortly after this a range of detachable lenses were developed to allow photographers to take all manner of shots from extreme wide angle (using a fish-eye lens) with maximal distortion, to extreme long shots (using a telephoto lens) with maximal compression, and capable of capturing images from hundreds of metres away.

Cont'd

1950s on: Television sets mass produced with the aim of having one in every living room. Graphic footage of the Vietnam War led to massive political activism.

1980s: Offset lithography printing introduced in newspaper production allowing for premium quality photographic reproduction.

1981: IBM launches home computers (the PC) and the digital race begins.

1988: Fuji FILM introduces the world's first digital camera, complete with removable media, known as the DS-1P.

1990s: The internet provides a way for computers to communicate with each other through a global system of interconnected computer networks; while the world wide web allows anyone with internet connection to view, share and upload hyperlinked documents, including images and videos.

2000s	2000s: Fully digitized news capture, design and production.

2.1 *Image as illustration*

The role of the press photograph in news discourse was initially seen as being an illustrative adjunct to the more important verbal reporting of newsworthy events. This probably had much to do with the fact that during the 1800s photographs were reinterpreted in woodcut engravings giving them more of an art feel. They were also mostly static portraits of prominent individuals (see Caple 2010b for examples). The verbal text took control of all of the description. However, to view portraiture (particularly of prominent figures in society) as merely illustrative would be a mistake. Portraiture became, and still is, a dominant means of establishing a rapport between the reading public and key figures in society. As noted by Welling (1987), putting a face to the names that frequently appear in the news helps the public not only to identify such figures, but also to humanize them, and then to empathize with them (we have talked about this with respect to the news value of Personalization). As early as 1860 Abraham Lincoln suggested that he was able to sway the public in the presidential election that saw him take office through the wide distribution of visiting cards, or carte-de-visite as they were called then, which were like small business cards that carried a portrait of the person (Welling 1987). This means that as well as having this illustrative function, such images also have the capacity to play a significant role in engaging both the public and their representative governments in ways that may bring about significant social, political and cultural change. At the same time, however, the professional rhetoric around the role of news images has remained sceptical, as noted by Zelizer:

For most journalists, news images have always taken a back seat to words. Since the photograph's inception in the mid-1800s, pictures have long been seen as the fluff of journalism, the stuff that **illustrates** but is adjunct to verbal descriptions. (Zelizer 2004: 118, bold face ours)

2.2 Image as evidence

The evidence status of press photography is tied to the notion that a photograph is a way of truth-telling and that indeed, the photograph 'never lies'. With this view we also encounter the notion of objectivity. This notion of objective truth is encapsulated in Barthes' (1977: 44) description of the photograph as record:

> In the photograph – at least at the level of the literal message – the relationship of signifieds to signifiers is not one of 'transformation' but of 'recording', and the absence of a code clearly reinforces the myth of photographic 'naturalness': the scene is *there*, captured mechanically, not humanly (the mechanical is here a guarantee of objectivity). (Barthes 1977: 44, italics in original)

This truth-telling role is also reflected in the Media/Journalism Studies literature, which describes press photographs as authoritative, as mirrors of the events they depict – what Zelizer refers to as 'photographic verisimilitude' (2005: 171). Examples can be seen in the documentary photography of the late nineteenth century, which was used to help galvanize governments to take action on social issues. Photographers in New York, Glasgow and London began photographing slum conditions in these cities and 'straight' photography, introduced by P. H. Emerson in 1889, showed images in sharp focus and free of manipulation or reinterpretation (Welling 1987). With this the notion of truthful, objective photography emerged and through such realistic images, governments began to take note of social and environmental conditions and how they impacted upon their citizens. Such work has continued throughout the twentieth century in the images of photographers such as Robert Capa, Dorothea Lange or Nick Ut. However, we can again see at least two functions present in such images. On the one hand, they do stand in evidence of the existence of dire situations, but on the other hand, they also have the capacity to elicit strong affective responses in the viewer (see Section 2.5 'Image as evaluation'), responses that have the potential to prompt governments to take steps towards remedying such situations.

2.3 Image as sensation

The notion of image as sensation is tied closely to the emergence of the tabloid and picture press of the early to mid-twentieth century. Tabloid newspapers like the *Daily Mirror* in the United Kingdom and the *Daily Graphic* in the United States emerged as newspapers that relied exclusively on photography to relay news (Gernsheim 1955). The tabloid press placed great emphasis on photography in newspapers, using large, sensational images that usually revolved around the themes of violence, sex, scandal and accidents. Photography historian Robert Taft labelled the reproduction of such photographs in the tabloids as 'trite, trivial, superficial, tawdry, salacious, morbid or silly' (1938, cited in Becker 1992/2003: 133). Thus the early twentieth century press photograph earned its reputation as sensational journalism, which made it increasingly difficult to view photography as a credible medium for serious news reporting. This view shifted considerably though, when images became central to the reporting of war.

2.4 *Image as icon*

Iconic images are images that function as symbolic representations of key moments in history. This iconic status comes through most clearly in war photography, with the many wars of the twentieth and twenty-first centuries providing key critical moments that have since become embedded in the national psyche, symbols of nationalism and even at times used for propaganda purposes. Iconic images of the twentieth century that came to represent an entire historical period/event include Joe Rosenthal's 'Raising the Flag on Iwo Jima' (World War II) and Nick Ut's image of Phan Thi Kim Phúc, as a naked 9-year-old girl fleeing a napalm attack during the Vietnam War. Both of these images won Pulitzer Prizes. 'The Tank Man', an image taken by Jeff Widener of the Associated Press, shows a man defiantly standing in front of army tanks in Tiananmen Square in Beijing, China, in June 1989. This is another example of an image that has come to symbolize an entire historical event. Ken Jarecke's shot of a dead Iraqi soldier, charred and ashen, still at the wheel of his vehicle stands as an iconic reminder of the first Gulf War in the early 1990s, while Richard Drew's '9/11 Falling Man' is an iconic image from a more recent event. Again, iconic images of this nature can be deployed to galvanize a particular social group to support or resist a particular action. For example, some of the most memorable and terrifyingly authentic images to come out of the Vietnam War were instrumental in swaying public opinion and fuelling antiwar protests around the world (Sontag 2003; for a comprehensive account of the role of press photography in bearing witness see Zelizer 2004).

However, this potential to provoke strong reactions may also mean that photographs are sometimes deliberately withheld. This was the case in 2011 when the president of the United States of America, Barack Obama, decided not to release images showing the body of Osama bin Laden, who was killed by US Navy Seals on 2 May 2011. His reason for doing so was based on the fear that they would become a propaganda tool. White House press secretary Jay Carney said, 'it is not in our national security interests to allow those images, as has been in the past been the case, to become icons to rally opinion against the United States' (as reported in Cowan 2011).

2.5 *Image as evaluation*

The ability for iconic images to have an enduring effect on our visual memories is not only because they capture a critical moment in the unfolding of an event, a moment that comes to represent the entire event, but also because such images carry huge emotional appeal. This strong emotional engagement with the viewer can be achieved in the capturing of dramatic, graphic or emotionally confronting images. Examples of such images in the news today can be seen in the winning portfolios in competitions like World Press Photo. In 2011, press photographer Daniel Morel won first prize in the category for 'spot news stories' for his images of the dramatic rescue of victims (with the dead alongside the living) of the Haiti earthquake. Guang Niu, of China, won second prize in the category 'general news' for his graphic depiction of the mass cremation of victims of an earthquake in Qinghai province, and Javier Manzano's emotionally confronting image of the head of a man by the roadside near Ciudad Juarez in northern Mexico gained third prize in the same category.

From a semiotic perspective, both Economou (2006) and Caple (2009a) have argued that news images, in combination with verbal text and layout, can function to establish an evaluative stance on the events retold in the story (Caple 2009a) or that they instantiate different evaluative 'voices' or 'keys' in relation to their role in the news discourse as record or interpreter (Economou 2008: 255).

2.6 *Image as aesthetic*

Aesthetics in news photography is somewhat of a controversial issue. At various points in recent history, academics have denied press photographers a hand in the aesthetic appeal or even composition of their images. For example, Bignell (2002: 98) suggests that 'photogenia and aestheticism **are rarely** seen in press photography' (bold face ours), and Schirato and Webb (2004: 96), in describing a photograph of a protest depicting police and protesters facing each other, make the claim that 'it is manifestly not a press photograph, because there is a concern with composition rather than action'. However, we argue in this book that press photographers are indeed concerned with composition and the choices they take up in relation to this are very much motivated by an aesthetic value. In other words, photographers are always conscious of the aesthetic potential of any news image they produce. We also believe that there is evidence of resurgence in valuing the aesthetic in news images on the part of editors. We explore the aesthetics of images in more detail in Chapter 7 so will say no more about this here.

3 Images and the organization of news

It has become clear in the above discussion that images perform many functions in news discourse and that these functions occur simultaneously. Images have the capacity to function as evidence at the same time as they are able to elicit strong emotional responses in the audience; and some of these images may enter the national psyche as icons.

It is important to note that considerations for page layout, the size of images on the page and the relations between the verbal and visual text are also significant in pointing to the functions of images as news discourse. Indeed, those working on a daily basis with the production of the news claim that today's newspapers are a 'designer's newspaper' (Stephen Clark, senior news designer with the Australian broadsheet the *Sydney Morning Herald*, 2006, personal communication). They suggest that stories are planned and packaged around the notion of visual design, taking into consideration how they are framed and how they relate to other stories and advertising spaces on the page. From a linguistic perspective, Bateman (2008: 157) refers to the rhetorical organization of image and text within a single page layout as 'page-flow'. He states that page-flow is of central importance for advancing the treatment of multisemiotic genres because it is the primary 'resource' that multisemiotic genres build upon (Bateman 2008: 198). Bateman further suggests that newspapers rely on the page-flow model because when we read the newspaper there are many chunks that can be read about many different topics and without any necessary order imposed (Bateman 2008: 226). How layout and typography impact on the ways in which we engage with images in the news is very clearly shown in Figure 5.2 (from Chapter 3). Here we see 'screamer' headlines with capitalization, exclamation marks superimposed onto the large-size images of bin Laden allowing for maximum bleed between the image and the typography.

Figure 5.2 Front pages on the killing of Osama bin Laden

In the context of broadcast news, Montgomery (2007) proposes that frameworks of consumption (the fixed/closed daily news bulletin in conventional TV news programming versus the free-floating/open structures of the dedicated 24-hour news channels) have different effects on news story organization. He suggests that features of the more open structure of news storytelling, such as updates, constant forward projection through time and to later moments in the programme are beginning to influence the whole of broadcast news, and as such are having a significant effect on the ways in which discourse, audience and news events interact (Montgomery 2007: 67). In relation to the visual, Montgomery (2007: 55) points to the distinct postural shifts enacted by the newsreader as s/he moves from addressing the audience to addressing the correspondent on the video screen in the studio, which are characteristic of this change in structure.

Furthermore, different rhetorical organizations and functions of images and text have emerged in new ways of reporting the news. For example, Knox (2007, 2010) investigates the role of thumbnail images in newsbites, the short headline-plus-lead-plus-hyperlink stories on newspaper website homepages. He argues that 'each home page is a complex sign, consisting of a range of visual and visual–verbal signs which function as coherent structural elements' (Knox 2007: 23). In particular, he suggests that the function of newsbites on newspaper homepages is very different to that of news texts on story pages in that they operate as 'independent texts in their unique contextual environment to construe actors and events according to the institutional goals and ideologies of the newspaper' (Knox 2007: 26). He goes on to state that:

> newsbites function to highlight the stories valued by the institution of the newspaper as most important on a given day. Their social purpose is to present the focal point of a news story with immediacy and impact. They afford the institutional authors of the newspaper the means by which to visually evaluate stories in terms of their *comparative* importance (including by size, relative positioning, headline font size and colour and inclusion of optional structural elements such as images), and are designed to attract readers to navigate to story pages in order to access longer (and/or modally different) versions of the 'same' story. Every reader's click on a newsbite provides another advertising opportunity for the newspaper. (Knox 2007: 26, italics in original)

Other new practices emerging in the online environment can be seen in the 'Multimedia' sections of newspaper websites. Here, audiences can engage with photo galleries, videos, interactives, graphics or audio slideshows that are often hyperlinked to written news stories elsewhere on the website. Audio slideshows are automated and run from the first image to the last and often include music, ambient sound and voice-over from a reporter offering commentary on elements of the story (which may or may not be depicted in the corresponding images), while interactives consist of maps or images, where readers activate the revelation of information by hovering the cursor over these figures and thus navigate their own pathway through the text; graphics are additional tables and figures that are linked to a news story elsewhere on the website. Further, major world events (e.g. The Royal Wedding of Prince William and Kate Middleton in the United Kingdom in April 2011) are not only streamed live on news websites, but are then packaged up into shorter 'themed' units (like 'the balcony kiss', 'the vows', 'the wedding procession'), for audiences to relive their favourite moments from the event. Other practices that are far less polished are also emerging where 'raw' (unedited) footage from an event is being released to the public without any verbal commentary (although with original ambient sound). This seems to be associated more with breaking news events such as the protests on the streets in Bahrain, Benghazi or Tripoli (in February 2011) or with footage taken in the aftermath of natural disasters like the massive earthquake and tsunami in Japan in March 2011, and certainly help to construe news values such as Timeliness and Negativity (see Chapter 3).

Whether or not we are looking at practices of telling news stories in print news, broadcast news or online news, any analysis of the way such stories are organized in these different media forms arguably benefits from taking into account the relations between the verbal and the visual text. Therefore, we now turn to an exploration of text–image relations in news discourse, and discuss the ways in which language and still and moving images relate to each other.

4 Text–image relations in news discourse

4.1 *Overlap, displacement and dichotomy*

One of the classic studies on the relations between visual and verbal text in the news is Meinhof's (1994) research into televisual news discourse.[2] This research focuses on the textual strategies deployed in TV news bulletins to elicit certain responses in the viewers. Meinhof takes as her unit of analysis three 'action components' in the news item: the actors, the activities/events and the affected/effect/outcome (1994: 215–16) and proposes three categories for relating these components to each other in the form of image/text relations: overlap, displacement and dichotomy (1994: 216–17) (see Table 5.2 on p. 121).

In our analysis below, we will examine the extent to which Meinhof's categories for analysing text–image relations can be applied to both still and moving news images. We begin with an investigation of moving images, before widening our discussion to include still images in print news discourse and we end with a brief look at sequenced images in online news galleries.

Table 5.2 Categories for analysing intersemiotic relations

Categories	Definitions
Overlap	– where the visual track and the verbal track share the same action component, either directly or metonymically
Displacement	– where the visual and verbal tracks represent different action components of the same event (e.g. text reports the causes, images the effects)
Dichotomy	– where the visual and verbal tracks represent action components of different events

4.2 Text–image relations in moving images

The relationship between moving images and the verbal text accompanying them (e.g. in the case of TV news: the voice of newsreaders in the studio, the voice-over of reporters, and 'talent' interviewed on camera) can be analysed for the ways in which they form an intersemiotic relationship. To clarify, by *intersemiotic relationship* we mean the relations between different semiotic systems such as language and image (e.g. the relation between the voice-over and what is depicted in a shot), whereas *intrasemiotic relationship* refers to relations within one semiotic system (e.g. relations between images/shots or relations between sentences/clauses).

To exemplify **inter**semiotic relationships in moving images in this section (overlap, displacement, dichotomy), we draw on shots from two video news bulletins that were published online by ABC News (Australia) and BBC News (UK) on 2 May 2011, in which the death of Osama bin Laden was confirmed. We will not describe the news event in detail here as these bulletins are the subject of our case study in the final chapter (Chapter 9) of the book.

The first category suggested by Meinhof is that of **overlap**, where the visual and the verbal track share the same action component. Indeed, news organizations are often berated for simply restating verbally what can be seen visually, although this may at times be necessary (e.g. to clarify that a group of people standing by the side of a road are victims rather than perpetrators of a crime). Such overlap can be achieved through shared reference between the verbal and visual tracks, for example, in the use of spatial deixis (*here*) and demonstrative reference (*this man*) (Montgomery 2007: 95). In Table 5.3 on p. 122, two shots (5 and 6) from the ABC bulletin exemplify overlap between the verbal and visual track. In shot 5, President Obama speaks directly to the camera, and the verbal track carries his exact words (in contrast to the BBC story, as described in Chapter 9). In shot 6, the verbal track indicates the effect of Obama's announcement (*scenes of jubilation*) and the visual track shows people cheering, punching the air and waving flags, that is, acting out this *jubilation*.

Table 5.3 Examples of overlap in text–image relations in moving images (ABC *News in 90 Seconds* bulletin)

Shot	Visual Track	Verbal Track	Text–Image Relations
5	[Fixed camera position. Shot duration: 56 sec.] President Obama speaking into a microphone	'Today, at my direction, the United States launched a targeted operation against that compound in Abbottabad Pakistan . . . We must and we will remain vigilant at home and abroad.' (President Obama)	**Overlap** Verbal track: direct speech – the words spoken by the President match the visual track Visual track: President speaking
6	[Fixed camera position. Shot duration: 15 sec.] Crowds of people waving flags, punching the air, very dark surrounding so location is vague.	**Newsreader:** The announcement sparked scenes of jubilation outside the White House with people gathering to cheer and celebrate the death of America's most wanted terrorist.	**Overlap** Verbal track: scenes of jubilation Visual track: people punching the air, waving flags

Another way in which the verbal and visual tracks relate to each other is through **displacement** where 'film footage and text represent different action components of the same event' (Meinhof 1994: 216). Meinhof suggests that displacement can be seen in the typical cause–effect type reporting of natural disasters. The cause, an earthquake or tornado or cyclone, may be restated in the verbal text while the pictures show the devastation, destroyed buildings, debris and loss of life. Another kind of cause–effect relationship can be seen in the example in Table 5.4 on p. 123, which is taken from the BBC news bulletin. In shot 8, the visual track depicts the site of the attacks on the World Trade Centre in New York, while the verbal track relates the number of people killed as a result of these attacks.

Sometimes, there may be no immediate relation between the visual and verbal track in a news bulletin. This occurs most frequently when no suitable vision is available for a story, or if archived footage is used. This can be very misleading and may lead the viewer to attempt to make connections where none are intended. Meinhof (1994: 217) uses the term 'dichotomy' to refer to instances where 'film footage and text represent action components of different events'. For instance, both the BBC and the

Table 5.4 An example of displacement in text–image relations in moving images (BBC *One-minute World News* bulletin)

Shot	Visual Track	Verbal Track	Text–Image Relations
8	[Fixed camera position. Shot duration: 3 sec.] Aerial shot of the remains of the towers, after they had collapsed.	. . . 2001 in which around three thee-thousand people were killed.	**Displacement** Verbal track: details on the number of people killed in these attacks Visual track: the smouldering ruins of the WTC

ABC show file footage of Osama bin Laden in their reporting of his death. In Table 5.5 we can see footage of Osama bin Laden crouching and firing a gun, very much alive and well, while the verbal text is an indirect speech act from President Obama explaining how he was killed. This is a clear example of **dichotomy**.

Table 5.5 An example of dichotomy in text–image relations in moving images (ABC *News in 90 Seconds* bulletin)

Shot	Visual Track	Verbal Track	Text–Image Relations
3	Osama bin Laden in a crouching position, fires a gun	**Newsreader:** . . . Obama has announced that Osama bin Laden was killed by US forces who now . . .	**Dichotomy** Verbal track: indirect speech of US president Obama on the killing of bin Laden Visual track: shows images of bin Laden alive and actively firing a gun

Apart from analysing the intersemiotic relationships that hold between visual and verbal track in moving images, it is also important to consider intrasemiotic relations, that is, the relations between shots in the visual track (shot sequencing) and between clauses and sentences in the verbal track. Van Leeuwen (1991: 76, 2005: 229) approaches such analysis through conjunction, and puts it that just as clauses and sentences can build up a structure through temporal, comparative, causal or conditional relations, similar logical relations can also be identified for sequences of images. For example, temporal relations are enacted through the shot sequencing of one event after another and typically provide narrative progression, while the transition from a long shot to a close shot (i.e. a zoom-in) of the same subject realizes 'Detail' in van Leeuwen's (2005: 229) terms and the transition from close-up to long shot (i.e. a zoom out) realizes 'Overview'. For instance, in the news bulletin on the death of Osama bin Laden, the BBC follows a shot of the burning towers of the World Trade Centre with a zoom-in on the rubble showing details of the effects of the attacks (Table 5.6).

Table 5.6 An example of a zoom-in shot sequence, from Overview to Detail (BBC *One-minute World News* bulletin)

Shot	Visual Track	Verbal Track
6		**Newsreader:** The US has been trying to track him down
7	 [camera zooming in on rubble]	since al Qaeda came to the fore in the late 1990s well before its September 11 attacks on the World Trade Centre and the Pentagon in . . .

In general, it seems that when engaging with moving images viewers often expect the shots to relate to each other and attempt to make sense of each shot in terms of its position in the sequence. Furthermore, synchronized editing, where the transition from one shot to another coincides with clause and sentence boundaries, may help to establish parallelism between the verbal and visual track and with this their reciprocal relevance: 'the words seem to be driving the pictures at the same time as the pictures seem to be driving the words' (Montgomery 2007: 104).

To conclude this section, when considering the relations that hold between elements in online videos or televised reports or indeed other types of news discourse where moving images are used, we need to analyse not just the relations between words and images/shots but also the relations between clauses/sentences and between shots. Hence, it might seem as if the relations that hold between text and **still** images (e.g. in print news) are less complex. However, here we can investigate the relations between images and different parts of the verbal text: the caption, headline and body text. In the following we will explore image/caption, image/headline and image/ body text relations and the extent to which categories like those suggested by Meinhof for text–image relations in **televisual** news (moving images) may be applied to similar relations in **print** news (still images).

4.3 Text–image relations in still images

To explore text–image relations in still images we will draw on an example story from the *Boston Herald* ('Children OK, jake injured in blaze', *Boston Herald*, 15 December 2010, p. 11; reporter: Renee Nadeau Algarin, photo by Mark Garfinkel). This story (represented in Figure 5.3) includes a press photograph with a caption and an extended story which we have already analysed in Chapter 4.

Children OK, jake injured in blaze

By RENEE NADEAU ALGARIN

A two-alarm fire sent the kids and staff at a Dorchester day care scrambling yesterday morning, but everyone made it out safely.

The fire broke out at 18 Boyden St. on the Dorchester-Mattapan line at 10:08 a.m. yesterday, said Boston fire department spokesman Steve MacDonald.

The blaze was caused by an electrical short circuit inside the walls of two-story wood-framed house.

"The fire got in the walls and just traveled throughout the house," MacDonald said.

Two adults at the Pride N Joy Day Care center on the building's first floor managed to get all 10 children out safely before the fire engines arrived at the scene, MacDonald said.

Residents of an upstairs apartment were not home at the time of the fire.

One firefighter suffered a hand injury fighting the flames. He was treated and released from Carney Hospital in Dorchester.

Damage was estimated at $350,000, MacDonald said.

— madeau@bostonherald.com

STAFF PHOTO BY MARK GARFINKEL
HOT AND COLD: Boston firefighters battle a fire at 18 Boyden St. in Dorchester yesterday that caused $350,000 in damage to a day care.

Figure 5.3 'Children OK, jake injured in blaze', *Boston Herald*, 15 December 2010, p. 11, reprinted with permission of the *Boston Herald*

Before we examine the relationship between the image and caption/headline/body text we will look at the image itself and see what is depicted here. The image focuses on the work of two firefighters (the *actors*, in Meinhof's terms): one is outside standing on a crane and is inspecting the roof of a building (*activities*) and the other, inside the building, is removing external wall panelling (*activities*). We can also see aspects of the damage caused to the building in the blackened walls (*affected/effect/outcome*). The depiction of uniformed firefighters in this image construes the news value of Prominence (see Chapter 3). As a professional elite they are trained to deal with dangerous situations, and carry with them a degree of gravitas that also construes Negativity (in the event they are attending). The walls of the building appear to be severely damaged and the inside of the room is blackened, which construe the news value of Impact. There are no flames in the image and only minimal smoke, which leads us to conclude that the major threat of the fire appears to be over.

Image/caption relations

We will now consider the relations between the image in Figure 5.3 and its caption: *HOT AND COLD: Boston firefighters battle a fire at 18 Boyden St. in Dorchester yesterday that caused $350,000 in damage to a day care*. The bold, capitalized minor clause (*HOT AND COLD*) at the beginning of this caption is a feature of caption writing that is becoming increasingly common. Briefly here, Caple (2008a: 129) has theorized this minor clause as a 'prosodic tail' in relation to its use in stand-alone stories (see Chapter 8). It is often playful and requires the reader to be familiar with the text as a whole (including the image) in order to decode its meaning. In this instance, it is possibly referring to the fact that the fire (*hot*) resulted in the children and staff inside the building having to evacuate into the *cold* December outdoors.

Turning now to the relationship between the rest of the caption and the image: In this caption the verbal text tells us who – the actors – (*Boston firefighters*) is depicted, what they are doing – the activities/events – (*battle a fire*), where this is taking place (*at 18 Boyden St. in Dorchester*) and when – the circumstances – (*yesterday*). In terms of text–image relations we can say that in general there is **overlap** between the caption text and the image. However, this may seem somewhat of a simplification of these relationships since in the verbal text we get clarification of which firefighters these are (*Boston*) and in the image we can also see their uniforms, including hard-hat, gloves, heavy boots, and the types of equipment (oxygen tank, ladders) these firefighters are deploying in their work. Thus, the text specifies who these firefighters are but the image also specifies what exactly they are wearing and the tools they are carrying and working with (attributes), which also serve to clarify that these are firefighters rather than paramedics. So this is a two-way relationship in which both words and pictures specify each other in very detailed ways. The caption text further summarizes the activities of the firefighters in the verb *battle*; however, the image offers a more nuanced depiction of one firefighter inspecting the roof section of the building from a crane and another (largely obscured) inside the building and removing wood panelling from the smoking walls. We could then say that there is **displacement** between the activities in the caption and the activities in the image, as *battle* seems to be pointing to an earlier stage in this event when the firefighters probably were battling to bring the blaze under control. The action in the image lacks the intensity implied in the verb (presumably used to increase news value), but the presence of smoke and the extent of the damage depicted in the image point to this intensity. Note also that the verbs in this part of the caption tend to be written in the simple present tense.

Sometimes, a caption may stop after the first stage of clarifying our understanding of what is going on in the image. Quite often, however, news image captions tell us more than just what is going on in the image, as is the case in the *Boston Herald* story in Figure 5.3. This leads us to the second function of the caption, which is to relate the image to the wider news event and its news value (Caple 2009b). Clauses here are also usually marked by a shift in time/tense choice. In the caption in the fire story (Figure 5.3) we get the following extra information attached to the main clause: *that caused $350,000 in damage to a day care*. In this relative clause we get a shift in tense from present (*battle*) to past (*caused*) and we get additional information relating to the financial impact/consequences of this fire event. Meinhof's category of **overlap** can again be deployed in that the damage visually depicted is specified in the verbal text. However, we also get additional information relating to the use of the building (as a *day care* centre), which cannot be recovered from the image alone. This information, then, extends the meanings presented visually. Caple (2009b: 116) terms the **function** of this part of the caption text *contextual extension*. In this sense, the second clause in this caption elaborates on the wider news context and focuses our attention on the news angle, contextualizing the story in a news sense; it answers the question 'why is this news?', justifying its place in the newspaper. This part of the caption also serves to position the event in the image in relation to other activities preceding or following it or in relation to the event as a whole. This is why such contextual extension features a shift in time/tense choice.

Image/headline relations

The relationship between headlines and images is typically a lot less direct than that between images and their captions. Indeed, in the majority of cases, the headline text has little or nothing to do with any images associated with the story. Rather, headlines are most often extrapolated from the lead paragraphs of the verbal text and hence form a very close relationship with the lead. This is also a reflection of the institutional practices of news writing, where headlines are usually written by subeditors not journalists or photographers (see Chapter 4). An example of a story where the headline and image are only tangentially related to each other can be seen in the story in Figure 5.3 from the *Boston Herald*. The headline to this story reads 'Children OK, jake injured in blaze'. The image does not depict any children and it is impossible to gauge from the image alone that this building is particularly associated with children (although readers may infer that *children* were the occupants of the building before the *blaze* mentioned in the headline). There is a further point of commonality between the headline and image in the mention of *jake* (Boston slang for firefighter) in the headline and the depiction of two 'jakes' in the image. However, neither of the firefighters in the image appears to be injured: rather, they are working. Further, the *blaze* mentioned in the headline is more or less over in the photograph, with only a little smoke still visible. Thus, we can analyse the relationships between headline and image in this story as **displacement**, as the words and the image point to different action components of the same event.

While it is rare for headlines and images to share close relationships of **overlap**, there are instances where images and headlines do attempt

Table 5.7 Examples of overlap in image/headline relations

Text–Image Relations	Example Stories
Overlap Person depicted named in the headline. Defiant facial expression in image reflected in 'vows to fight' in headline.	**Example 1** DeLay, sentenced to 3 years, vows to fight Look of defiance (*Seattle Times* (US), 11 January 2011, p. A4)
Overlap Both the headline and subheadline specify the place 'Brisbane' which is visually depicted in the image. The 'floods' in the Issue Header are depicted in the image.	**Example 2**  Brisbane forgets the lessons of 1974 (*Press* (NZ) 14 January 2011, p. A5)

to do this. Examples are where a person depicted in an image is named in a headline (see Example 1 in Table 5.7 on p. 128) or where a facial expression is rendered verbally in the headline (also in Example 1). This verbal labelling is also used with place names: a place is visually depicted and named in the headline, as in *Brisbane* in Example 2, Table 5.7. Example 2 also makes use of what journalism professionals call an Issue Header. Issue headers are used when several stories on a page all relate to the same topic (see 'Gang wars' in Figure 3.9 in Chapter 3), in this case the *Queensland floods*. Sometimes, this header may be the main (or only) way in which connections are established between images and headline text.

To conclude, it would seem as if most news stories do not enjoy very close intersemiotic relationships between image and headline, although particular kinds of stories may do so – an example is the stand-alone (Caple 2010a) which we will discuss in Chapter 8. Here, we will continue our discussion of intersemiosis by examining the relationship between photographs and the body text of a news report.

Image/body text relations

We can also use Meinhof's categories of overlap, displacement and dichotomy to examine the relationships between image and body text. Indeed, it is likely that all three of these relations are present as the image will often capture a particular moment in the unfolding of an event while the story text will also relate to the happenings on either side of the captured moment as well as point to other matters of news value in the event. Let us continue with our examination of the fire story from the *Boston Herald* for image/body text relations (in Table 5.8 on p. 130).

We have already established above that the major threat of the fire appears to be over in this image; rather the image focuses on the work of the firefighters in inspecting the roof of the building and removing wail panelling, which reveals the extent of the damage to the building. The caption also points to the impact/consequences of the fire by putting a dollar figure to the damage depicted and the headline evaluates the situation in terms of human safety and injuries sustained. In terms of image/body text relations a clear pattern emerges in relation to time. The verbal text mostly retells action components that occurred before the one shown in the image (**displacement**) and emphasizes that the building occupants are safe; however, there was an injury sustained by a firefighter. Since the headline refers to the safety of the building occupants and the injury to the firefighter, it seems that the relationship between the headline and the body text is much closer than that between image and body text. It is possible to also state that there is limited **overlap** between the body text and image in the verbal mention and visual depiction of the building.

Table 5.8 Image/body text relations in 'Children OK, jake injured in blaze', *Boston Herald*, 15 December 2010, p. 11

Image/Caption	Story Text	Text–Image Relations
HOT AND COLD: Boston firefighters battle a fire at 18 Boyden St. in Dorchester yesterday that caused $350,000 in damage to a day care.	**Children OK, jake injured in blaze** A two-alarm fire sent the kids and staff at a Dorchester day care scrambling yesterday morning, but everyone made it out safely.	**Displacement**
	The fire broke out at 18 Boyden St. on the Dorchester-Mattapan line at 10.08 a.m. yesterday, said Boston fire department spokesman Steve MacDonald.	**Displacement** (**Overlap** – mention of the building and building is pictured)
	The blaze was caused by an electrical short circuit inside the walls of two-story wood-framed house [*sic*].	**Displacement**
	"The fire got in the walls and just traveled throughout the house," MacDonald said.	**Displacement**
	Two adults at the Pride N Joy Day Care centre on the building's first floor managed to get all 10 children out safely before the fire engines arrived at the scene, MacDonald said.	**Displacement**
	Residents of an upstairs apartment were not at home at the time of the fire.	**Dichotomy**
	One firefighter suffered a hand injury fighting the flames.	**Displacement**
	He was treated and released from Carney Hospital in Dorchester.	**Displacement**
	Damage was estimated at $350,000, MacDonald said.	**Displacement**
	Reprinted with permission of the *Boston Herald*	

Table 5.9 An example of overlap in image/body text relations

Text/Image Relations between Image and Body Text	Example Story
Overlap Direct reference made in the lead paragraph to the moment captured in the image in: *BLEEDING profusely from a head wound, **this is the dramatic moment** an alleged car thief was arrested after ramming a police car in a desperate bid to get away.*	

Daily Telegraph (AUS), 15 March 2010, p. 13,
image © Newspix/Lindsay Moller

An unusual instance of direct **overlap** between an image and the body text of a print news story can be seen in Table 5.9. In this example (also discussed in Chapter 3), the story leads with the moment captured in the image and makes direct reference to the image in the verbal text *this is the dramatic moment . . . .* The use of the demonstrative *this* in the lead paragraph is reminiscent of TV news reporting where shared reference between the verbal and visual track is achieved through spatial deixis, and demonstrative reference in the verbal track overlaps the visual track (Montgomery 2007: 95). Indeed, the fact that there is a photograph (originally published in colour) of *the dramatic moment* could be the reason why this story has achieved such prominence on the page (rather than being included in a simple newsbrief).

With respect to the relations in print news between image, caption, headline and body text, we may ask whether or not it is necessary to analyse all of these relations and in what order they should be analysed. This is pertinent to studies that investigate how we 'read' news stories. For example, eye-tracking studies seem to suggest that readers of print newspapers engage first with the largest headlines and image on the page, and captions to such images (especially depicting action) are also more likely to be read before the main story (Quinn and Stark Adam 2008). Thus it may be prudent to analyse the relationship between image, caption and headline first and then relate the three together to the remainder of the story text.

4.4 Text–image relations in sequenced images

The relationships described in the previous sections between headline, image and caption are also relevant to emergent online practices in which news organizations are taking advantage of the abundance of visual material to create photo galleries or online news galleries (see Caple and Knox in press). Such galleries typically include a headline, and a caption with each image; however, they are also **sequences** of images. This means that they also have things in common with moving images where we can find sequences of shots. We briefly explore such galleries in the following section.

At their most basic, online news galleries (Caple and Knox in press) are authored sequences of images and captions constructed around a news event (e.g. Deep Water Horizon Oil Spill in the Gulf of Mexico) or according to themes (e.g. Weather) or time (e.g. This Week in Images). They are 'authored' in that photographers and editors select from a number of images and write captions (and often headlines) for these images. They are numbered and sequenced and when opened one enters the gallery at the first image. A scroll tool usually allows the viewer to move forwards or backwards once the sequence has begun. This ordering of images has led researchers like Caple and Knox (in press) to question the extent to which galleries with a *sequential* beginning, middle and end have the potential to also be guided by narrative norms with a *rhetorical* beginning, middle and end. This is driven by the fact that news reporting is often defined in terms of its storytelling nature (see for example Tuchman 1973/1997, Schudson 1978, van Dijk 1988b, Bell 1991). Thus, online news galleries add to the range of possibilities for online news storytelling. Since such galleries involve image/verbiage complexes of still image and caption (and often headline) and are at the same time sequences of images, they can be analysed both for the relations that hold between each still image and its accompanying verbal text (**inter**semiotic relations), as well as for the relations that hold between images (**intra**semiotic relations).

To illustrate this point briefly we will look at one online news gallery where both inter- and intrasemiotic relationships are employed to produce a cogent story.[3] The gallery concerns the *Oktoberfest* in Munich (see Chapter 8 for a detailed explanation of this festival) and was published on the *Guardian* (UK) newspaper website (www.guardian.co.uk/) on 21 September 2009. The gallery can be accessed at www.guardian.co.uk/travel/gallery/2009/sep/20/oktoberfest-festivals-munich?INTCMP=SRCH#/?picture=353206027&index=0 and we therefore do not reproduce the whole gallery here. Rather, we draw on four examples from the beginning, middle and end of the gallery to exemplify inter- and intrasemiotic relations (in Table 5.10; see Caple and Knox in press for a complete analysis of this gallery). There are fourteen images in the gallery: five from the parades, five from inside the beer tents, two from the fairground, one of drunken

Table 5.10 Inter- and intrasemiotic relations in the online news gallery 'Oktoberfest starts in Munich' (www.guardian.co.uk/, 21 September 2009)

Slide	Image	Caption	Text–Image Relations	Conjunctive Relations	
				Between Images	Between Captions
1		Children play drums and march during the marksmen's parade on the second day of the Oktoberfest beer festival at the *Theresienwiese* in Munich	Overlap	n/a	n/a
2–5	More images of people parading				
6		Visitors clink beer mugs	Overlap	Next event	Addition/next event
7–10	More images of people drinking in the beer tents				
11–12	Visitors at the fairground				
13		After drinking, what better than a rest against a wall	Overlap	Next event	Next event
14		Crowds flock to the beer tents at night	Overlap	Next event/ overview	Next event/ conclusive event

revellers sitting/lying on the floor, and one of a night view of the whole venue, including fairground rides, beer tents and the crowds on the street. From the ordering of these images, we can already detect a temporal and spatial progression as we move through the gallery (from day to night, and from outside to inside to outside again). The headline 'Oktoberfest starts in Munich' is consistently displayed above every slide and each image has its own caption.

In terms of text–image (**inter**semiotic) relations, the caption texts remain closely descriptive of the images and there is clear **overlap** between caption and image. Indeed, all of the images and captions relate to each other in this way throughout this gallery. Turning to the (**intra**semiotic) relations between the images, sequential meaning is afforded by the mechanical requirement of clicking through the sequence of images in the gallery. This is also a temporal sequencing (i.e. relating to each other as the next event), which is reinforced by the transition from daytime to night time in the final image. Also, in van Leeuwen's (2005) terms, the shot type (long shot of the beer tents, the parade ground and the fairground rides) of the final image can be read as a conjunctive relation of Overview between the final image and **all** of the preceding images. A similar pattern emerges for the **intra**semiotic relations between the captions in this gallery. The captions are generally related by addition and/or temporally as next event. In this way, intra- and intersemiotic relations are employed to tell a cogent news story about 'things that happen' at the Oktoberfest.

5 Conclusion

In this chapter, we have examined the important contributions that images in and of themselves make to the ways in which readers and viewers engage with major news events, for example, as evidence, evaluation or aesthetic. We have also explored the relations between elements in news stories that include still or moving images. We have drawn primarily on Meinhof's framework and have shown how it can be applied to moving images, print news stories and online news galleries. Other frameworks that draw more explicitly on linguistic concepts such as cohesion (see n. 2) may allow a more in-depth analysis but have so far not been applied to news discourse. Our discussion has demonstrated the complexity of relations that hold between different elements of news stories and have shown the need for systematic analysis that takes into account the fact that words and images work together to create meaning. Images can be regarded as partners in the retelling of newsworthy happenings and capable of allowing for the multiplication of meaning at the intersection of words and images (Caple 2009b). We thus need to develop specific frameworks not just for analysing relations between the verbal and the visual, but also for systematic analysis of meanings made in the language and meanings made in the image so that we can bring both together. In the next two chapters, we introduce two specific frameworks for analysing language (for evaluation) and images (for composition), before again bringing the analysis of language and image together in two case studies.

Directions for further reading

For discussion on intersemiosis see:

Caple, H. (in press), *Photojournalism: A Multisemiotic Approach*. Basingstoke: Palgrave Macmillan. Explores inter- and intrasemiotic relations in print and online news discourse.

Royce, T. (2002), 'Multimodality in the TESOL classroom: exploring visual–verbal synergy', *TESOL Quarterly*, 36 (2), 191–205. Investigates intersemiotic complementarity from a systemic functional linguistic perspective.

van Leeuwen, T. (1991), 'Conjunctive structure in documentary film and television', *Continuum*, 5 (1), 76–114. Examines conjunctive relations between sequences of images in documentaries.

— (2005), *Introducing Social Semiotics*. London/New York: Routledge. Chapter 11 deals specifically with 'information linking' in the multimodal environment.

For discussion of TV news and the relationship between words and images:

Meinhof, U. H. (1994), 'Double talk in news broadcasts: a cross-cultural comparison of pictures and texts in television news', in D. Graddol and O. Boyd-Barrett (eds), *Media Texts: Authors and Readers*. Clevedon: Open University Press, pp. 212–23. Investigates intersemiosis in televisual news discourse.

Ray, V. (2003), *The Television Handbook: An Insider's Guide to being a Great Broadcast Journalist*. London: Macmillan. Investigates the relationships between words and images in televisual news discourse from a professional perspective.

Notes

1   This is different to Peirce's notion of icon, where the signifier represents the signified through likeness (see Rose 2007: 83, Sturken and Cartwright 2009: 28–9).

2   In Social Semiotics, the main focus of research has been on intersemiosis (the relationship between visuals and verbal text) in a wide variety of contexts. While this research has not focused specifically on text–image relations in news discourse, it has provided the basis for other researchers investigating intersemiosis. Royce (2002: 194) bases his interpretation of ideational, or representational, meanings encoded in a multimodal text in high school science textbooks in lexical cohesion (after Halliday and Hasan 1985), including

synonymy, antonymy, hyponomy, meronymy and collocation. Van Leeuwen (1991) looks at conjunctive relations both within and between the verbal and visual tracks in documentary film and television. Building on this work on conjunctive relations, Martinec and Salway (2005) develop their approach to componential cohesion in text–image relations by combining logico-semantic and status relations (Halliday 1985) with text relations (Barthes 1977). With regard to *news* discourse, social semiotic research in this area includes investigation of newspaper texts (Macken-Horarik 2003), newspaper front pages (Kress and van Leeuwen 1998), stand-alones (Caple 2006, 2008a, 2010a, in press), longer-form news features (Economou 2006, 2008), newsbites (Knox 2007, 2010) and online news galleries (Caple and Knox in press).

3 It must be noted that many galleries do not (or may not even attempt to) achieve such cogent storytelling. Indeed, it is those based on a particular news event rather than a theme that will try to tell a cogent story through the gallery (see Caple and Knox in press for further discussion of these issues).

CHAPTER SIX

Evaluation in the news

1 Introduction

In this chapter and the following, we outline two specific frameworks for analysing aspects of language and image in news discourse. This chapter deals with a linguistic framework for analysing evaluation in the news, while Chapter 7 introduces a semiotic framework for analysing composition in images. Chapter 8 then offers a case study that applies both of these frameworks. Our objectives for this chapter are:

- to introduce readers to the notion of evaluation
- to outline one framework for analysing evaluation
- to discuss some of the functions of evaluation in news discourse
- to explore some of the issues that arise when analysing evaluation.

We will start by discussing evaluation in general before we move to the specific framework for analysis that we describe in this chapter.

2 What is evaluation?

What, then, is evaluation? By way of introduction consider the following three examples from radio news discourse:

(1) He [President Obama] also said the Libyan government must be held accountable for its **brutal** treatment of protesters. (NPR Hourly News Summary, 27 February 2011)

(2) 'There is **a lot of confusion on the ground so that is often difficult for us to sort through to get to what the actual facts are**' (NPR Hourly News Summary, 4 March 2011)

(3) Newspapers and news reels saw in the young queen a photogenic
    star, everything her father had had no wish to be. **How unexpected
    that** almost six decades later a movie is making George VI a star as
    well. (BBC Radio NewsPod, 7 January 2011)

These examples all contain various expressions of subjectivity or opinion.
For example, President Obama is reported as expressing a condemnation
of the Libyan government's treatment of protesters (Example 1); another
source is heard making a judgement about the difficulty or complexity
of a situation (Example 2) and a journalist evaluates a state-of-affairs as
unexpected (Example 3). In other words, the three examples all contain
evaluations. Generally speaking, then, evaluation is concerned with the
expression of speaker/writer opinion or subjectivity. As Examples 1–3
show, such evaluations can involve quite different meaning dimensions or
parameters, such as disapproval (Example 1), complexity (Example 2) or
unexpectedness (Example 3). That is, we can evaluate some aspect of the
world as more or less positive or negative, easy or complex, expected or
unexpected. In fact, we can distinguish a wide range of such *evaluative
parameters* and will introduce these further below. Examples 1–3 also
show that evaluations in news discourse can be employed by different kinds
of speakers, for example, they can be part of a source's quoted speech,
or part of what a journalist (e.g. newsreader, correspondent . . .) says –
remember the complexity of authorship in news discourse (Chapter 2) and
its integration of source material (Chapter 4). The examples also illustrate
that such evaluations can relate to different aspects of the world in terms of
what is evaluated by speakers/writers – ranging from someone's behaviour
(Example 1) to a situation (Example 2) or an event (Example 3). There
are also many other aspects of the world that we can evaluate through
language.

In this chapter we introduce one particular approach to analysing
evaluation in news discourse. It must be noted at this stage that there are
alternative theories and conceptualizations of evaluation and evaluative
language, including notions such as *subjectivity* (e.g. Pounds 2010),
evaluation (e.g. Hunston and Thompson 2000), *appraisal* (e.g. Ben-Aaron
2005, Martin and White 2005, Thomson and White 2008) and *stance*
(e.g. Conrad and Biber 2000, Lombardo 2004). Bednarek (2006c, 2008b)
provides more detail about relevant research and the rationales behind the
particular framework that will be introduced below (see also the 'Directions
for further reading' section at the end of this chapter).

One of the reasons why it is worthwhile to focus on evaluation when
analysing news discourse from a linguistic perspective is its multifunctionality
(Thompson and Hunston 2000: 6). For instance, evaluations in the news
can express the evaluative stance, ideological or political position of the
principal (cf. Chapter 2); they can construe news values (cf. Chapter 3);
they can establish relationships with readers/audiences; and they can be

used to structure or organize news stories. In fact, evaluation in news discourse has a range of functions that are worthy of further investigation (see White 1997, 2000, 2003b, 2006, Lombardo 2004, Bednarek 2006c, 2010a), especially the usage of evaluation in different genres or text types. While the main focus in this chapter is on the introduction of a particular framework for categorizing evaluation, we will comment on the potential functions of evaluations in the examples we use and also point to some of their key functions in news discourse in general, particularly concerning the construal of news values. As we have seen in Chapter 3, evaluation is one of the main ways in which newsworthiness is discursively construed in the news. We will explore this in more detail in this chapter.

3 Parameters of evaluation

As suggested above, evaluations can relate to different meaning dimensions such as disapproval, complexity and unexpectedness. Following Thompson and Hunston (2000), we can call such dimensions *parameters of evaluation* or *evaluative parameters*. Evaluative parameters refer to the standards, norms and values according to which we evaluate something through language. For example, speakers and writers can evaluate situations as good or bad, expected or unexpected, important or unimportant, and so on. Bednarek (2006c, 2010a) – the basis for this chapter – has explored the kinds of parameters that can be found in British print news discourse and has suggested a number of core and peripheral parameters (Figure 6.1). It must be stated that this framework is conceptualized as open-ended and organic, with clear potential for further redevelopment and refinement as it is applied to more and more data.[1]

In this chapter we use data from radio news discourse to provide illustration for each parameter – this is partially because we have not yet made much use of examples from radio news discourse in this book, and partially because most existing analyses of evaluation (appraisal, etc.) have

P	*The parameter of Un/importance:* 'how important or unimportant?'
a	*The parameter of In/comprehensibility:* 'how comprehensible or incomprehensible?'
r	*The parameter of Im/possibility or In/ability:* 'how possible or impossible?'
a	*The parameter of Un/necessity:* 'how necessary or how unnecessary?'
m	*The parameter of Emotivity:* 'how positive or negative?'
e	*The parameter of Un/genuineness or In/authenticity:* 'how authentic or artificial?'
t	*The parameter of Reliability:* 'how likely or unlikely?'
e	*The parameter of Un/expectedness:* 'how expected or unexpected?'
r	*The parameter of Evidentiality:* 'how do we know?'
s	*The parameter of Mental state:* 'how do people feel (about this)?'

Figure 6.1 Parameters of evaluation

focused primarily on print news. Indeed, the analysis of evaluation in online, TV and radio news is an area delineated for future research, with attention needed both to similarities/differences to print news as well as internal differences, for example, between news bulletins and news podcasts. Examples in this chapter are taken from the morning news programmes broadcast live on ABC News Radio, Australia (recorded between December 2010 and January 2011, 8–9 a.m.) as well as from online news podcasts by national public radio broadcasters in Canada (CBS), Ireland (RTÉ), New Zealand (Radio New Zealand), United States (NPR) and the United Kingdom (BBC) downloaded between December 2010 and April 2011.

We include both evaluations that originate in journalists (whether correspondents, newsreaders, etc., see authorship roles in Chapter 2) and those that originate in (quoted) sources. Evaluations by the latter are indicated through single quotation marks ('. . .') around the example. Evaluations that occur in interviews with affiliated journalists are not marked by quotation marks, as they are still seen here as originating in a journalist rather than a source. In fact, as Example 5 on p. 141 illustrates, broadcast news often features live interviews between the in-studio newsreader and an affiliated representative (e.g. in-field correspondent) (see Tolson 2006: 61, Montgomery 2007). The following sections will provide examples for each evaluative parameter. In transcribing examples, hesitation phenomena (such as *erm*) and paralinguistic information (e.g. laughter, coughing) have not been transcribed. For ease of readability, we discuss only one parameter of evaluation (**bolded**) per example, even when other parameters are present.

3.1 *The parameter of Un/importance*

Evaluations along the parameter of Un/importance evaluate the world and discourse about it according to a subjective evaluation of its status in terms of importance, relevance, significance and related notions. A useful paraphrase for such evaluations is 'how important or how unimportant does this appear?' For instance, in Example 4, the evaluation is produced by a correspondent who is live in action so to speak, and who evaluates her position in terms of its significance location-wise, thus arguably increasing her eyewitness status.

(4) . . . I'm standing at one of the **major** checkpoints . . . (RTÉ Radio 1 News at One, 25 February 2011)

In Example 5 below, a newsreader and correspondent together construe an army statement as important (increasing its newsworthiness), and in (6) a source makes a prediction concerning whether or not the impact of a weather phenomenon will be significant for local news consumers. In fact, evaluations of Unimportance as seen in Example 6 are rare in news discourse, presumably because they decrease news value.

(5) [Newsreader]: Can you please tell us about some news that's come in recent times, a statement from the army reported by the state news agency that the army has stressed it will not use force against the demonstrators. How significant is that? [correspondent Nathan King]: I think that's **very significant** . . . (Radio New Zealand Morning Report, Top Stories for 1 February 2011)

(6) . . . the bureau's hydrologist, Jimmy Stewart, thinks the rainfall is **unlikely to have a major impact,** at least around Rockhampton (ABC News Radio, 6 January 2011)

We could also include notions of stardom/famousness (*celeb, star, famous, celebrity, largely unknown*), influence/authority (*leading, senior, top*), that is, the importance of people, in this parameter (or, alternatively, set this up as its own parameter), considering statements that relate to how well-known, influential or powerful news actors and sources are said to be, as in Examples 7 to 9.

(7) Well, it [attempted robbery and kidnap] started at about half nine last night when about four armed and masked men entered the home of Liam O'Sullivan, now Liam O'Sullivan is **a very senior executive,** and I'm [unclear] he's **one of the top ten executives** in the company (RTÉ Radio 1 News at One, 5 April 2011)

(8) Professor David Howard from the University of York is **an expert** in the science behind sound (BBC Radio NewsPod, 6 March 2011)

(9) Newspapers and news reels saw in the young queen a photogenic **star,** everything her father had had no wish to be. How unexpected that almost six decades later a movie is making George VI **a star** as well. (BBC Radio NewsPod, 7 January 2011)

Again, explicit references to news actors as senior, experts or stars increase news value (of Prominence, or Attribution – cf. Chapter 3). Indeed, the reporting of events involving 'important' people or stories about stars, and the use of quotes attributed to the powerful elite are one of the mainstays of news discourse. News workers assume that news consumers are interested in such reporting and evaluations are a way of enhancing such aspects of reported events.

3.2 The parameter of In/comprehensibility

Evaluations of In/comprehensibility in news discourse have to do with the degree to which journalists, news actors or sources evaluate entities, situations, states-of-affair, or statements in stories as being within or outside the grasp of their understanding. In/comprehensibility encompasses the related concepts of vagueness and explicitness: what is vague is less easily comprehensible; what is explicit is more easily comprehensible. It also incorporates the concepts of inexplicability and mystery, including unsolved problems, and states of affairs that are unknown to us and hence remain mysterious. It also takes in questions of ease and difficulty. A useful paraphrase for such evaluations is 'how comprehensible or easy, or how incomprehensible or difficult, does this appear?' Examples from radio news programmes are:

(10) It was a moment that everyone had known would have to come but, as the mayor Bob Parker said yesterday afternoon, that **didn't make it any easier.** 'Today we transition from rescue to recovery. And those are the words that nobody in this city, none of the families, none of the friends here and overseas, I would imagine nobody anyb-anywhere wanted to hear.' (Radio New Zealand Morning Report, Top Stories for 4 March 2011)

(11) . . . but what scientists are trying to do is to **pin down** exactly what it is in their [choir boys] voice that gives it this really **unmistakeable** quality (BBC Radio NewsPod, 6 January 2011)

(12) Yes, **it's very difficult to get accurate information** because all communication had-has been cut off in Libya for the last couple of days (CBC News Hourly Edition, 18 March 2011)

As can be seen, such evaluations are sometimes connected to notions of undesirability (e.g. in Example 10); they can be used to create a slight aura of mystery (e.g. in Example 11) and/or drama. Further, news discourse strives to be authoritative, yet at the same time it often reports on events before all details are confirmed as different news organizations strive for scoops (cf. Example 12 and Chapter 3 on competition in the news process). It appears as if evaluations of In/comprehensibility are used to balance these contrasting constraints. Such evaluations may also be used because of the journalistic code (the values of objectivity, fairness, truthfulness and accuracy – cf. Chapter 2), that is, in order to be accurate about the limits of the reported information.[2]

3.3 *The parameter of Im/possibility or In/ability*

The parameter of Im/possibility or In/ability is related to the linguistic concepts of (deontic and dynamic, not epistemic) modality,[3] and concern evaluations of what is (not) possible. A useful paraphrase for such evaluations is 'how possible or how impossible does this appear?' Examples 13 to 15 include journalists' and sources' evaluations of behaviour as impossible (flying; firing a staffer) and possible (minimizing risks).

(13) We'll talk more about the roads later but first to the skies and another fifteen thousand people who **haven't been able** to fly today after Dublin airport suspended flights at around half past nine this morning. (RTÉ Radio 1 News at One, 23 December 2010)

(14) NDP MP Pat Martin says Jason Kenney **can't** just fire his staffer. (CBC News Hourly Edition, 4 March 2011)

(15) '. . . so although, as I say, you **can't** eliminate risks, [unclear] the possibilities of an incident happening here entirely but you **can** minimize them, I think we are doing that' (BBC Radio NewsPod, 6 January 2011)

Again, we can see that the force or effect of such evaluations may vary. For instance, in Example 13 the evaluation seems to imply an undesirable or difficult state-of-affairs for the passengers involved (cf. the news value of Negativity); in Example 14 a source uses the evaluation to express his disapproval, whereas in Example 15 a source appears to evaluate the risks of a nuclear incident in the United Kingdom as not very high.

3.4 *The parameter of Un/necessity*

The parameter of Un/necessity deals with what linguists have traditionally described as deontic and dynamic modality or modulation (see n. 3). It relates to the use of modal verbs, nouns, adjectives, or adverbs and other linguistic items that express evaluations of what is (not) necessary. A useful paraphrase for such evaluations is 'how necessary or how unnecessary does this appear?' Consider Examples 16 to 18 in this respect.

(16) He [Public security minister Vic Toews] repeated that new rules **are needed to** deal with people who sneak migrants into the country (CBC News Hourly Edition, 19 January 2011)

(17) President Obama acknowledged that so long as Muammar Gaddafi remains in power Libyan civilians will **need** protection from the international community (NPR Hourly News Summary, 23 March 2011)

(18) Well, this is the most recent update from Foreign Affairs here in Ottawa. This new warning says that Canadians who **don't need to** be in Egypt **should** get out. What it says is Canada-Canadians in Egypt should consider leaving if their presence is **not necessary** (CBC News Hourly Edition, 30 January 2011)

These examples show that sources frequently comment on current affairs in terms of the necessary actions they imply. This may be used to justify political decisions (Examples 16 and 17) or to inform citizens about actions to undertake (Example 18). Such evaluations can also be tied to expressing dis/approval (conceptualized as Emotivity below), commenting 'that what **is** shouldn't be (thereby implicitly evaluating it as bad) and what **isn't** should be (thereby implicitly evaluating it as good)' (Martin 1992: 363, bold face ours).

3.5 *The parameter of Emotivity*

The parameter of Emotivity is concerned with the journalist's or source's evaluation of events, things, people, activities, or other evaluated entities as positive (good) or negative (bad). Evaluations of Emotivity are expressed by a range of linguistic items that vary enormously in their evaluative force and are situated on a cline ranging from more or less positive to more or less negative (see Bednarek 2006c: 46–8). However, a useful general paraphrase for such evaluations is 'how positive or how negative does this appear?' Look at these examples of positive (*welcome*) and negative (*inappropriate*, *irresponsible*) Emotivity:

(19) 'The other aspect, and that's very **welcome** is that beds are being re-opened that had been closed . . .' (RTÉ Radio 1 News at One, 5 January 2011)

(20) 'The number one goal for an energy strategy in the 21st century is fossil fuel, it's **worse than inappropriate**, it's **irresponsible**' (Radio New Zealand Morning Report, Top Stories for Monday 4 April 2011)

Here sources' (rather than journalists') evaluations of positive and negative Emotivity are quoted in the news programme. This is in fact common for many types of print and broadcast news programmes, as it allows for the appearance of objectivity, yet permits the inclusion of evaluations (in sources' speech) that are newsworthy (cf. Chapter 4).

We can also identify a number of subsets of positive and negative Emotivity if necessary for more detailed textual analysis (as does Appraisal Theory; see Martin and White 2005), such as morality (*brutal* in Example 21) or aesthetics (*unsightly* in Example 22), while some words express only very general positivity or negativity (*bad* in Example 23):

(21) He [President Obama] also said the Libyan government must be held accountable for its **brutal** treatment of protesters. (NPR Hourly News Summary, 27 February 2011)

(22) There must be thirty or forty bags [of rubbish] here, spilling out all over the street and as I look up the road it's the same picture, and here, like in many other parts of the city it's been waiting

to be collected for up to three weeks. It's **unsightly,** it smells and
that's not the worst of it (BBC Radio NewsPod, 6 January 2011)

(23) 'It's a **bad** bill, built on **bad** assumptions and **bad** ideology' (BBC
NewsPod, 4 April 2011)

Evaluations of Emotivity often relate to the evaluative stance of a particular
news organization, whether political or ideological. They are also used
for construing and attracting a target audience with whom the news
organization aims to 'bond' and establish solidarity (Martin and White
2005, Caple 2008a). Newspapers, for instance, will aim to construe a
story 'which is in line with what they think are the opinions, attitudes, and
feelings – hence, the evaluative stance – of (the majority of) their readers'
(Bednarek 2006c: 203). We can tie this to the concept of *audience design*
(see Chapters 1 and 2), and this, therefore, is one of the ways in which news
discourse discursively construes a readership.

3.6 *The parameter of Un/genuineness or In/authenticity*

Evaluations of Un/genuineness or In/authenticity relate to the journalist's or
source's evaluation of how genuine or how artificial social actors or aspects
of the news event are. A useful paraphrase for such evaluations is 'how real,
true, and authentic or how fake, false, and artificial, does this appear?'
While no such evaluations could readily be found in the downloaded radio
podcasts, which may mean that they are relatively infrequent, they do
occasionally occur, at least in print and online news discourse, and are
often associated with evaluating the authenticity of emotional relationships
or behaviour, as is also the case in these four examples from Australian and
British newspapers and news websites:

(24) 'Hefner says the relationship developed into a **genuine** love affair'
('Oh boy, the party's over', *Sydney Morning Herald*, 18–19
October 2008, p. 13)

(25) 'Ai Wei Wei, former bad boy made good, who was closely involved
in the design of the Bird's Nest stadium in Beijing, says the
Olympics are a **fake** smile hiding China's deep troubles' ('A market
for creativity', www.theaustralian.com.au, 28 July 2008)

(26) The sense of shock felt among Britain's senior police officers
yesterday was **genuine.** ('The shaming of Britain's racist
policemen: five quit after documentary shocks the force',
Independent, 23 October 2003, p. 3)

(27) Scores of defiant delegates sat on their hands rather than be
whipped into a mood of **artificial** enthusiasm. ('It's a fake and
flop', *Sun*, 10 October 2003, p. 11)

Clearly, journalists and their audience/readership are particularly interested in whether or not emotional behaviour is real or feigned. However, there may be an argument for incorporating this parameter under Emotivity because frequently evaluating someone or something as 'genuine' equals a positive evaluation and evaluating someone or something as 'fake' equals a negative evaluation (White 2002: 12). But at this stage it is questionable whether or not this is always and exclusively the case. In other words: if evaluations of Inauthenticity are always negative and evaluations of Authenticity are always positive, they are clear subsets of Emotivity – if not, it may be worthwhile investigating them as a separate parameter.

3.7 *The parameter of Reliability*

Evaluations of Reliability are connected to what is generally described as epistemic modality or modalization in Linguistics, that is, matters of reliability, certainty, confidence and likelihood (see n. 3). They relate to evaluations of how probable it is that future events will happen. A useful paraphrase for such evaluations thus is 'how likely or how unlikely does it appear that this will happen?' For instance, the forecasters mentioned in Example 28 below predict a future snow storm (*will*), while the NPR newsreader in Example 29 predicts no further legislative action for a repeal measure, and Example 30 reports an official's estimate of the probable length of an evacuation.

(28) Some spots could be hit with as much as one to two feet of snow by Monday morning with the heaviest snow fall in South Eastern New York and in New England, but forecasters say a huge sweep of the East Coast **will** see flakes (NPR Hourly News Summary, 25 December 2010)

(29) The house has approved two hundred and forty-five to one eighty-nine a bill to repeal last year's health law but, as NPR's Julia Rovner reports, the repeal measure **is not likely to** see any further legislative action (NPR Hourly News Summary, 19 January 2011)

(30) . . . an official says it will **probably** take several flights over several days to take care of everyone who wants to leave [Egypt] (NPR Hourly News Summary, 30 January 2011)

These three examples suggest that such evaluations are frequently used by journalists in news stories to express hypotheses as well as to predict happenings and to speculate about future events. As mentioned in Chapter 4, the development of a news story may include information about potential consequences of a news event. Predictions using evaluations of Reliability may be a typical way of referring to such consequences or impact: In live exchanges on TV news, reporters have been shown to use *will* frequently to make predictions (Haarman 2004: 84), and researchers have argued that BBC radio news discourse 'is largely oriented towards making predictions, speculations and statements about the future' (Jaworski et al. 2003: 61).

3.8 *The parameter of Un/expectedness*

The parameter of Un/expectedness involves evaluations of aspects of the world (including statements) as more or less expected or unexpected. A useful paraphrase for such evaluations is 'how expected or how unexpected does this appear?' We can also include in this parameter the notion of contrast expressed by conjunctions, adverbs (e.g. *but, while, still, although, though, even*) and negation (e.g. *no, not, only*). In fact, much linguistic research has shown that negated statements (statements with *no, not, only,* etc.) are connected to notions of counter-expectation and are used to refer to deviations from what we would expect to be the case. A more implicit way of creating Unexpectedness would be to single out actions that deviate from those that we normally or typically associate with particular groups of people, for example, schoolboys and rape (see Montgomery 2007: 79 for this example).

In Example 31, we can see an evaluation of an event as to be expected – this may be relatively rare in news discourse, perhaps because it decreases the news value of Unexpectedness (even while construing Consonance, cf. Chapter 3).

> (31) It was a moment that **everyone had known would have to come** but, as the mayor Bob Parker said yesterday afternoon, that didn't make it any easier (Radio New Zealand Morning Report, Top Stories for 4 March 2011)

In the other examples below, events are evaluated as Unexpected (Examples 32 and 37), and we can also find contrasts between what we would normally expect or not expect to be the case (e.g. that people have donated parrot seeds in Example 33, that the heavy rain will impact on people in Example 34, that Sudden Oak Death affects more than just oaks in Example 35). This sets up a dialogue with the reader in terms of common ground and expectations. We can also see the juxtaposition of positive and negative evaluations in Example 36.

> (32) In an **unexpected** development no bodies have been found inside Christchurch's quake-ravaged cathedral (Radio New Zealand Morning Report, Midday News for 5 March 2011)
>
> (33) 'People from this community who weren't affected by the floods have just brought anything and everything. You'll see boxes of carrots, boxes of pumpkins, you'll see baby food, you'll see dog

food, you'll **even** see seed down here for parrots' (ABC News Radio, 18 January 2011)

(34) The bureau of meteorology has issued a severe weather warning with heavy rainfall and flash flooding in South East Queensland. **But** the bureau's hydrologist, Jimmy Stewart, thinks the rainfall is **un**likely to have a major impact, at least around Rockhampton (ABC News Radio, 6 January 2011)

(35) **Despite** its name [Sudden Oak Death] it affects a variety of species, in particular, large species are susceptible. (BBC Radio NewsPod, 7 January 2011)

(36) . . . investing in that kind of infrastructure [roads] in Africa might be expensive **but** it's **not** complicated. Some of the other challenges, **though**, are politically very difficult. (BBC Radio NewsPod, 24 January 2011)

(37) . . . in many parts of the city [Birmingham], **believe it or not, nothing** [i.e. no rubbish] has been taken away since the middle of last month (BBC Radio NewsPod, 6 January 2011)

Functions of evaluations of Un/expectedness in news discourse that are also apparent in these examples include increasing the newsworthiness of what is reported by appealing to the news value of Unexpectedness (*an unexpected development*; *believe it or not*), providing logical structure to the news story (*despite*, *but*, *though*) and contributing to negative evaluation (***nothing has been taken away since the middle of last month***). With respect to the last example here, negation works to state that something (unexpectedly) did **not** happen or does **not** exist, which can then be evaluated by readers negatively or positively, depending on their reading positions, beliefs and values. For example, the fact that no rubbish had been taken away (Example 37) is likely to be evaluated negatively by a majority of readers (on the assumption that we share the desire for our streets to be sanitary – though we might imagine a fictitious filmic scenario where animated cats, dogs or rats would rejoice in rubbish on the streets). However, while a textual analysis can be used to classify evaluations of negative statements as evaluations of Unexpectedness, only audience studies can tell us whether or not these are interpreted positively or negatively by the audience.

3.9 *The parameter of Evidentiality*

With the evaluative parameter of Evidentiality, we are starting to move into the important area of sourcing in journalism. As its name suggests, expressions of Evidentiality give information about the bases (or 'evidence') of statements and information. 'Evidential' expressions answer questions such as 'How do we know? What is the basis of journalists' and others' knowledge? What kind of evidence do we have for this?' Because such questions and their answers are frequently tied to judgements about the reliability of such knowledge, it is useful to consider them as part of evaluation. We can make a subdistinction between at least seven different possible bases of information.[4] Compare Table 6.1 (the examples are invented for the sake of a systematic overview, but authentic examples from radio news discourse are provided below).

Table 6.1 Bases of information

Basis	Examples
Speech	He **said** that they were wrong.
Thought or feeling	He **thought** that they were wrong.
Expectation	He **expected** them to be wrong.
Emotion	He **hoped** that they were wrong.
Perception	There are **signs** that they were wrong.
Proof	**Evidently**, they were wrong.
General knowledge	It's **well-known** that they were wrong.
Unspecified basis	It **emerged** that they were wrong.

The category of **speech** relates to the many occasions (cf. Chapter 4) when statements are attributed as having been expressed by sources at a particular time:

(38) CBC meteorologist Jackie Johnstone **says** there is still the possibility of storm surges and more snow (CBC News Hourly Edition, 28 December 2011)

With respect to the Evidentiality subcategory of speech, we also need to look at what sources said and how they said it. This relates to the use of different types of attributing or reporting expressions such as *say* versus *admit* versus *insist* versus *claim*, and a guiding question could be 'how was it said by sources?' (called the parameter of Style, see Bednarek 2006c: 56–8). This has already been explored in Chapter 4 so no more will be said about it here.

The category of **thought or feeling** is about attributing information to what sources think, feel or experience:

(39) Some Conservatives have now complained that their coalition partners are being treated too softly, but, as our chief political

correspondent Norman Smith reports, some at Westminster **think** these difficulties may actually have strengthened the coalition. (BBC Radio NewsPod, 23 December 2010)

Because journalists do not have insights into sources' minds, such evaluations may be followed up by a quote from the sources or other evidence demonstrating such an evaluation. Example 40 illustrates this phenomenon.

> (40) '. . .' The former Conservative cabinet minister Peter Lilley who
> **believes** the coalition is still on a steep learning curve. 'The
> Liberals, and indeed, new ministers on the Conservative side
> who've never been ministers before, have got to learn at a rather
> more rapid pace than people like me had to do when we were
> junior ministers . . .' (BBC Radio NewsPod, 23 December 2010)

In other cases, such an evaluation may simply rephrase what sources said to journalists in an interview ('*I think*' → X *thinks* . . .). They can also occur in the form *I think/believe*, and so on, usually in quoted speech. But *I* and *think* are also key words in reporter speech in TV live exchanges and used for personal assessments (Haarman 2004: 81). In any case, evaluating something as a belief incorporates an element of doubt or mitigation with respect to the reported information.

The category of **expectation** describes what sources and other news actors expect to happen, as in Example 41.

> (41) The same storm that caused hundreds of flight cancellations and
> gave people in the South Eastern US a white Christmas could
> cause major headaches for travellers trying to get home. As
> NPR's Tamara Keith tells us, the MidAtlantic and Northeast **are**
> **expected to** get a heavy dose of snow tomorrow. (NPR Hourly
> News Summary, 25 December 2010)

This again can be related to the attribution of predictions, similar to evaluations of Reliability. In other words, saying that something is *expected to* happen is another way of saying it is likely to happen, and is a concise way of attributing a prediction to someone other than the journalist.

The category of **emotion** describes sources' and other news actors' positive or negative emotional stance to what is attributed to them.

> (42) . . . there were growing **fears** that the government forces would
> wreak a horrible revenge on Benghazi for weeks of rebellion there
> (RTÉ Radio 1 News at One, 18 March 2011)

In Example 42, not only are we told that some people think that revenge might follow, this prediction is also shown to cause a negative emotion (*fear*) and is hence negatively evaluated, at least by the unnamed sources to which this emotion is attributed here through the noun *fear*. Using *hope* achieves the opposite effect. Like the reporting of emotions in general, such expressions can be tied to a range of news values (e.g. Negativity, Personalization).

The category of **perception** encompasses different kinds of perception that can be reduced to one general parameter for methodological purposes, including 'mental perception' (Greenbaum 1969: 205) (*seem, appear*) and sensory perception (*look, see, show, visibly, audibly*).

(43) The army has not intervened in the latest clashes but further gunshots have been fired into the air in the past few hours, **seemingly** a warning to all present (CBC News Hourly Edition, 3 February 2011)

(44) Tokyo water bureau officials first began **to see** increased radiation levels a few days after the Fukushima nuclear power complex began to have problems earlier this month . . . (NPR Hourly News Summary, 23 March 2011)

Such evaluations allow journalist to draw conclusions (Example 43) and to provide sensory, that is, highly reliable evidence for any information they report on (Example 44).

Similarly, the category of **proof** relates to an evaluation of a statement as being based on some sort of 'hard proof', such as tests, polls, and other kinds of evidence:

(45) '. . . **there is clear evidence that** since the Gulf of Mexico incident last year extra measures that have been taken by the industry in the UK to bring more capping and containment equipment to the UK . . .' (BBC Radio NewsPod, 6 January 2011)

(46) . . . but now **testing has found** the amount of radioactive iodine is at twice the recommended limit for infants (NPR Hourly News Summary, 23 March 2011)

These kinds of evaluations are very common, especially where scientific information is reported and/or in electoral reporting (cf. Appendix 2). But they may also be used more argumentatively, as in Example 45 to provide backing or support for a statement.

With the category of **general knowledge**, information is evaluated based on what is regarded as part of the communal epistemic background shared by the audience and the journalist:

(47) Tokyo is a city **well-known for** its work ethic but for another day company owners told some employees to stay home to conserve electricity. (NPR 7 a.m. News Summary, 18 March 2011)

This allows the journalist to express a subjective evaluation (here: that people in Tokyo work hard), while appearing not to be the source of this subjectivity but rather stating a commonly known fact.

The last category, **unspecified basis**, encompasses cases where information is attributed to some basis, but where that basis remains unspecified, although it may at times become clear from the preceding or following text or might be inferred:

> (48) It's **emerged that** the Pyne Gould and Canterbury TV buildings were both given green stickers following last September's quake, which means they were cleared by council inspectors using an external check only. (Radio New Zealand Morning Report, Top Stories for 1 March 2011)

Expressions of Evidentiality abound in news stories. They are used by journalists to give bases for subjective statements and to evaluate the reliability of different kinds of information. This is because we attach different degrees of reliability to different bases. For instance, proof carries more reliability than sources' speech, thoughts or expectations. Expressing Evidentiality also increases facticity or objectivity: eyewitness reports and quotations belong to the most important strategies employed in news stories to give 'the illusion of truth' (van Dijk 1988b: 86).[5]

3.10 *The parameter of Mental State*

The final evaluative parameter discussed in this chapter is that of Mental State. Here the question we are asking is: 'how do people feel (about this)?' As we cannot directly experience others' mental states ourselves, such descriptions cannot be considered factual and non-evaluative but rather 'introduce a subjective element' (Lombardo 2004: 233) into news discourse. The subcategories of this parameter are associated with the different kinds of mental states actors can experience: emotions, volition (wishes and intentions), beliefs, expectations and knowledge. As we have seen, some of these mental states can be used to attribute statements to sources (cf. Section 3.9 'The parameter of Evidentiality'), but they can also be used without necessarily attributing a statement to a source. Indeed, Semino and Short (2004: 140–1) found that in the British press it is more often the case to find beliefs, opinions or emotions about specific states of affairs (e.g. . . . *doubts grew over M Delors's candidacy*) than to introduce a thought act (e.g. *Les Gore . . . thought it was someone shooting rabbits*).

In Examples 49 to 56 we can see how the mental states of belief (49), knowledge (50), various emotions (51, 52, 53), non-volition (54) and volition (55, 56) are attributed to different news actors.

(49) 'We may have differences in policy but we all **believe in** the rights enshrined in our constitution' (NPR 7 a.m. News Summary, 26 January 2011)

(50) 'Because it's-there's no Maori front, this is the, Auckland is the capital of Polynes- the capital of-more Maori live here than anywhere else in the world. People **know** of Maori, it's through the Haka with the rugby and they come here, they expect to see something Maori here.' (Radio New Zealand, Morning Report, Top Stories for Wednesday 6 April 2011)

(51) He [Congresswoman Gabrielle Giffords's husband] says his wife continues to interact with him and she's **surprising** her doctors at almost every turn (NPR 7 a.m. News Summary, 19 January 2011)

(52) There's growing **frustration** along the Gulf Coast with the pace at which claims [following the oil spill] are being handled (NPR 7 a.m. News Summary, 22 March 2011)

(53) Alabama's Republican Attorney-General Luther Strange says **anxiety** has reached a boiling point. (NPR 7 a.m. News Summary, 22 March 2011)

(54) Mr Gbagbo **is refusing** to relinquish power even though most people think he lost last year's presidential election (BBC NewsPod 4 April 2011)

(55) 'People are finding it very difficult to-to move around which-which gives us a problem as well because we [Medecins Sans Frontières]'re not able to move around as much as we'**d like**' (BBC NewsPod 4 April 2011)

(56) The fourteenth amendment to the constitution grants citizenship to anyone born on US soil. But a group of state legislators say that's an improper interpretation. The legislators from more than a dozen states say they'll push for laws to create different birth certificates and legal status for those children. The legislators admit, though, that what they really **want** is for immigrant rights and civil rights groups to sue them and push the issue to the Supreme Court. (NPR 7 a.m. News Summary, 6 April 2011)

Some common functions here are to increase the news values of Personalization, Negativity or Unexpectedness (emotion of surprise). More generally, references to news actors' emotions are of immense importance in news discourse, providing colour and human interest. Ungerer suggests that it is not likely 'that the reader can process emotional descriptions without any kind of emotional response' (1997: 319). Attributing emotions to news actors hence sparks audience interest and triggers an emotional response. Thus, journalists try to elicit mental state descriptions from interviewees, especially in witness interviews where the interview focuses on telling the viewers/listeners '**what it felt like as it happened**' (Montgomery 2007: 168, bold face in original). Mental state descriptions can also evoke positive or negative evaluations of the audience. For example, if someone voluntarily (volition) commits a negative act, they will be evaluated more negatively than if they commit that act involuntarily, for example, by accident.

3.11 Resources for expressing evaluation

What has become apparent so far is that in the above framework no distinction is made between lexical (vocabulary) and grammatical (e.g. modality) means of evaluation, and that this framework thus follows a 'combining' (see Thompson and Hunston 2000: 4–5) approach to evaluation. In fact, resources for expressing evaluation include both lexical and grammatical means and vary in the way in which they relate to evaluation and the extent to which they might be semantically classifiable as expressing 'opinion'. For instance, evaluative parameters may be directly and explicitly referred to through language, such as when speakers/writers use terms like *great, fantastic* or *brilliant* to evaluate something positively (Emotivity) or when modal expressions (*may, perhaps, possibility* . . .) are employed. In contrast, the same parameter may be more indirectly implied; for example, via an utterance such as *petrol prices were raised*, which does not include any explicitly evaluative language but may imply positive or negative evaluation depending on the reader's or writer's position, values and background (see Martin and White 2005: 61–8, Bednarek 2006d).

We also need to look at the text itself and our cultural/background knowledge to consider aspects such as irony, or sarcasm, where a positive evaluation is insincere and turned into a negative evaluation (Example 57).

> (57) 'Whoever wins today, nothing fundamental will change in the ACT because it will still be run by a jumped-up local council playing at being a government. **Fortunately, it is such a wonderful place to live**' ('On mediocre territory, Greens may crown king of the pygmies', *Sydney Morning Herald*, 18–19 October 2008, p. 4)

Here readers familiar with the Australian context will readily recognize the ironic comment on Canberra, which has a reputation for Sydneysiders of not being somewhere that people want to live.

As seen, evaluation includes different kinds of resources and it may not always be easily identifiable. To identify evaluation, Thompson and Hunston suggest looking for 'signals of comparison, subjectivity, and social value' (2000: 13), including 'indications of the existence of goals and their (non-) achievement' (2000: 21). Other techniques that can be used to identify evaluative expressions include trying to paraphrase, find synonyms for, or look up the dictionary meanings of these expressions. In fact, some dictionaries now include information on the evaluative meanings of items. For example, the definition for *crony* in the *Longman Dictionary of Contemporary English* reads 'one of a group of people who spend a lot of time with each other—used to show disapproval'. We can also survey previous research to identify potential evaluative items, both lexical and grammatical, and ask native speakers for their input.

Concerning the identification of evaluation, it also needs to be pointed out that several parameters can be expressed simultaneously by just one evaluative item. For example, certain reporting expressions combine evaluations of Evidentiality with Mental State (*fear that, expect that, believe that*), or Reliability (*claim that*). Similarly, some lexical items (*serious, critical, grave*) realize Emotivity and Importance, evaluating something as both important and negative (for further examples see Bednarek 2006c, 2008b). In such cases we need to double- or even triple-code instances of evaluation in the analysed text.

There are also other issues that need to be taken into account when analysing evaluation in the news, and Section 4 below discusses these to some extent.

4 Further issues for analysis

The first issue concerns the origin of the evaluation – is the journalist expressing his or her own opinion or is s/he quoting a source? There are clear differences in the effect this has on the reader and on the subjectivity of the news report, and it is interesting to analyse whether journalists express their own opinion at all, when they do so, and who does so (e.g. newsreader or correspondent?). For example, much research has argued that the journalistic 'hard news' voice – what Feez et al. (2008: 201) call the objective 'reporter voice' – aims to project objectivity, hence minimizing elements of subjectivity (such as evaluations), but incorporates this subjectivity in the use of quoted contributions, for instance, in order to increase newsworthiness. This applies to both print and broadcast news where evaluation occurs in interviews or exchanges rather than the discourse around it (see Montgomery 2007: 122–3). In the context of radio news, Montgomery notes that:

> The facticity of news kernels can be related to their use of unmarked modality and the absence of the speaker's point of view in the utterance: averalls that take the form of categorical assertion without obvious modal features or sharply evaluative lexis accrue to themselves the value of objectivity. However, a further way of 'doing objectivity', or

impartiality, is by harvesting quotations from a range of representative viewpoints while aligning with none of them. (2007: 87)

With respect to the sourcing of evaluations, we also need to look at how such Other-evaluations are embedded in the news discourse (e.g. as more direct or indirect, cf. Chapter 4). Are contrasting points of views presented? Are both points of view presented in similar ways or is preference given to one point of view? And so on. It is also interesting to analyse where in the typical structure of news discourse (see Chapter 4) such evaluations, whether by journalists or by sources, occur. For example, while evaluation in British political TV news reporting occurs throughout the report, it tends to cluster in the newsreader's introduction with assessment and predictions found in the final parts before closing (Lombardo 2004: 233).

A second issue for analysis concerns the kinds of entities, situations, states of affairs, people, behaviour, and so on that are evaluated – what has alternatively been called 'evaluated entity' (Thetela 1997: 103) and attitudinal 'target' (White 2004: 233). Here an analysis could either be detailed and specific, listing all evaluated targets in the analysed text, or it could try to come up with a more general categorization of such evaluated targets – for example, dividing them into people and their behaviour or entities/situations (as done in Appraisal Theory; see Bednarek 2009: 128; see also n. 2). It can also be useful to scan the surrounding text for prospective/retrospective evaluation to identify what/who is evaluated. Compare Example 58, where the evaluation in the first sentence, *bring out the best*, works prospectively to positively evaluate the Canadian tourist and his actions that are described only later in the text.

> (58) 'Traumatic situations **bring out the best** in some people. Most
>   of those helping with the recovery were volunteers. I met one, a
>   Canadian tourist, dressed in protective gear from head to toe, who
>   was helping to move dead bodies. Underneath, he was still in his
>   swimming shorts' ('The moment: Khao Lak, Thailand – January
>   5, 2005', *Sydney Morning Herald, Good Weekend*, 11 October
>   2008, p. 23)

A third issue for analysis concerns the intensity of the evaluation (what is variously called intensification, up-/down-scaling, modulation or graduation). For example, is something evaluated as very positive, very important or very unexpected, or slightly positive, slightly important or slightly unexpected? A related issue concerns the linguistic environment in which an evaluation is placed and the degree of 'reality' that it is imbued with. For instance, in relation to the parameters of Evidentiality and Mental State, texts can refer to 'speech and thoughts events that are presented as future, possible, imaginary or counterfactual' (Semino and Short 2004: 159). In the examples below, while all instances include an evaluation of

Mental State (the emotion of happiness), the linguistic environment changes the way this evaluation is presented:

> *He was happy.*
> *Was he happy?*
> *Why are you happy?*
> *Be happy!*
> *If he was happy ...*
> *He will be happy.*
> *He could be happy.*
> *If he had any ice-cream, he'd be happy.*
> *... in order to be happy*
> *He wanted to be happy*
> *He should consider whether he is happy.*
> *He might be happy.*
> *He looks happy.*

Such differences clearly need to be taken into account and are currently an area of focus for research in evaluation (Taboada and Trnavac 2011), and its quantitative and qualitative analysis.[6] More generally, it may be important to consider how evaluation interacts with other linguistic features to produce specific rhetorical effects and fulfil particular discourse functions.

Once evaluations have been identified (and, perhaps, quantified as instances per 100/1,000 or 10,000, etc. words), analysis can focus on interpreting possible reasons behind and functions of their use: Why do journalists or sources express evaluations; in other words, what are their possible motivations? Is the use of evaluations related to journalistic practice, to ideology, to bias, to editorial policy, to house style? In our own research we investigate the functions of evaluations mainly in the context of journalistic practice, and especially their key contribution to the construal of news values, but other research may want to tie them to ideology or hegemony. Another strand of research might investigate the influence of speakers'/writers' and hearers'/readers' backgrounds, such as their beliefs and values (e.g. the use of inferencing and other cognitive processes) and draw on research in the area of Response Theory (see Chapter 1). In any case, the framework introduced in this chapter is offered to be used in different linguistic approaches to news discourse (cf. Chapter 1), whether Critical Discourse Analysis, practice-focused, corpus or otherwise. We hope that it may also be useful for research in Media/Journalism and Communications Studies (cf. Chapter 1), as the analysis of evaluation ties in with research on media and ideology (e.g. Althusser, Gramsci, and others). It may also be useful for detailed textual/discourse analysis and content/framing analysis. For instance, Koteyko et al. (2008) have shown how linguistic analysis, including that of evaluation, offers an interesting way of studying the framing of MRSA (a bacterial infection) in UK news discourse.

To conclude, in this chapter we have described and illustrated key parameters of evaluation that can be found in news discourse (see Table A1.2 in Appendix 1 for an overview), hypothesizing also as to the potential functions they may fulfil. It is important to note that analyses of evaluation in the news need not always focus on all of the above parameters. It may well be that limiting the analysis to selected parameters, say Evidentiality or Emotivity, or even subparameters (e.g. Mental State: emotion) will help answer a particular research question or throw light upon a particular issue in the analysed data (cf. Appendix 2).[7] Since evaluation is such a complex matter, we would suggest that additional readings are consulted before starting an in-depth investigation of evaluation in the news. This chapter, however, provides a useful starting point for analysis.

Directions for further reading

Bednarek, M. (2006). *Evaluation in Media Discourse: Analysis of a Newspaper Corpus*. London/New York: Continuum. This book analyses evaluation in British news discourse, comparing tabloid and broadsheet newspapers.

Martin, J. R. and White, P. R. R. (2005), *The Language of Evaluation. Appraisal in English*. Basingstoke/New York: Palgrave Macmillan. This book introduces Appraisal Theory, an alternative approach to evaluation used in Systemic Functional Linguistics.

A bibliography of research on evaluation and related concepts can be accessed at www.monikabednarek.com/10.html

Notes

1   In fact, different versions of this framework exist, proposing slightly varying lists of parameters to experiment with refinement and redevelopment as well as to establish connections with Appraisal Theory. This chapter draws largely on Bednarek (2010a).

2   Note also that evaluating something as incomprehensible may at times imply a comment on the person for whom it is incomprehensible. For example, if something is said to be difficult for someone, this can arguably be construed as a comment on that person's competence. Koteyko et al. note that '[o]ne is rarely blamed for not accomplishing a task which is recognized to be complex and difficult, but the failure to do something which is perceived to be easy inevitably incurs judgement' (2008: 231). There are other examples where such overlap exists, often relating to metonymic relations – for example, evaluating a semiotic product such as a letter also implies an evaluation of its author (see Bednarek 2008a: 75).

3   The distinction between epistemic, deontic and dynamic modality is widely used in Linguistics. Broadly speaking, epistemic modality conveys the speaker's

degree of confidence in the truth of the proposition, deontic modality is defined as 'the possibility or necessity of acts in terms of which the speaker gives permission or lays an obligation for the performance of actions at some point in the future' (Hoye 1997: 43), and dynamic modality is mainly concerned with the ability and volition of subjects as well as with some kinds of objective possibility (Perkins 1983, Palmer 1995, Hoye 1997). In Systemic Functional Linguistics, the terms *modulation* and *modalization* are used to distinguish different kinds of modality (Halliday and Matthiessen 2004: 147).

4   Bednarek (2010a) includes a further category, mental process, incorporating expressions such as *decide*, *imagine* and *speculate*, which can be used to attribute statements to sources (e.g. *Somebody working in the post room was injured in the hands and face as another parcel exploded. Some **speculated** it was linked to recent bomb scares.* (ABC News Radio, 24 December 2010)). But it may be possible to include these under speech or thought/feeling.

5   However, both modality and evidentiality may not feature equally in all parts of the news item; for instance, Montgomery (2007) argues that both do not normally occur in the routine discourse of news presentation. Lombardo (2004) on the other hand finds that mental verbs make up 22 per cent of all reporting verbs in the language of newsreaders and reporters in British political TV news reporting (excluding interviews and newsreader–reporter live exchanges).

6   It is worth pointing out that the analysis of evaluation in news can proceed both with recourse to computerized analysis (e.g. Corpus Linguistics or computational sentiment analysis – see Hunston 2011 for an overview), and 'manual', close-reading type analysis or indeed, a combination of the two. There are by now many examples of such investigations; to give just a few examples for research into news discourse drawing on Corpus Linguistics (sometimes together with) discourse analysis, compare Bednarek (2006b) and Koteyko et al. (2008) for analyses of evaluation, and Semino and Short (2004) and Garretson and Ädel (2008) on Evidentiality.

7   There are other aspects of evaluation that we have not yet touched upon; for instance, should evaluations of causality (making judgements about who is responsible or what causes an event) be counted as a parameter of evaluation? What about comparison (comparing one event to another)? These do seem to involve elements of subjectivity and have been included in some approaches to evaluation (see White 2003a, Feez et al. 2008: 230–6, Bednarek 2010a, Pounds 2010). Further parameters as well as combinations of parameters may also be included (Bednarek 2006c). As said above, the parameter-based framework is conceptualized as open-ended and organic with clear potential for further redevelopment and refinement.

CHAPTER SEVEN

Balancing act: image composition

1 Introduction

As noted in Chapter 6, our focus has now shifted to outlining specific frameworks for analysing aspects of language and image in news discourse. In this chapter we take up image analysis. The analytical framework that we introduce here deals quite specifically with the composition of images and is based on the argument Caple (2009b, in press) makes in relation to composition, balance and the aesthetics of news images. She suggests that in composing their images press photographers do consider the aesthetic quality of the news images they produce and that for some news organizations, the decision to publish an image (and with it a story) can be based primarily (indeed solely) on this aesthetic quality. It must be noted, however, that there are many elements that contribute to the aesthetic quality of a photographic image, including lighting, colour, shutter speed and composition. This chapter will explore one of these in considerable detail: the role of balance as a feature of composition and its relation to aesthetics in news photography.[1]

The *Balance Framework* (Caple 2009b, in press) that will be introduced in this chapter for analysing composition in images was originally conceptualized within a social semiotic paradigm (Kress and van Leeuwen 1990/1996, 2006). It is also informed by visual arts (see for example Arnheim 1954, 1982, Dondis 1973) and film theory (see for example Bordwell and Thompson 2008), as well as by Caple's professional practice and training as a press photographer. We have simplified the framework somewhat for this chapter with the aim of making it applicable to scholars and researchers from a number of disciplines to work with effectively. Our objectives for this chapter are to enable readers to understand:

- how images can be analysed for their compositional meaning

- how compositional meanings can contribute to the aesthetic quality of an image

- what role composition and aesthetics play in the news.

2 Composition is a balancing act

We have already established (see Chapter 5) that there is a basic need in news reporting for an image to function as an 'illustration' of a particular news event. It achieves this by providing an image that consists of (usually) people engaging in some kind of activity, and located in a particular place at a particular time. In social semiotic terms (Kress and van Leeuwen 2006), we can label this the 'representational' function of the image. Images are also able to engage an audience on an interpersonal (or interactional) level. This can be achieved through the depiction of emotions in the facial expressions and gestures of the represented participants or through more technical aspects such as camera angle, lens or distance between subject and photographer. At the same time, photographers are also concerned with where these represented participants are placed within the image frame and the extent to which they will be singled out or shown in relation to other participants also within the frame or even beyond the frame. These are **compositional** considerations that a photographer uses to present a balanced image, and, as we argue below, balancing the arrangement of participants within the image frame contributes to the aesthetic appeal of images.[2]

The connections that we make between composition, balance and aesthetic appeal come from work on composition within Gestalt psychology (as applied to photography by Arnheim 1954), and from the idea of the Golden Ratio, as it applies to film and photography studies. Arnheim explores not only the workings of perception but also the quality of individual visual units and the strategies for their unification into a final and complete whole. In his view, the human organism seems to seek harmony in what it views, a state of ease, of resolution, what the Zen Buddhists speak of as 'meditation in supreme repose' (Dondis 1973: 85). As a result, humans attempt to organize all stimuli into rational wholes (Dondis 1973: 85, Stroebel et al. 1980: 164, Zakia 1997: 31) and Gestaltists have argued that the eye, and for that matter the brain, 'will not be deterred in its endless pursuit of resolution or closure in the sensory data it views' (Dondis 1973: 89). This resolution or closure is most easily achieved through regularity, symmetry and simplicity, that is, absolute balance.

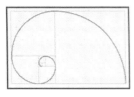
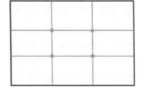
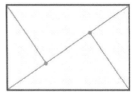

Example 1: Golden Ratio   Example 2: Rule of Thirds   Example 3: Dynamic Asymmetry

Figure 7.1 Visual representations of the Golden Ratio, Rule of Thirds and Dynamic Asymmetry

The idea of symmetry and regularity is also visible in the concept of the Golden Ratio, which is theorized in film and photography studies as the Golden Mean or the Rule of Thirds (see Examples 1 and 2 in Figure 7.1 for visualizations of these concepts) (Altengarten 2004). The Golden Mean is based on the Fibonacci sequence, where the ratio of each successive pair of numbers in the series approximates to the Golden Number (1.618034), identified by the Greek letter Phi φ. The Golden Mean is a division based on the Golden Number proportion and can be used as a method for placing the subject in an image or of dividing a composition into pleasing proportions (Präkel 2006: 22). The reason why it produces reliably balanced compositions is because the Golden Number is calculated from the physical proportions of naturally occurring life forms such as flowers, shells and even the human body (as shown in Figure 7.2)

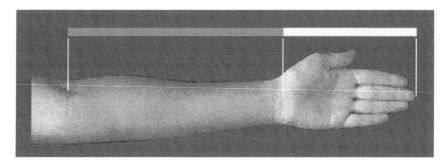

Figure 7.2 The hand creates a golden section in relation to the arm, as the ratio of the forearm to the hand is also 1.618, the Golden Number

As far as composition in art and photography is concerned, the Golden Mean is represented as follows in Example 1 in Figure 7.1. Here, each rectangle is at a ratio of 1:1.618 with the next and as they are joined at the corners they form a spiral. A simpler version of the Golden Mean more commonly used in photography is the Rule of Thirds (see Example 2 in Figure 7.1). This allows a photographer to organize information in the frame around four points, or 'hot spots', that are located away from the centre of the frame. This is a useful aid in composing reliably well-proportioned images where information placed on these hotspots is generally of equal weight, though it does not necessarily produce very 'exciting' images. A more challenging and dynamic approach to the organization of information in the frame is exemplified in Example 3 in Figure 7.1, due to the potential to unbalance the image by placing information on the diagonal axis rather than on the horizontal or vertical axis as is the case in Example 2 in Figure 7.1. Diagonal lines in photography are said to produce more dynamic compositions. By placing participants in the image on or near one of the hot spots (in Example 3 in Figure 7.1), they can be counterbalanced by placing other information on or near the other hot spot on the same diagonal axis. The use of the diagonal creates tension, especially if one of the hot spots is left empty. This stimulates the eye to resolve the potential imbalance and the resulting asymmetry is highly valued in photography as an aesthetically pleasing form of composition (Altengarten 2004, Präkel 2006).

As humans, then, we have a tendency to attempt to find resolution or closure in the sensory data we encounter. This is most easily achieved when images organize the visual information into regular or symmetrical patterns. We would argue that any sense of balance in this organizing of visual information also has aesthetic potential. This is the basis for the creation of the *Balance Framework* for analysing composition in images, and it is to this framework and how we apply it to image analysis that we now turn.

3 The *Balance Framework*

Press photographs are not random snapshots of news events. A concern for composition and balance in the image frame is central to the work of any press photographer. Equally as strong is the need to provide a complete visual unit of information (VUI) that can also be viewed as being representative of the news event photographed. This relates well to Dondis' (1973: 91) idea that the human perceptual system needs to find resolution in what is viewed, that is, we perceive images as 'organised configurations rather than as collections of independent parts' (Stroebel et al. 1980: 164). This compositional balancing of elements within the image frame will be introduced below. But first we need to clarify and define the terminology that we will be using in this section: image frame, elements and visual unit of information (Table 7.1 on p. 164).

The framework that we will be using for analysing composition/balance in images is visualized as a taxonomy in Figure 7.3, categorizing the various ways in which balance can be achieved in images. In the following we will discuss this taxonomy in more detail, giving examples of images that use these compositional features and assessing the kinds of meanings that such features bring to our understanding of images.

Table 7.1 Key terminology for discussing composition and the *Balance Framework*

Term	Explanation
Image Frame	For the purposes of the analyses presented here the *image frame* is the boundary of the image that the reader is working with. This means that the initial capturing of the event by the photographer and subsequent editing process is subsumed in this definition, since semioticians generally do not have access to the capturing and editing process but analyse what is finally presented as a photograph in the newspaper.
Elements	The *elements* of a photograph are the people (represented participants), places (circumstances) and activities depicted within the *image frame* and through their interactions with each other.
Visual Unit of Information (VUI)	The combination of these *elements* makes up the *visual unit of information* depicted in the *image frame* (e.g. an image of a man walking his dog in the park would be made up of one VUI, whereas an image of a man walking his dog in the park while six boys are playing soccer in the background would be made up of two VUIs). Generally, press photographs have only one VUI within an image, as they tend to single out one aspect of an event to represent the entire event (cf. Painter et al. 2011 on composition in children's picture books).

Figure 7.3 The *Balance Framework*

3.1 Focusing or relating?

When we look at (or indeed take) a photograph, we can usually detect two basic patterns of organizing elements within the image frame to create a visual unit of information. Either we single someone or something out and make that element the focus of our attention (*isolating*), for example, in a portrait; or we find regular, repeated patterns between several elements and show them in the image frame in relation to each other (*iterating*), for example, a group of friends all raising their glasses to cheers. These are the two main categories in the *Balance Framework: isolating* and *iterating*. In Table 7.2 we show two images that are either *isolating* or *iterating*. These are what we might call 'typical' examples of images that are *isolating* or *iterating* because they conform quite stereotypically to the compositional arrangements of the *Balance Framework*, in that Example 1 in Table 7.2 has one element in the centre of the frame, so it is focusing our attention on one element (*isolating*); and Example 2 shows several elements regularly arranged in the image frame and in relation to each other (*iterating*).

To help us to decide whether an image is *isolating* or *iterating* we could ask the following questions:

Is the image focusing our attention on one element in the image?

Is the image depicting more or less stable relations between several elements in the image?

Table 7.2 Examples of typical *isolating* and *iterating* compositional configurations

Compositional Configurations	Examples
Example 1: *Isolating* – shows one element in the centre of the frame	
Example 2: *Iterating* – shows several elements regularly arranged in the image frame and in relation to each other	

These questions will help us in the most typical cases, but we must be aware that certain categories in the *isolating* branch may also show relations, albeit dynamic/unequal (*axial*) relations, and categories in the *iterating* branch can also construe unstable relations (in the *scattered* configuration). So these questions have to come with qualifications. This means that *iterating* is typically, but not always, stable and *isolating* is typically, but not always, 'one element' only. We will exemplify these points as we explain the framework in more detail below.

3.2 Isolating (centred, single)

In general, images such as portraits or close-ups have a single element in the centre of (or filling) the image frame and in such images, the viewer is expected to focus on/engage with that single element. In our *Balance Framework*, we could analyse such images as *isolating, centred, single*. This section of the framework is demonstrated in Example 1 in Table 7.3 and

Table 7.3 Examples of the *isolating* compositional configurations

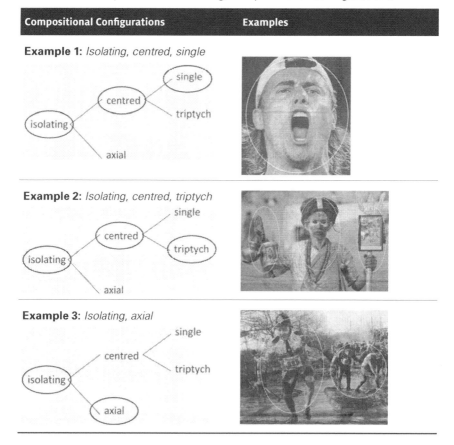

includes an example photograph. Equally, a wide-angle shot of a person standing in the centre of the frame with a lot of the background visible would also be considered *isolating, centred, single*.

3.3 *Isolating (centred, triptych)*

Another type of *isolating* relationship in images is the *triptych*. In a fine arts context, a triptych is typically a carving or a painting consisting of three panels, hinged together, where the two outer panels relate to but are subordinate to the larger central panel. We can adapt this notion to the configuration of elements in the image frame in photography, in that the main focus of attention may remain on the centrally located element (thus it is *isolating*) but this central element is also shown in relation to two separate elements either side of it. Table 7.3 gives an example (2) of a *triptych* in photography. Note that the Hindu ascetic fills the centre of the frame, but is holding religious relics to either side of him. So, while we focus our attention on him, we also see him in relation to the two other significant elements in the frame.

3.4 *Isolating (axial)*

Another, more dynamic *isolating* relationship in photography is the *axial* configuration of elements in the image frame. This is where all elements in the frame are located away from the centre of the image frame, and one element is shown in relation to other elements in the frame but along the diagonal axis (see Example 3 in Figure 7.1 for a schematic representation of this). We see this configuration as an *isolating* one, because one element, which usually dominates (in size, focus, fore-/backgrounding) the image frame, is clearly singled out and focused on. Example 3 in Table 7.3 illustrates this *axial* configuration.

Here we can see one race participant (dressed as a police officer) in focus, foregrounded and dominating the left side of the image frame, while some of his competitors are shown much smaller and slightly out of focus to the right of the frame. Thus, while the policeman is singled out in terms of size, focus and position in the frame, he is also shown in relation to other elements in the frame. Given that this story is about a race over an obstacle course, this *axial* configuration works particularly well to not only focus the viewer's attention on the leader, but to also tell us something about the state of his opposition.

These examples (in Table 7.3) demonstrate that the *isolating* category in the *Balance Framework* operates not only to focus our attention on a single element in the image frame, but may also establish dynamic, unequal relationships between a dominant element and other less significant elements in the frame. Images with elements arranged in these ways can be said to be balanced; however, whether images compositionally organized along the *centred single* configuration are aesthetically stimulating is open to question. According to Gestalt theory (Dondis 1973), centred, formally balanced images offer no visual surprise, while elements organized axially within the image frame create an unequal relationship between elements and therefore offer more visual stimulation because of the need to counterbalance the elements on the diagonal axis. This is one reason why the asymmetry in axially composed images is highly valued in photography as an aesthetically pleasing form of composition (Altengarten 2004, Präkel 2006).

3.5 *Iterating*

Now we turn our attention to the *iterating* category in the *Balance Framework*. The notion of *iterating* comes from the repetition or regular/symmetrical patterning of elements within the image frame. This can be a relationship between just two elements in the frame (*dividing*), or many (*serialising*), as Examples 1 and 2 in Table 7.4 demonstrate.

As can be seen in the examples in Table 7.4, no single element dominates the image frame. Instead, the elements are equal in size; typically they are evenly/symmetrically arranged within the image frame and are therefore shown in relation to each other. The two principle distinctions in the *iterating* category lie in the number of elements that are included in the image frame. If there are two elements in the frame, then this configures with the *dividing* category, but if there are more than two elements,

Table 7.4 Iterating images demonstrating two or more than two elements

Number of Elements	Examples
Example 1: Two elements – *iterating, dividing, matching*	
Example 2: More than two elements – *iterating, serialising, matching*	

the configuration is *serialising*. We will explain and exemplify these compositional configurations in the *iterating* category below.

3.6 Iterating (dividing, matching)

When two elements in the image frame are captured doing the same thing, this can be taken as a *matching* relationship. Example 1 in Table 7.5 shows two guitarists playing together. The position of their heads, bodies, arms, hands and guitars match each other. Their postures, however, do not need to be exactly identical, as we discuss further below.

3.7 Iterating (dividing, mirroring)

The notion of *mirroring* in this framework does literally refer to the reflecting of elements in a surface, be it in an actual mirror, water, glass or another surface. Example 2 in Table 7.5 shows two flamingos and their

Table 7.5 Examples of the *iterating, dividing* compositional configurations

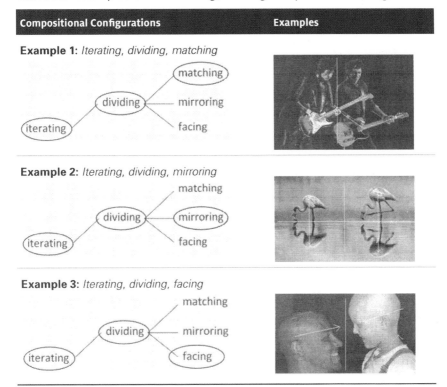

reflections in the water in which they are standing. Technical manipulation of an image to create artificial mirroring may also be classified as mirroring, however, such techniques are unlikely to be used in news discourse. It could be further argued that the stance of the flamingos is also matching. This means that this image could be analysed both as *iterating*, *dividing*, *mirroring* **and** *matching*. Such images (including Example 2 in Table 7.6), it seems, can be analysed along more than one compositional configuration and this could contribute to making them more special or interesting (such instances are explored in more detail in Caple in press).

3.8 Iterating (dividing, facing)

When two elements are turned towards each other, this can be taken as a *facing* relationship. In Example 3 in Table 7.5, two people are photographed facing each other and side on to the camera. It is important to note here that *facing* and *mirroring* are different from each other. Two quite distinctive elements (such as a man and horse) or two identical elements (twins) may be photographed facing each other (and side on to the camera) and both would be considered *facing*, while *mirroring*, as noted above, is meant in the literal sense of being reflected in a surface. Also, *matching* relations would be going in the same direction or directed towards the camera, which are different again to both *facing* and *mirroring*.

3.9 Iterating (serialising, matching/mirroring/ facing/scattered)

Similar relations can also be detected in the *serialising* category, where *matching*, *mirroring* and *facing* relations are the same as those noted above but involve more than two participants. The examples in Table 7.6 illustrate each of these compositional configurations in turn.

As can be seen in all of these *iterating* examples, the elements in the image frame are shown in relation to each other. They are very similar to each other in shape and size, and are organized along more or less the same dimensions. Such regulated configurations can be said to emphasize the relationships between the elements in the frame, rather than relationships between these elements and the viewer. These are also stable relations. However, there is one configuration in the serialising category where unstable relations are demonstrated. This is the *serialising*, *scattered* category. Here elements in the image frame are somewhat randomly configured and seem to be fairly unstable or chaotic in their organization, as exemplified in Example 4 in Table 7.6, where locusts fill the skies.

Again, we can state that images that adhere to these *iterating* configurations above are said to be balanced. However, the extent to which they are also

Table 7.6 Examples of the *iterating, serialising* compositional configurations

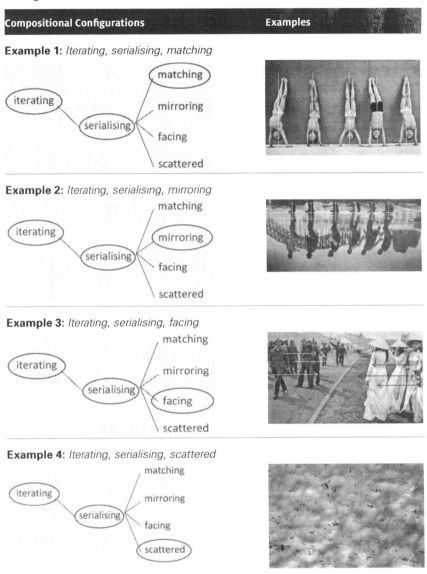

Compositional Configurations	Examples

Example 1: *Iterating, serialising, matching*

Example 2: *Iterating, serialising, mirroring*

Example 3: *Iterating, serialising, facing*

Example 4: *Iterating, serialising, scattered*

aesthetically stimulating can be questioned in the same way as *isolating, centred, single* images. To put it quite bluntly, such configurations can be boring. They are predictable, static and unimaginative, and professional photographers are very much aware of these criticisms. Again, we can draw on Gestalt theory, in stating that *iterating* compositions rarely offer any

Table 7.7 Iterating images demonstrating more or less visual stimulation

Types of Stimulation	Examples
Example 1: Somewhat predictable serialising configuration – *iterating, serialising, matching*	
Example 2: A more visually stimulating serialising configuration – *iterating, serialising, matching*	

'visual stimulation' (Dondis 1973: 85) or surprise. The eye/brain enjoys a challenge in attempting to organize visual stimuli into rational wholes and the two examples (in Table 7.7) will be used to illustrate this point.

As has already been demonstrated in Table 7.6, the first example image (Example 1, repeated in Table 7.7) shows the very regular arrangement of five boys practicing handstands (*iterating, serialising, matching*). They are not perfectly symmetrical in their positions; one boy has his head turned towards the other boys rather than at the camera and another boy is wearing dark shorts, imperfections that serve to add visual stimulation to the image. This makes the image appear more natural rather than contrived (slight imperfections in the arrangement of elements in the image frame make an iterating image appear more natural). Otherwise, the arrangement of the boys, while producing a well-balanced final image, is somewhat 'predictable' (from a professional photographer's perspective). In the second image (see Example 2 in Table 7.7), however, the inclusion of the window to break up the regular arrangement of another group of boys practising handstands has the potential to unbalance the image, and thus adds visual stimulation, as the eye has to work harder to reach the same sense of balance and closure as in the image in Example 1 in Table 7.7.

A similar phenomenon can be observed in the two mirroring images in Tables 7.5 and 7.6. The photograph of the tap dancers (Example 2 in Table 7.6) is, like the flamingos, symmetrically iterating, mirroring and therefore balanced; however, the image of the dancers is cropped in close at the knees, leaving the viewer to fill in the remainder of the picture to make it fully symmetrical. Extra visual stimulation, like that in these two shots, is said to add to the aesthetic appeal of images (Dondis 1973: 85, Stroebel et al. 1980: 164, Zakia 1997: 31, Berdan 2004).

4 'Ugly' or unbalanced images

There are, of course, also instances where it is difficult to analyse the elements in the image frame according to the *Balance Framework*. This typically occurs where the scene is cluttered or confusing, or where an image contains more than one VUI competing equally for the attention of the viewer. In such instances, it takes too much time for the viewer to figure out the content and relationships depicted – sometimes to the extent that clear communication is hindered and the image may be described as 'aesthetically ugly' (Dondis 1973: 93). Again, this is best explained in an example image (Example 1 in Table 7.8 on p. 174). The story depicted in Table 7.8 concerns the Sydney Body Art Ride, a charity bike ride where competitors ride naked (save their underpants). The main problem with this photograph (originally published in colour) appears to be that there are two VUIs competing for the viewer's attention and it is difficult to reconcile compositionally how these two VUIs relate to each other. This is made more difficult because of the competing colours of the red participants on the left and the pink participants on the right, and because there are two different activities taking place – posing for a photo and painting their bodies. Is this configuration isolating or iterating? Matching or facing? Or are they scattered? None of these categories seem to apply.

However, if we were to remove one of the VUIs, then we could more easily detect compositional relations: an *isolating*, *axial* configuration in Example 2: Cropped Section A in Table 7.8; and *iterating*, *dividing*, *facing* between the visible participants who are touching up their paint job in Example 3: Cropped Section B in Table 7.8. Dondis (1973) would probably describe Example 1 in Table 7.8 as ambiguous because it is 'sloppy and inferior on any level of the criteria of visual communication' (Dondis 1973: 93). Example 2: Cropped Section A in Table 7.8 has a marginally better composition simply because it makes use of just one VUI, thus focusing the viewer's attention on one activity, the taking of a group photograph. We could analyse this as an *axial* configuration, as the photographer fills the bottom left corner of the image, while the other participants radiate out from his position along the diagonal. Their gaze is also directed back towards him.

Table 7.8 Unbalanced images and rebalancing effects

Un/balancing Images	Examples
Example 1: An unbalanced image Two VUIs compete for reader attention	
Source: ('Barely there', *Sydney Morning Herald*, 14 February 2005, p. 3, Fairfax Syndication)	
Example 2: Cropped Section A Rebalancing the image by focusing on one VUI	
Example 3: Cropped Section B Rebalancing the image by focusing on one VUI	

In summing up the general points introduced above, any press photograph that can be analysed as representing one of the above ways of creating balance can be considered as well proportioned or balanced. Through the use of regularity, symmetry and simplicity, resolution/closure/balance is achieved. The results are well-proportioned images. However, not all of these proportioned or 'balanced' images are equally 'exciting' or even beautiful. For example, isolating, centred images are too readily resolved, whereas asymmetric but balanced images (e.g. axial configurations) are highly valued aesthetically because they are more stimulating. Similarly, images that are not perfectly regular/symmetrical (while clearly being balanced compositionally) add visual stimulation, as the eye has to work harder to reach the same sense of balance and closure. In other words, extra visual stimulation adds to the aesthetic appeal of images. In addition, how we perceive the events represented in the image in terms of aesthetics may interact with what is represented (e.g. a beautiful natural landscape, or a beautifully made up actor or model), or with colour, lighting and other techniques, like film speed/graininess. Compositional balance, then, is a necessary but not a sufficient condition for a 'beautiful' image. At the same time, all balanced pictures are well proportioned and hence satisfy criteria for a visually appealing image.

5 The role of composition, balance and aesthetics in the news

Communications scholars such as Schirato and Webb (2004) claim that composition and aesthetics are not the concern of press photography. In describing a photograph of a protest depicting police and protesters facing each other, they state:

> But it is manifestly not a press photograph, because there is a concern with composition rather than action: the balance between the barren sky and barren concrete; the asymmetry between the police and the protesters; the line of shadows falling from the police balanced by the regular vertical lines of posts, staffs and arms to create a sense of stasis. Time seems to be frozen; everyone is waiting for something to happen. This provides a very different sense of meaning and value than we might expect from a press photograph, where a conventional (conservative) paper might focus on individuals with dreadlocks and torn jeans, or protesters engaged in violence; or a left-wing paper would be more likely to focus on a police charge, or random violence against unarmed youths. But in any case, something is being told, and a point of view is being 'sold' to viewers. (Schirato and Webb 2004: 96)

However, based on Caple's research into the balance of news photographs as well as her professional experience as a former press photographer in the United Kingdom, we would argue instead that balance, composition and aesthetics in fact do play a major role in press photography (see also Hartley 2007, or Hartley and Rennie 2004 on art and the aesthetic at the interface between fashion and photojournalism).

First, press photographs will generally be well proportioned, and hence balanced. For example, Caple's (2009b) analysis of balance in 1,000 stand-alone images in the *Sydney Morning Herald* found overwhelming consistency in the compositional balance of these images in that 99 per cent of the images could be easily analysed using this framework. In other words, nearly all of the 1,000 images were well composed and balanced. Press photographers are, after all, members of a professional community who share professional practices and discursive conventions (see also Chapter 4 on news writing conventions). This would suggest that in composing their images press photographers do consider the aesthetic quality of the news images – although this research needs to be complemented with further quantitative studies concerning a variety of news genres. For example, 85 per cent of Caple's stories concern soft news and it is thus not clear yet whether other news genres would produce similar results.

Further, there may be occasions where press photographs appear not to be balanced. This would include occasions when the photographer is present at the unfolding of critical events, where the magnitude of the event and limited access to the event may impede a photographer in getting the kinds of shots they would like. Zakia (1997: 64–5) suggests that 'those images that don't conform to the Gestalt laws of perceptual organization would include those that have strong emotional appeal'. Some news photographs may be so strong in their construal of the event as newsworthy in terms of news values such as Negativity or Superlativeness, that this aspect overrides the concern for balance (a good example of this can be seen in Figure 3.5, in Chapter 3). As Mike Bowers, former photographic editor of the *Sydney Morning Herald*, notes 'The gravity of the event is inversely proportional to the quality of footage. If there's grainy and difficult footage from a major accident or disaster, it will get a run despite poor quality' (Rau 2010: 34), but in most other cases quality is needed – and this quality includes not just lighting, colour and 'graininess', and so on but also balance/composition. As a former press photographer, Caple would moreover argue that even in the most difficult of circumstances a good press photographer will still know when and how to capture that critical moment in the unfolding of an event: critical in terms of the nature and newsworthiness of the event itself, critical in its power to stand in evidence of the entire event, and critical in its *compositional* power to attract and hold our attention to form a memory that will last long after the words have been forgotten. This is what Cartier-Bresson would refer to as the 'decisive moment': 'one in which all the elements come together to form a compelling psychological

Figure 7.4 A well-balanced image taken in difficult circumstances ('Going against the grain', *Sydney Morning Herald*, 20 November 2004, p. 16, Fairfax Syndication)

and visual statement' (Rosenblum 2007, see also Chapter 5). An example of such critical moment photography can be seen in Figure 7.4.

If we analyse this image using the *Balance Framework*, we would get an *isolating, axial* compositional configuration, which is arguably the most aesthetically pleasing of the compositional choices for its ability to stimulate visual appeal while using the dynamic, asymmetrical axis to demonstrate unequal relations. The facial expression of the protestor aside, the drama in this image is also enhanced by the visual weight of the riot police that far outnumber the single protester positioned in the bottom right-hand corner of the image frame. This configuration of meanings is clearly enhanced by the composition of the image. Thus, while this photograph of a protestor and riot police has clearly been taken in difficult circumstances and is certainly newsworthy in terms of Negativity, there is also an aesthetic quality to the photograph that demonstrates a concern for composition that press photographers are rarely acknowledged for. Given Caple's experience as a press photographer, we argue that even in a situation like that depicted in Figure 7.4, photographers would still attempt to negotiate the best possible position within the restrictions imposed on them from which to compose the image. They would also have an idea of what they would like to have in the frame and what is likely to be in the frame as they thrust their hand in the air and angle the lens at the target. Thus even in the most trying of circumstances, composition counts.

Figure 7.5 A dramatic event that is also construed as 'beautiful' through composition and aesthetic appeal ('Waves on the line halt trains', *Sydney Morning Herald*, 29 October 2004, p. 14, Fairfax Syndication)

Secondly, when composition and other factors come together to create beautiful images, we have argued that the newsworthiness of the event is enhanced, through construing it as beautiful (cf. Chapter 3). To give another example, in the story in Figure 7.5 (originally published in colour) a commuter train is stranded on a rail track that is being battered by huge waves. If we just focus on the elements in the image frame, the train and the huge waves, there is no doubt that this construes Negativity and Superlativeness. However, added to this are the low lighting conditions, which necessitate the use of a slower shutter speed. This gives the effect of both graininess and enhances the movement of the waves because of the longer exposure time needed. In addition, the warm colours of the train and its headlights starkly contrast with the white spray from the waves. This, combined with the axial configuration of the train juxtaposed with the mighty waves, adds further visual stimulation/aesthetic appeal to the image. Thus we could say that this image also construes the event as 'beautiful'.

Thirdly, aesthetic concerns can have an impact on the selection of news stories as well as on the emergence of new genres. The examples in this chapter are from stand-alones: a unique news story genre in which a large, striking image that also carries aesthetic appeal along with its ability to illustrate the news event to which it relates is combined with a headline that is often allusive or playful and a caption text. Figure 7.6 on p. 179 shows how they look on the page, including the size of the space that they often occupy (spanning up to seven columns in most instances). Often, the image dominates the story (and the page). We can see that these are not stories that need to be told, they are stories that need to be *shown*.[3] Furthermore, being 'packaged' as stand-alones, these stories are not swamped by too

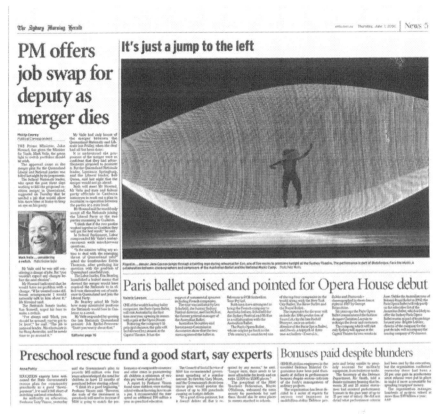

Figure 7.6 An example stand-alone dominates the page ('It's just a jump to the left', *Sydney Morning Herald*, 1 June 2006, p. 5, Fairfax Syndication)

much text. The images are given the space to speak for themselves and ultimately, they make the newspaper look better. We explore such stories fully in the next chapter.

6 Conclusion

In this chapter we have introduced the *Balance Framework* for analysing compositional choices in still images. We argue that press photographers are acutely aware of the power of compositional choices to arrest the attention of the newspaper reader. They are concerned not only with composition but also with other technical elements such as lighting, colour, shutter speed, and the choices they take up in relation to these are very much motivated by an aesthetic value. Press photography is not simply a matter of information relay, or standing in evidence of the existence of an event. Meaningful compositional choices are being made every time a photographer puts her eye to the viewfinder and such choices are highly motivated for their aesthetic value.

Directions for further reading

Dondis, D. A. (1973), *A Primer of Visual Literacy*. London: MIT Press. Explores composition from the point of view of Gestalt psychology, taking into consideration other factors such as colour and texture.

Kress, G. and van Leeuwen, T. (2006), *Reading Images: The Grammar of Visual Design* (2nd edition). London: Routledge. Offers a comprehensive social semiotic analysis of the 'grammar' of visual design, including colour, perspective, framing and composition.

Präkel, D. (2006), *Composition*. London: AVA. Explores composition from the professional photographer's point of view.

Notes

1 The data in this chapter comes from a 1,000-image/story dataset from Caple (2009b) of stand-alone images used in the metropolitan broadsheet newspaper the *Sydney Morning Herald* between 2004 and 2006. As previously mentioned, stand-alones are news stories that focus on a dominant image, with a headline and caption text only.

2 It must be noted, however, that aesthetic appeal is not solely based on compositional configurations. As mentioned, other factors, including subject matter, colour, light, contrast, and so forth, also contribute to the aesthetic of the image.

3 This was also confirmed by a news values analysis, which showed that apart from Timeliness, the events construed in these stories were not particularly newsworthy, for example, in terms of Negativity, Prominence or Proximity. Indeed, many of the stories did not carry much cultural significance to an Australian audience. Furthermore, 83 per cent of these stories were exclusive to the *Sydney Morning Herald* (rather than also occurring in competitor publications in the Sydney region) and hence clearly not stories that *needed* to be told (see also Chapter 8).

CHAPTER EIGHT

The big picture: a case study of stand-alones in print news

1 Introduction

In the previous two chapters, we have introduced specific frameworks for analysing aspects of news discourse: namely, compositional configurations in images (Chapter 7) and evaluations in language (Chapter 6). Both of these analytical frameworks have the potential to tell us a lot about the ways in which news discourse is constructed and the potential effects of such a construction. In this chapter we will demonstrate how these frameworks can be put to use in analysing a particular type of print news story – the 'stand-alone'. We will begin by introducing the stand-alone before analysing some of these news stories for balance in the image and for the use of evaluations in the captions and headlines. We will discuss instances of both *soft* news and *hard* news events, before concluding the chapter with a discussion of this journalistic practice. Our objectives for this chapter are thus to enable readers to understand:

- what a 'stand-alone' news story is
- the types of compositional configurations that may occur in stand-alones
- the types of evaluations that may occur in stand-alones
- what role composition and evaluation play in stand-alones
- how soft news and hard news stand-alones are similar or different to each other.

2 Stand-alone stories in print news

First of all, what is a stand-alone? This is a type of news story where the image dominates – both the verbal text and often the page (see Figure 8.1) – this is why they have also been called *image-nuclear* news stories (see Caple 2009a, in press). These images are usually very well *balanced* (see Chapter 7) and thus have the potential to construe a news event as aesthetically appealing. There is also typically a headline with the image, which relates directly and often playfully to the photograph through the use of pun or allusion to other discourses (Caple 2008a, 2009b, 2010a).[1] An extended caption (Layton 2011: 48), up to two to three sentences, is also included with the image and headline. There is no other verbal text with such stories.

To illustrate, Figure 8.1 is a typical example of the way that stand-alones are used in the *Sydney Morning Herald*, an Australian broadsheet newspaper published by Fairfax Media (a leading media company in Australia and New Zealand), which services the metropolitan area of Sydney and New South Wales. As can be seen, the striking image is used quite large on the page and the headline makes an allusion to a popular 1995 Hollywood

Figure 8.1 'Dry hard with a vengeance': An example stand-alone story in the *Sydney Morning Herald*, 24 July 2004, p. 21, Fairfax Syndication

movie, *Die Hard: With a Vengeance*. We will not discuss this story in detail here, as we will return to it in our qualitative analysis below.

The fact that the images in such stories are well composed (according to the *Balance Framework*) and that their verbal text is so concise makes them good examples for a case study. Further, stand-alones are worthy of attention as they represent a not uncommon method of storytelling in newspapers. Indeed, as pointed out in Chapter 5, this is a prime example of a more visual way of telling a (news) story or 'packaging' the news. Indeed, newspapers such as the *Guardian*, *The Times* and the *Independent* in the United Kingdom, the *New York Times* in the United States, the *Sydney Morning Herald* in Australia, as well as English-language newspapers in other parts of the world including *China Daily* and *Jakarta Post*, frequently feature such stories in their news pages. This type of story also regularly occurs in freesheets aimed at 18- to 36-year-old professionals working in the city such as *mX* in Australia and *Metro* in the United Kingdom.

The data that we use in this chapter for exploring these news stories come from a study Caple (2009a) completed on a collection of 1,000 stand-alones. These stories were collected during the period from June 2004 to December 2006 from the *Sydney Morning Herald*. Every instance of a stand-alone that was published in this newspaper was collected during this period and was analysed in a database written specifically for the project. Other competitor newspapers in the Sydney region, as well as the *Sydney Morning Herald*'s sister newspaper the *Age* in Melbourne, were monitored on a daily basis throughout the same period with regard to whether these publications carried the same stories (in any format).

Focusing on key aspects of stand-alones as well as on composition, evaluation and news values we will discuss these stand-alones both quantitatively and qualitatively, with the dual aim of describing this special kind of news story, and of illustrating how some of the frameworks introduced in this book can be applied in the study of news discourse.

3 Stand-alones in the *Sydney Morning Herald*: quantitative and qualitative analyses

3.1 *Quantitative analyses of all stories*

General statistics

In Table 8.1 on p. 184, we present first some of the general results from our analysis. One of the most interesting findings is that there is a near 60/40 split between stories that were internationally sourced and stories that were sourced from within Australia (mostly from staff photographers employed by the newspaper). Further, all of the international stories were provided by agencies (as demonstrated in Table 8.2 on p. 185). One of the reasons for the high percentage of agency-sourced stories could be due to the fact that newspaper companies often have contracts with agencies that are based on quotas (e.g. ten stories per week) and this may be one of the ways in which a newspaper may try to 'use up' its quota in a given week (Peter Kerr, Commissioning Editor and former Foreign Editor, *Sydney Morning Herald*, 2006, personal communication). Table 8.1 also demonstrates that 83 per cent of the stories were exclusive to the *Sydney Morning Herald* (based on monitoring other newspapers, as noted earlier). This may also confirm that the *Sydney Morning Herald* was indeed filling agency quotas, as suggested above, but it also indicates that many news events that may otherwise go unreported in the news did get exposure in the *Sydney Morning Herald*.

Stand-alone stories were also occasionally used on the front page of the *Sydney Morning Herald* and in such instances (5 per cent) they often served to link the reader to a more in-depth version of the story on the inside pages. This works very much in the same way that a hyperlink would work on the homepage of the online version of the newspaper where a newsbite (Knox 2007: 20) would be hyperlinked to a longer version of the story elsewhere on the website. Furthermore, most stories (84.5 per cent) dealt in human interest type events, such as festivals, sporting events and the arts, while the remaining 15.5 per cent of stories focused on destabilizing or hard news events, such as accidents, protests or natural disasters. We will investigate the soft/hard news split in more detail below.

Table 8.1 General quantitative results on the stand-alone corpus

Total Number of Stories	1,000
	Percentage of total database
Published in colour	88
Stories sourced from within Australia	38
Stories exclusive to *Sydney Morning Herald*	83
Stories published in weekend edition	23
Stories sourced from agencies	63
Story used on front page and linking to another story inside	5
Human interest (soft news) stories	84.5
Hard news stories	15.5

Table 8.2 Stories sourced from agencies (63 per cent)

Agency	Percentage of All Agency Copy
AP	38
Reuters	36
AFP	21
Others	5

Another important finding from this study of stand-alones in the *Sydney Morning Herald* is the extent to which the headlines and images enter into a playful relationship with each other. Nearly all headlines (95 per cent) in this dataset make use of pun or allude to other discourses. Puns (approximately 33 per cent) include the kind of play on words that involves idioms, colloquial phrases and conventionalized expressions and that relies on linguistic knowledge, such as *burn the midnight oil, don't look now,* or *give the low down on.* Allusions (approximately 66 per cent) include play on words that draws on cultural knowledge of other discourses in the form of formulaic expressions, long quotations and proper names or titles, such as *mission accomplished, he ain't heavy, he's my brother* or *Jurassic Park.* This playful relationship extends across both words and images and leads to quite a complex integration of figurative and allusive representations in the wordings with their often literal representations in the images. The effects of such complex play can present quite a challenge to readers who are able and willing to engage with this and has been discussed in terms of community building among newspaper audiences (e.g. Caple 2009b, 2010a). Interestingly, other newspapers using stand-alones (e.g. the *Guardian* in the United Kingdom) tend not to engage in such play to the same extent as the *Sydney Morning Herald* does.

Composition and evaluation

Apart from the general statistics on sourcing, story placement, type of news (soft/hard) and type of play (puns/allusions) reported above, the stand-alones in the database were also systematically analysed for the compositional meanings made in the images. What became apparent from this analysis was the fact that nearly all (99 per cent) of the images were balanced according to the *Balance Framework* introduced in Chapter 7. Further, two-thirds of all images (67 per cent) were composed along the isolating configuration, with an almost even split between images where elements were centred or arranged on the more dynamic axial configuration (see Figure 8.2). As already noted in Chapter 7, such axial configurations create an unequal

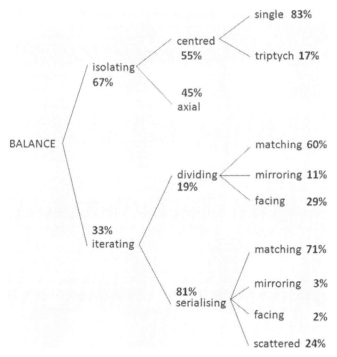

Figure 8.2 Compositional configurations in stand-alones from the *Sydney Morning Herald*

relationship between elements and therefore offer more visual stimulation because of the need to counterbalance the elements on the diagonal axis. This is regarded as aesthetically pleasing and highly valued (Altengarten 2004, Präkel 2006). Thus, many of the images in Caple's database have the potential to construe the depicted news events as aesthetically appealing (in interaction with other techniques and aspects of content, as discussed in Chapter 7).

Further, while it was beyond the scope of our analysis to exhaustively analyse all verbal text (headlines and captions) in the 1,000 stories for evaluations, we used a corpus linguistic software programme (*Wordsmith*, Scott 2011) to produce lists of the most frequent words and word combinations in headlines and captions. We then went through these lists 'hunting' for possible pointers to evaluations.[2] Table 8.3 on p. 187 shows the analysis of the captions (51,538 words in total).[3]

A number of points become apparent from this analysis. First, there is not much evaluative language per se (i.e. *explicitly* attitudinal language, cf. Chapter 6). However, evaluations are occasionally expressed in other ways, for example, through negative lexis (potentially construing the news value of Negativity) or through contrast/negation (potentially construing

Table 8.3 Pointers to evaluations in the caption text in stand-alones from the *Sydney Morning Herald*

Parameter	Pointers in Captions
Reliability (high reliability/likelihood)	*will* (158) *will be* (54)
Evidentiality (speech, general knowledge, expectation)	*said* (131) *said the* (28), *known as* (20), *expected to* (19)
Unexpectedness (mainly through contrast, negation, comparison)	*but* (119), *first* (111), *new* (68), *not* (55), *just* (38), *only* (34) *the first* (61), *a new* (23), *but the* (21) *the first time* (13)
Negative Emotivity (only negative lexis, no evaluative language)	*police* (62), *fire* (41), *killed* (34), *military* (32), *war* (32)
Intensification/quantification (not a 'parameter' per se)	*world* (114), *more* (110), *years* (75), *million* (59), *all* (52), *thousands* (46), *most* (43), *high* (40), *kilometers* (35), *many* (33) *more than* (90), *the world* (70), *thousands of* (34), *up to* (25), *world's* (23), *hundreds of* (22), *the most* (20), *at least* (19) *the world's* (23), *in the world* (14)

Novelty). The fact that not much explicitly attitudinal language is present in the captions can again be tied to the projection of objectivity that happens in much news discourse (cf. Chapters 4 and 6). Similarly, it can be argued that the frequent usage of the neutral reporting verb *said* (131 instances) and of references to general knowledge *known as* (20 instances) – expressing Evidentiality: speech and Evidentiality: general knowledge respectively – background the journalistic voice and instead foreground communality and objectivity. In general, there are many words in the frequency list that are not easily linked to evaluations, many pointing instead to soft news (e.g. *anniversary, festival*, etc.) – which we can associate with the fact that most of the stories deal with human interest type events as mentioned above.

On the other hand, Table 8.3 also illustrates that intensifying language does occur in the captions – while this is not seen as a 'parameter' of evaluation (as the parameters themselves can be intensified), this type of language is counted as evaluative or appraising by some researchers (e.g. Martin and White 2005). Interestingly, though, at least with respect to quantification (e.g. through numbers: *hundreds, thousands*) the occurrence of such language may not contradict the journalistic projection of objectivity and may be allowed to occur precisely because it could potentially be justified (e.g. by reference to official 'counts'). It nevertheless fulfils a specific rhetorical function and increases newsworthiness. For example, in Chapter 9 we will discuss two examples reporting on Osama bin Laden's death, one of them referring to *hundreds of people* cheering upon hearing this news, the other report simply mentioning *people* but not quantifying them. Only the example including quantification would construe Superlativeness. Considering the results presented in Table 8.3 in terms of news values, both the evaluations that do occur as well as the intensifying and quantifying expressions seem to indicate that the captions partially construe the news values of Novelty, Negativity and in particular Superlativeness – and possibly also Timeliness (*will*, *expected to*). The latter hypothesis is confirmed by the fact that *yesterday* also occurs frequently in the captions.

Considering now headlines (5,204 words in total), these feature few evaluations and/or other devices that increase news value(s) – note, for example, the unexpected occurrence of *a little* in Table 8.4,[4] which might actually downplay newsworthiness. News values that might be construed through headlines might be Novelty (through evaluations of unexpectedness) and Superlativeness (through intensification/quantification), but the frequencies are not very high. This finding can be related to the fact that the headlines function to play with readers (through puns/allusions), rather than to increase newsworthiness. We will now look at both compositional meanings and evaluations in further detail in a more qualitative analysis of selected stories below.

Table 8.4 Pointers to evaluations in the headline text in stand-alones in the *Sydney Morning Herald*

Parameter	Pointers in Headlines
Unexpectedness	*no* (18), *but* (15), *not* (14), *new* (11), *just* (10)
Expectedness	?*another*? (10)
Mental state	?*ready to*? (6)
Intensification/quantification (not a 'parameter' per se)	*all* (20), *big* (10), *the top* (5) *a little* (7)

3.2 Qualitative analyses of selected soft and hard news stories

Since the news stories can be split into those dealing with human interest events (soft news) and those dealing with destabilizing events (hard news), we will in turn discuss selected examples falling into these two general types of news. We will analyse both compositional meanings and evaluations as well as other relevant aspects of these stories that give us insights into the construction of news in such stand-alones.

Soft news

As noted above, the vast majority of stories analysed in this study involve human interest events (84.5 per cent). These are stories that tend to focus on stable events in a society, like festivals, seasonal or religious happenings (Christmas, Easter and Ramadan), or events that appear regularly in the calendar like anniversaries or sporting competitions (the Olympics and World Cups in various sporting codes). These types of stories tend to reflect and comment on the established social order (Feez et al. 2008). Often they serve to remind us of the prevailing moral values both within our own culture and to exemplify those of other cultures. These may sometimes come across as quite stereotypical, or may merely reflect the way that other nations are typically construed.

The two examples of soft news stand-alones that we will look at both concern a festival, the *Oktoberfest* (see Table 8.5 on p. 190). The *Oktoberfest* is a widely known festival that occurs annually over a two- to three-week period at the end of September in Munich, southern Germany. The festival includes street parades where participants dress in traditional Bavarian costumes, like Lederhosen or Dirndls, a fairground with rides and amusement arcades and the very famous beer halls. The two Oktoberfest stories in Table 8.5 appeared in the *Sydney Morning Herald* in successive years, 2004 and 2005.

If we look first at the content of the images, in Example 1 ('Queasy riders') in Table 8.5 we can see people on one of the more thrilling amusement park rides, the big dipper, and a famous Munich landmark in the background, the *Frauenkirche* (Church of our Blessed Lady). In Example 2 ('Hans'), we can see a row of puppets dressed in traditional Bavarian costumes and an artist working on one of them. The content of these images construes the news value of Consonance, as we expect to see fairground rides and traditional costumes at the *Oktoberfest*, alongside less family-friendly aspects such as beer and breasts (see Chapter 5; Caple and Knox in press).

In terms of compositional configurations, we can analyse Example 1 as *isolating*, *axial*, juxtaposing the ride with the historical building and heightening the sense of size of the ride, and Example 2 as *iterating*, *serialising*, *matching*, since all of the puppets are lined up and facing the same direction. The more dynamic composition in Example 1 ('Queasy riders') emphasizes the excitement of the fair (as opposed to the more traditional aspects), the scale and daring of the big dipper. On the other hand, the repetitive, static nature of composition of the puppets in Example 2 ('Hans') along with the concentration of the artist at work (who is barely distinguishable) focus our

Table 8.5 Two 'soft news' stand-alone stories about the *Oktoberfest*

	Example 1 ('Queasy riders')	Example 2 ('Hans')
Date of publication/ page	20 September 2004, p. 9	13 August 2005, p. 20
Image		
Headline	**Queasy riders . . . or they soon will be**	**Hans, knees und boomps-a-daisy**
Caption	Early visitors of the 6 million expected to attend Munich's Oktoberfest over the next six weeks soared high on a big dipper when Germany's annual beer-swilling event, the 171st, opened on Saturday.	A worker puts the finishing touches onto puppets dressed in traditional Bavarian costumes in preparation for the Oktoberfest in Munich, southern Germany, next month.
Compositional configurations	Isolating, axial	Iterating, serialising, matching
Play (allusion/ pun)	Allusion to cinematic discourse: *Easy Rider*: 1969 film (road movie), directed by Dennis Hopper, starring Peter Fonda, Dennis Hopper and Jack Nicholson (www.imdb.com/title/tt0064276/)	Reference to 'Hands, knees and boomps a daisy' an old British music hall song from late nineteenth to early twentieth century and word play across languages (*Hans/hands, und/and*).

attention on the traditions behind the festival rather than the more modern aspects depicted in Example 1.

Looking at the language in the captions, Example 1 shows both the use of intensification/quantification (*6 million, soared high*) and of Evidentiality: expectation (*expected to*), which our corpus analysis has already indicated as occurring across some of these stories. The latter is used to make a prediction enabling the newspaper to include a reference to the *6 million* envisaged visitors and thus construing Superlativeness. In contrast, the caption of Example 2 is very descriptive and does not feature any evaluations. Further, the only evaluations in the headlines occur in Example 1 (*will* – Reliability; *queasy riders* – possibly negative Emotivity of the ride that causes riders to feel sick). With respect to news values we could thus argue that intensification and evaluations in Example 1 establish newsworthiness more than in Example 2, at least with respect to Superlativeness.[5]

However, in both examples the main point of the headline is not necessarily the establishment of newsworthiness (although the headline of Example 1 may incidentally do so); rather they make use of other devices to attract readers – play on words and image and/or allusion (cf. Chapter 4 on headlinese). The image in Example 1 shows the big dipper ride, which is well known for making riders feel sick. The headline confirms this through the use of *Queasy riders*, which could also be said to enhance the Consonance in this story, since many typically associate fairground rides with nausea. However, this headline also points to another text, the 1969 Hollywood movie, *Easy Rider*, directed by and starring Dennis Hopper. Certain readers would detect the allusion to this film in the headline and may laugh/groan or congratulate themselves on deciphering the play. This may attract readers through challenging them intellectually as well as through community building (see Caple 2010a). Similarly, the headline in Example 2 alludes to a very old British music hall tune, 'Hands, knees and boomps a daisy'. It also plays on the similar sounds of the German and English *Hans/hands*, *und/and*. Again, readers are challenged to detect both linguistic and cultural clues in the play in this headline, which has similar implications in terms of community building among those who choose to engage with and decipher the play. This is complex play and is not reserved only for use in soft news contexts in this newspaper, as we shall now see in discussing selected stories reporting hard news events.

Hard news

As mentioned, approximately 15 per cent of the stories in Caple's database of stand-alones can be categorized as *hard* news. Generally, hard news concerns newsworthy events that are likely to have a material impact on a person's life (Tuchman 1973/1997). Bell (1991: 147–8) uses both the terms *hard news* and *spot news*, and defines this kind of news as 'tales of accidents, disasters, crimes, coups and earthquakes, politics or diplomacy', while White (1997: 101) describes the domain of hard news as being 'typically associated with eruptive violence, reversals of fortune and socially significant breaches of the moral order' (see also Chapter 4). While information about hard news events is often packaged in a typical structure that we have described in Chapter 4, they can also be packaged in more visually dominating ways (cf. Chapter 5) as in the stand-alone. In the following we will examine two stories that report on negative environmental happenings: a drought and an oil spill (see Table 8.6 on p. 192).

Table 8.6 Two 'hard news' stand-alone stories about the environment

	Example 1 ('Dry hard')	Example 2 ('Trouble')
Date of publication/ page	24 July 2004, p. 21	16 October 2004, p. 15
Image		
Headline	**Dry hard with a vengeance**	**Trouble on oiled water**
Caption	Workers walk across the dried bed of the Hongyashan reservoir in Minqin, north-western China. The reservoir, which is the largest in Asia and can hold 98 million cubic metres of water, dried up last month for the first time since 1958, bringing hardship to the thousands of families depending on it.	An oil spill, dispersed by tides and winds, creates a multi-coloured sheen on water lapping the beaches of Vashon Island, Washington state. Department of Ecology officials and spill contractors were trying to use booms to protect sensitive marine habitats.
Compositional configurations	Isolating, axial	Iterating, serialising, matching
Play (allusion/ pun)	The heading alludes to the 1995 film *Die Hard: With a Vengeance*, starring Bruce Willis, Samuel L. Jackson and Jeremy Irons	Idiomatic phrase: *to pour oil on troubled waters* Allusion to song 'Bridge over troubled water' 1970: Simon and Garfunkel

Example 1 ('Dry hard') in Table 8.6 is also reproduced with the entire page in Figure 8.1 on p. 182. Figure 8.1 shows that the story spans five columns and dominates the upper half of the page. The image itself is very well composed, juxtaposing the workers in the top left side of the image frame with the dry, cracked earth that dominates the lower right-hand side of the image, in an *axial* configuration.[6] Technically, the photographer has utilized the low-lying sunlight to emphasis the contrast between light and shade and has used a wide-angle lens to accentuate the size of the cracks in the land. Together these juxtapositions and technical elements increase the intensity of the problem (the arid land) and construe the news values of Negativity, Superlativeness and Personalization (these workers represent all of the people suffering as a result of this drought). At the same time, this composition creates a visually impressive/appealing image of the event, thus possibly construing the event as aesthetically pleasing.

Considering evaluations, the caption shows instances of lexis that describe a negative event (*dried bed, dried up*), and its consequences (*hardship*), and also features instances of intensification/quantification and comparison (*the largest in Asia, 98 million, thousand, the first time since 1958*). This illustrates – as already indicated through quantitative analysis – that evaluations in the captions are expressed through resources such as negative lexis rather than evaluative language and that Negativity is one of the news values construed. We can also see the establishment of Superlativeness through intensification, quantification and comparison. As in Example 1 in Table 8.5, the headline features some expressions that may be tied to the increase of newsworthiness (e.g. *with a vengeance* arguably combines intensification with negative Emotivity). However, similar to the soft news examples in Table 8.5, the point of the headline is its play with the reader in its allusion to the 1995 film *Die Hard: With a Vengeance*, starring Bruce Willis, Samuel L. Jackson and Jeremy Irons. However, the play between *dry/die* and the drought situation explained in the caption to this story may be viewed as being somewhat insensitive, as may be the aforementioned potential construal of this event as aesthetically pleasing through compositional choices in the image (see further our discussion in Section 4).

Turning to Example 2 ('Trouble') in Table 8.6 now, this is an aerial photograph looking down on the Vashon Island coastline (Washington State, US), where the colours in the water, caused by an oil slick, form the same linear pattern as the beach/coastline (this image was reproduced in colour in the newspaper). These patterns, the contrast in colours and the unusual camera angle arguably make the scene look beautiful. This is a landscape image (with no sentient participants represented in the image). To date, images that are landscape only have not been analysed using Caple's *Balance Framework*. However, there may be a case for analysing this configuration of oil slick and coastline as *iterating, serialising, matching*, which reflects the linear patterning, emphasized by the technical aspects of this image noted above. In any case, we would argue that this environmentally hugely damaging event is very clearly construed as aesthetically pleasing in the image.

Considering evaluations, the caption is relatively descriptive, although we might argue that *multi-coloured sheen on water lapping the beaches* is associated with positivity (beauty, tranquillity) – especially in connection with the beautiful accompanying image – and that *oil spill* labels a negative event and *trying to use booms to protect sensitive marine habitats* describes its negative consequences. None of these expressions are explicitly evaluative, however. In the headline, *trouble* is again an example of negative lexis. But, as in the other stories, the headline asks the reader to decipher the play, in making reference to both the 1970 song 'Bridge over troubled water' (by Simon and Garfunkel), and to the idiom *to pour oil on troubled waters*. Together with the beautiful image this play is again somewhat problematic in that it is at odds with the negative environmental event that is reported on. In fact, this event was a very serious environmental disaster that attracted the maximum possible penalty under state law. Within two days of the spill, authorities had already spent US$750,000 on the clean-up, and by 19 October 2004 $1.25 million had been spent (Polar Texas Oil Spill 2006). The spill damaged the winter nesting grounds of the grebe, and other bird, shellfish and fish populations along the coastline and halted the harvesting of clams, oysters and other intertidal species, including seaweed. The final cost of the oil spill clean-up operation exceeded $2.2 million. What was also remarkable with this case was that it was the equivalent of a hit-and-run incident in that no company or individual claimed responsibility for the spill and its origin remained uncertain for some time. The source of the leak was eventually discovered to be an oil tanker (the *Polar Texas*), and the company responsible, ConocoPhillips, was compelled to pay a $540,000 fine levied by the Washington Department of Ecology. At that time, this was the largest fine Ecology had ever issued for a spill in marine waters (Polar Texas Oil Spill 2006). Yet, despite the seriousness of this event, it is represented as beautiful and reported on playfully in the *Sydney Morning Herald* story.

In sum, we can see clear similarities between the hard news and the soft news stories, not just in their use of composition and evaluation, but also in their play with the meanings between the headlines and images and the events. However, while this may be unproblematic in soft news, in both of the hard news stories the playfulness of the headlines and the beauty in the images could be viewed as somewhat at odds with the seriousness of the environmental disasters that have taken place in both of these stories, as retold in the captions. We will discuss this issue further in Section 4.

4 Standing up for stand-alones: why use them?

As we have noted above, images that appear in the stand-alone format tend to be very well composed and technically of a high standard. This means that such images have the potential to be classified as beautiful images. Equally, the playful relationship between headline and image also dominates. As we have already suggested, these are stories that need to be shown rather than told. For soft news stories, this is an attractive format, and as Caple (2010a) has argued, it creates opportunities for a news organization to bond with its readers. Where it may be viewed as problematic, however, is when this format is used with hard news reporting. This is particularly true when the headlines are playful, the images are 'beautiful' and the captions retell the seriousness of the news event (e.g. through negative lexis and intensification/quantification). We have termed this an 'evaluative clash' (Bednarek and Caple 2010: 14), when very serious and damaging events are packaged in this aesthetic/playful stand-alone format. However, we have also challenged the extent to which this is an inappropriate practice, since 'the dominance of the image and the play in these stories may draw . . . readers to this kind of story' and the stand-alone represents 'a novel way of getting readers that may not normally have read a "boring" environmental story to engage with environmental reporting' (Bednarek and Caple 2010: 14). And, as our statistics also showed, this format meant that a lot of news did get reported in the *Sydney Morning Herald* that would otherwise have gone unreported in the Australian news media, thus placing it on the news agenda and making audiences aware of these events. Consequently, it is possible to view this practice **both** critically **and** positively.

In this chapter, we have examined one particular type of news story (the stand-alone) both in terms of the compositional choices made in the images used in such stories and in terms of the evaluations in the verbal text accompanying such images. Since we only investigated stand-alones in one newspaper for this case study, our findings can only be generalized in so far as they apply to one particular publication in one particular context. However, such analyses could be extended to cover other publications in other countries, to provide cross-cultural comparisons, or to include other types of stories to discover the particular types of patterns that may be present in the use of words and images in these contexts. Equally, analyses of this type could examine the many different types of stories that report on one particular issue or event (such as the environment or an election). Such comparative analysis is able to tell us something about reporting practices in news institutions and the ways in which various issues/events are covered.

Directions for further reading

Caple, H. (2010), 'Doubling-up: allusion and bonding in multi-semiotic news stories', in M. Bednarek and J. R. Martin (eds), *New Discourse on Language: Functional Perspectives on Multimodality, Identity, and Affiliation*. London/New York: Continuum, pp. 111–33. Discusses play on words and images in stand-alones from a systemic functional linguistic perspective and explores the implications of such play for bonding and community building among newspaper audiences.

Lennon, P. (2004), *Allusions in the Press*. Berlin: Walter de Gruyter. Offers a comprehensive corpus-based analysis of allusions in the British press and explores the demands placed on readers to understand such allusions.

Piazza, R. and Haarman, L. (2011), 'Towards a definition and classification of human interest narratives in television war reporting', *Journal of Pragmatics*, 43, 1540–9. Explores a corpus of American and British Iraq war news items and how the element of narrativity is interlaced with that of human interest to produce 'human interest narratives'.

Notes

1 Allusion is a concept from literary theory that is based on the idea of texts making reference to other texts. Allusions are characterized as containing a short stretch of discourse that is recognized by the reader as 'a deliberate play on a piece of well-known composed language or name so as to convey implicit meaning' (Lennon 2004: 1). See Caple (2010a) for a discussion of allusion and intertextuality.

2 We call them *pointers* because we have not examined each occurrence in its co-text (although we have done so for *new*, excluding instances such as *New York* from the frequency count, as they are clearly not related to evaluation).

3 We considered word forms with a raw frequency of at least 30 (= top 181), the top 100 two-word combinations with a raw frequency of 18 or more and the top 20 three-word combinations with a raw frequency of 12 or more. The number in brackets refers to the raw frequency of the respective word form/ word combination.

4 We considered word forms with a raw frequency of at least 10 (= top 50) as well as the top 25 two-word combinations with a raw frequency of 5 or more. Three-word combinations were not analysed because they are too infrequent in this small-size corpus. The question marks indicate that it is less clear whether or not these can be categorized as pointers for the relevant parameters.

5 We could also compare other devices to construe newsworthiness; thus, temporal references and tense construe Timeliness in both news stories.

6 The workers themselves are also arguably configured as *iterating, serialising, matching* – a case for double-coding, as outlined in Chapter 7.

CHAPTER NINE

Killing Osama: a case study of online news

1 Introduction

In this final chapter we want to turn to moving images and online news, specifically video news summaries posted on news websites. By examining a case study of two online news bulletins in some detail we hope to enable readers to:

- apply the concepts introduced in this book to the analysis of news discourse
- use the concepts to discuss online video news stories
- appreciate how we can use such analysis to arrive at particular interpretations of news discourse.

We will describe our source data before discussing our analyses in detail. We will finish this chapter by offering conclusions relating to the case study as well as to the book overall.

2 Introducing the data

2.1 Data selection

Many major newsworthy events occurred during the time of writing this book (late 2010 to late 2011).The wedding of Prince William to Catherine

Middleton in the United Kingdom; severe floods and cyclones in parts of Queensland, Australia; severe earthquakes in Japan and New Zealand; the 'Arab Spring' in the Middle East; the shooting of more than 80 young people in Norway; riots in the United Kingdom; and the killing of Osama bin Laden in Pakistan all received considerable coverage in the news media. It is often a good idea to focus a case study on the reporting of such significant events, even while remaining aware of the fact that such special events also result in 'special' (often breaking news) reporting. For the case study in this chapter we decided to look at the reporting of Osama bin Laden's death in two online news video bulletins in the United Kingdom and Australia. The two news bulletins that we will look at in this study are taken from BBC *One-minute World News* (UK) and ABC *News in 90 Seconds* (Australia).

There are several reasons why we decided to examine the reporting of this event in these video summaries. First, the event (the death of bin Laden) was chosen because it was an event of global significance, with Osama being identified as 'the face' of terrorism since the 9/11 attacks. It was seen as an important event not just for a single country but also for a large part of the world and was front page news all over the world (see Moos 2011 for a gallery of 45 international front pages).

Secondly, we focused on the BBC and the ABC as news media institutions because of the roles that they play as national public service broadcasting corporations in their respective countries. Both are well established, are subsidized by government funding, and are arguably considered as authorities in news reporting. Both of these organizations are also strictly regulated at industry level and through their own internal editorial guidelines and codes of practice. Significantly for this analysis, neither is a US-based institution; thus to a certain degree both are reporting on the event as 'outsiders'. At the same time, both the United Kingdom and Australia maintain strong cultural and military links to the United States, and have been involved in supporting recent wars initiated by the United States.

Thirdly, we decided to focus on online news stories because they offer an opportunity to examine this media form in detail while at the same time looking at some of the aspects of new media in general (e.g. 'sharing'). Furthermore, both the ABC and the BBC appear to have established a presence for themselves as internet news providers. While a target audience for their internet services is not easily identifiable, as websites are generally accessible to anyone with unrestricted internet access, we would see the audience for the BBC as more global/international than the ABC.[1] This is because the BBC is a well-known and established international news authority that users from around the world will turn to (Paganoni 2008: 337). This is less true for the ABC, although it has been called Australia's 'most important cultural institution' (Simons 2011: 26) and is 'the biggest single employer of journalists in Australia' (Simons 2011: 28). General numbers for the online services of both BBC and ABC indicate a significant amount of users: for example, by 2008 the BBC website was receiving an average of 3.6 billion hits per month (no breakdown available for 'News' services, but see www.bbc.co.uk/aboutthebbc/ for further details). ABC news and current affairs websites were visited by an average of 4.3 million users a month between 2009 and 2010 (ABC Annual Report 2010: 55).

2.2 Data collection

The two video news summaries, our data for this case study, were broadcast on the relevant websites (the BBC news website at www.bbc.co.uk/news/ and the ABC News 24 website at www.abc.net.au/news/abcnews24/) on 2 May 2011, and we collected them at roughly the same time (6.15 p.m. Australian time). This is important because these news bulletins are updated regularly throughout the day – for example, there are ten ABC *News in 90 Seconds* bulletins daily. Table 9.1 gives an overview of the data collection according to Bell's (1991) categorization introduced in Chapter 1.

Table 9.1 Data collection from BBC/ABC for the case study

Genre	News (rather than opinion, advertising)
Outlets	BBC news website (www.bbc.co.uk/news/)
	ABC News 24 website (www.abc.net.au/news/abcnews24/)
Outputs	News report about Osama's death from *BBC One-minute World News* (online video, viewed 2 May 2011, 6.15 p.m. Australian (EST) time)
	News report about Osama's death from *ABC News in 90 Seconds* (online video, viewed 2 May 2011, 6.12 p.m. Australian (EST) time)

As can be seen from Table 9.1, the summaries are readily comparable with respect to genre, outlet and output. They are also comparable in terms of their purpose of providing summaries of news events online, and are both located in the multimedia section of each website, accessible either via a link on the home page or via the 'video' tab (see Table 9.2 on p. 200).

As Table 9.2 shows, the BBC offers audiences options for sharing the BBC *One-minute World News* segment on social media such as Facebook, Twitter and via email. Figures displayed on the website suggest that on a daily basis, this segment is shared by an average of 6,500 people. The ABC *News in 90 Seconds* segment does not display figures on the number of views or how many people have shared it; however, it can also be emailed and shared across a wide range of social media platforms (also shown in Table 9.2).

Table 9.2 Screenshots of BBC *One-minute World News* and ABC *News in 90 Seconds*

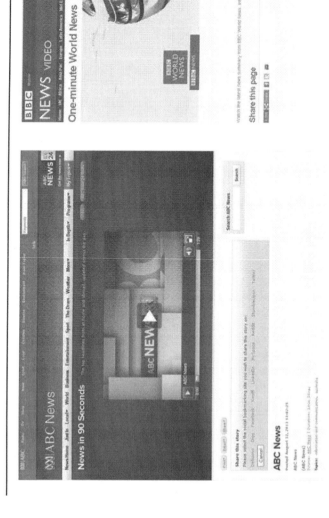

(screenshot of BBC *One-minute World News*, 2 September 2011)   (screenshot of ABC *News in 90 Seconds*, 12 August 2011)

Table 9.3 Transcript of the ABC's *News in 90 Seconds* video summary

Shot	Length	ABC News 24, Online News Vodcast, *News in 90 Seconds* (accessed 2 May 2011, 6.12 p.m. Australian (EST) time	
1	2 sec.		ABC intro music and logo
2	4 sec.		**Newsreader:** The world's most wanted man is dead. US president Barack
3	4 sec.		Obama has announced that Osama bin Laden was killed by US forces who now
4	5 sec.		have his body. The president made the announcement in a dramatic late-night address to the nation.
5	56 sec.		**Barack Obama:** 'Today, at my direction, the United States launched a targeted operation against that compound in Abbottabad Pakistan. A small team of Americans carried out the operation with extraordinary courage and capability. No Americans were harmed. They took care to avoid civilian casualties. After a firefight, they killed Osama bin Laden and took custody of his body. For over two decades, bin Laden has been al Qaeda's leader and symbol and has continued to plot attacks against our country and our friends and allies.

Table 9.3 Contd.

Shot	Length	ABC News 24, Online News Vodcast, *News in 90 Seconds* (accessed 2 May 2011, 6.12 p.m. Australian (EST) time
		The death of bin Laden marks the most significant achievement to date in our nation's effort to defeat al Qaeda. Yet his death does not mark the end of our effort. There is no doubt that al Qaeda will continue to pursue attacks against us. We must and we will remain vigilant at home and abroad.'
6	15 sec.	**Newsreader:** The announcement sparked scenes of jubilation outside the White House with people gathering to cheer and celebrate the death of America's most wanted terrorist.

These summaries were first recorded from the website using screen recording and video editing software and then transcribed. For the transcription, the text was segmented around shot boundaries – the point at which the visual track transitions from one shot to the next. This means that the verbal track often spans two shots. Further, even though we analyse the shot as a whole, to save space we have only included one (initial) frame from each shot in our transcript (see Tables 9.3 and 9.4).

Table 9.4 Transcript of the BBC's *One-minute World News* video summary

Shot	Length	BBC Website, Online News Vodcast, *One-minute World News*, 2 May 2011, accessed 6.15 p.m. Australian (EST) time
1	2 sec.	 BBC logo
2	6 sec.	**Newsreader:** To a summary now of these amazing events that have been unfolding over the last hour. President Obama

Contd.

Table 9.4 Contd.

Shot	Length	BBC Website, Online News Vodcast, *One-minute World News*, 2 May 2011, accessed 6.15 p.m. Australian (EST) time	
3	8 sec.	[camera steadily zooming in on Osama's face to extreme close-up]	has announced that the American Forces have killed the founder and leader of al Qaeda Osama bin Laden. The news came in a dramatic late-night address to the American
4	3 sec.		people live from the White House
Trns		[Part of BBC logo moves across shot] 	
5	16 sec.	[Obama walking towards camera, and camera zooming in on Obama]  [end of zoomed-in shot:] 	**Newsreader:** President Obama said a small team of Americans killed Osama bin Laden at a compound in Pakistan and took possession of his body. He said co-operation with Pakistani forces led the US to the hiding place of the world's most wanted man.
Trns		[BBC logo used to transition to next shot:] 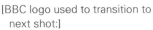	

Contd.

Table 9.4 Contd.

Shot	Length	BBC Website, Online News Vodcast, *One-minute World News*, 2 May 2011, accessed 6.15 p.m. Australian (EST) time	
6	3 sec.		**Newsreader:** The US has been trying to track him down
7	11 sec.	[camera zooming in on rubble]	since al Qaeda came to the fore in the late 1990s well before its September 11 attacks on the World Trade Centre and the Pentagon in
8	3 sec.		2001 in which around three thee-thousand [*sic*] people were killed.
Trns		[BBC logo used to transition to next shot:] 	
9	15 sec.	[a lot of camera movement: camera zooming out and moving sideways to show people, back to sign, back to people]	**Newsreader:** Hundreds of people have gathered outside the White House in Washington to celebrate the death of Osama bin Laden. The attacks on 9/11 traumatized the American people and led to the so-called War on Terror. [Sounds of crowds screaming and cheering audible behind the newsreader voice-over.]

A key difference between the two segments that becomes clear immediately is length – the ABC segment is 1.26 minutes long and comprises 206 words whereas the BBC segment is 1.07 minutes long and comprises only 180 words. In our analysis of these two news stories we will first discuss how both reflect established news practice in their use of language and images (shots) and then explore how differences between them can be interpreted in terms of news authority and voice.

3 Reflecting established news practices

3.1 Parts-of-speech, figures/numbers and evidentiality/intertextuality

From a linguistic analysis of the verbal text in the two stories, we can see some similarities to other kinds of news discourse described in Chapter 4. For example, nouns and noun phrases are used to refer to relevant countries and people (e.g. *Osama bin Laden, President Obama, the American People*) as well as to indicate time (e.g. *in a dramatic late-night address*), and place (e.g. *in Abbottabad Pakistan, at a compound in Pakistan, outside the White House*); to label news actors and sources (e.g. *US president Barack Obama*); and to include intensification (e.g. *the world's most wanted man*) and evaluation (e.g. *these amazing events*). The two extracts predominantly include lexical rather than modal verbs, although the ABC video, with its direct quote from the US president, Barack Obama, does feature a number of modal verbs in the quote (***will** continue to pursue, **must** and **will** remain*), which refer to the future (evaluations of Reliability and Necessity).

As with print news, the lexical verbs are used to introduce reported speech (e.g. *has announced, made the announcement, said*) and to report events (e.g. *killed, sparked*). They are used primarily in the active voice, although two examples of the passive voice occur in the ABC report with reference to the American actions (*was killed, were harmed*), one of them in the Obama quote. This does not obscure agency – that it is the Americans who killed bin Laden is made clear through use of a *by*-structure (*Osama bin Laden was killed **by** US forces*) and the surrounding text. Finally, the analysis of adverbials in the two reports shows the frequency of time adverbials (e.g. *now, today, over the last hour, in a dramatic late-night address, in the late 1990s, in 2001*) and place adverbials (*outside the White House, live from the White House, at a compound in Pakistan*) which are also commonly found in newspaper writing. These refer both to the time and place of current events (e.g. Obama's speech, people celebrating) and past events (e.g. the 9/11 attacks, the killing of bin Laden).

Further similarities with news writing can be seen in the use of figures/numbers, with numbers in the bulletins representing dates (*1990s, 2001*) and others being used for intensification (*for over two decades, three-thousand people, hundreds of people*). Finally, reference to other texts (evidentiality/intertextuality) is also present. First, the sign 'Ding Dong Bin Laden is Dead' held by celebrating Americans outside the White House (shown in the BBC report) is an allusion to the 1939 American film *The Wizard of Oz*, which clearly draws on cultural knowledge and would only be interpreted by those online users with such knowledge.

Secondly, both reports explicitly name a key discourse for this story – Barack Obama's address to the nation, first mentioning the announcement, then its circumstances (*in a dramatic late-night address to the American people live from the White House; in a dramatic late-night address to the nation*). The ABC report primarily relies on the same (illocutionary) lexis throughout to refer to the speech (*has announced, made the announcement, the announcement*), while the BBC version is more varied with both illocutionary and neutral lexis (*has announced, said, said*). This is because the BBC version uses indirect, rather than direct, speech to represent the contents of Obama's speech (part of the input material for the story) and therefore needs to use a variety of such lexis to introduce the reported speech (*President Obama said . . .; He said . . .*). The following section considers the use of input material more generally.

3.2 *Use of input material*

As with other news stories, various types of input material are used by a newsroom team to put a news story together. For example, the ABC's *News in 90 Seconds* is produced by the *Continuous News Centre* (CNC) comprised of a specialist production team under the direction of Gaven Morris, National Editor Continuous News. CNC journalists are principally responsible for the digital, server-based online news feed, which has its own studio space to produce presented bulletins. They work in two shifts, from 5 a.m. and from 1 p.m., and have to source content, write their stories, edit their pictures, present to camera in the studio, post-produce their segment and then post online (Gaven Morris, 2009, personal communication). This means that these journalists fulfil the producer roles of author, editor and animator and are a clear example of the multiskilled journalist we identified in Chapter 2. We have already seen how the outcome of this process reflects some of the linguistic characteristics of other types of news discourse, but will look more closely now at the main input material that has been used in these two stories.

Visual input material

First, looking at visual input material, the ABC story uses five shots: three of Osama bin Laden (all of which show him animated in some way – talking, firing a gun, walking), one of Barack Obama speaking to camera and one of the people gathered outside the White House. The BBC story, however, despite being shorter in length, uses a total of eight different shots: one of the newsreader, two of bin Laden, one of Barack Obama, three of the World Trade Centre and one of the crowds at the White House. It is worth noting that although the topic of these bulletins is the death of Osama bin Laden, no footage of either the killing or of bin Laden's body are shown. This is because this footage was not made available by the US military/ president because of its perceived potential to be used as propaganda (see our discussion of this in Chapter 5). Both stories thus had to resort to standard news practice in announcing the death of a prominent figure by using file footage of bin Laden collected prior to his death.

In terms of the communicative functions (cf. Chapter 5) of the shots used, both the ABC and the BBC segments begin with the logo (and signature music) which perform the function of 'channel-identification' (Montgomery 2007: 43) of the ABC/BBC and establish both in terms of their institutional authority. The BBC also has a shot of the newsreader, which we will further discuss below. The principle communicative functions of the remaining images are similar in both stories and mainly illustrate who the participants in the story are and provide evidence of happenings described in the verbal text (*scenes of jubilation, September 11 attacks on the World Trade Centre*).[2] There are also elements of evaluation in both stories – in shot three in the ABC story, Osama bin Laden fires a gun, an action that could be construed as an aggressive action; and in the final shot in both stories, crowds are screaming, cheering, whistling and displaying extreme emotions and gestures.

Compositionally (cf. Chapter 7), there is also a lot of similarity between the ABC and BBC footage. The visuals focus on two main participants, Barack Obama and Osama bin Laden, and both are centrally located in the image frame throughout. This serves to maintain attention on the key participants in the story. Further, the final shots in both stories contain many participants who are all similarly cheering, punching the air and waving flags/holding up signs (one of them stating 'Ding Dong Bin Laden is Dead'), analysed as *iterating, serialising, matching*. Some of the footage is of poor quality indicating that the construal of the reported event as aesthetic is not emphasized in these stories. In other words, the shots are balanced but not necessarily beautiful, and function to construe news values in other ways (see further below).

Verbal input material

The key verbal input material for the report in the ABC story is Obama's address. Seventy per cent of this report consists of a direct quote from Obama's address, with one sentence further incorporating indirect speech (*that Osama bin Laden was killed by US forces who now have his body*) and only two sentences of the report not featuring either direct or indirect speech. In contrast, the BBC report does not include any directly quoted speech at all and only introduces the content of Obama's address indirectly. Table 9.5 shows a direct comparison of Obama's address and the way it has been incorporated into the two reports.

Table 9.5 Barack Obama's address with its recontextualization in the BBC and ABC bulletins

Extracts from Obama's address	BBC	ABC
Tonight, I can report to the American people and to the world that the United States has conducted an operation that killed Osama bin Laden, the leader of al Qaeda . . . . Today, at my direction, the United States launched a targeted operation against that compound in Abbottabad, Pakistan. A small team of Americans carried out the operation with extraordinary courage and capability. No Americans were harmed. They took care to avoid civilian casualties. After a firefight, they killed Osama bin Laden and took custody of his body. For over two decades, bin Laden has been al Qaeda's leader and symbol, and has continued to plot attacks against our country and our friends and allies. The death of bin Laden marks the most significant achievement to date in our nation's effort to defeat al Qaeda. Yet his death does not mark the end of our effort. There's no doubt that al Qaeda will continue to pursue attacks against us. We must – and we will – remain vigilant at home and abroad. . . . But it's important to note that our counterterrorism cooperation with Pakistan helped lead us to bin Laden . . . . (full speech available from www. whitehouse.gov)	President Obama has announced that the American Forces have killed the founder and leader of al Qaeda Osama bin Laden. President Obama said a small team of Americans killed Osama bin Laden at a compound in Pakistan and took possession of his body. He said co-operation with Pakistani forces led the US to the hiding place of the world's most wanted man.	US president Barack Obama has announced that Osama bin Laden was killed by US forces who now have his body. 'Today, at my direction, the United States launched a targeted operation against that compound in Abbottabad Pakistan. A small team of Americans carried out the operation with extraordinary courage and capability. No Americans were harmed. They took care to avoid civilian casualties. After a firefight, they killed Osama bin Laden and took custody of his body. For over two decades, bin Laden has been al Qaeda's leader and symbol and has continued to plot attacks against our country and our friends and allies. The death of bin Laden marks the most significant achievement to date in our nation's effort to defeat al Qaeda. Yet his death does not mark the end of our effort. There is no doubt that al Qaeda will continue to pursue attacks against us. We must and we will remain vigilant at home and abroad.'

Obama's speech itself has over 1,300 words, but only selected content has been integrated into the two news reports: The BBC does not include much specific detail about the event itself, and does not include the president's evaluation of the event, although it does include information that can be found in Obama's speech at a later stage, that is, the cooperation with Pakistan, which is not mentioned in the ABC report. The ABC, on the other hand, has taken a chunk of the address verbatim and simply incorporated it into its report with the representation of indirect speech working as an introduction to Obama's speech. This quote includes specific information on the event as well as the president's evaluation. In this way, we can see how the use of selected input material is used to present a particular version of this story. This is also tied to the different structure of the two stories to which we will now turn.

3.3 *Structure*

If we analyse the structure of the stories, we can see from Table 9.6 on pp. 210–11 that both can be subdivided into lead and lead development (as introduced in Chapter 4). However, the BBC lead is preceded by a piece-to-camera by the newsreader in the newsroom, which is very similar to the way that TV news bulletins begin. Montgomery (2007: 39) labels this initial stage in the news bulletin the 'news kernel' and considers it to be a structurally obligatory element as it serves to introduce and link into the news item proper.

Both leads are similar in first mentioning what they see as the most significant aspect of Obama's announcement: the killing of Osama bin Laden by American forces. Both clearly treat this as the point or newsworthy element of the story and use it to begin the report. Both leads are short but informative, and provide the same angle to the story. Turning to the lead development, we can see the different types of information that this usually adds (further details, background/context, attribution, consequences, etc.). Both lead developments include attribution (direct and indirect speech) and consequences (celebrations), although only the BBC includes further background and contextualization:

- *The US has been trying to track him* [Osama bin Laden] *down since al Qaeda came to the fore in the late 1990s well before its September 11 attacks on the World Trade Centre and the Pentagon in 2001 in which around three thee-thousand people were killed.*

- *The attacks on 9/11 traumatized the American people and led to the so-called War on Terror.*

Why does the BBC include this background information? We would argue that its audience can be expected to know what happened on '9/11' and its results. One answer might lie in the established use of

Table 9.6 The structure of the BBC and ABC segments (language only)

BBC		ABC	
To a summary now of these amazing events that have been unfolding over the last hour.	news kernel by newsreader	—	—
President Obama has announced that the American Forces have killed the founder and leader of al Qaeda Osama bin Laden.	intro/lead	The world's most wanted man is dead. US president Barack Obama has announced that Osama bin Laden was killed by US forces who now have his body.	intro/lead
The news came in a dramatic late-night address to the American people live from the White House.	intro/lead development adding further details	The president made the announcement in a dramatic late-night address to the nation.	intro/lead development adding further details
President Obama said a small team of Americans killed Osama bin Laden at a compound in Pakistan and took possession of his body. He said co-operation with Pakistani forces led the US to the hiding place of the world's most wanted man.	indirect attribution	'Today, at my direction, the United States launched a targeted operation against that compound in Abbottabad Pakistan. A small team of Americans carried out the operation with extraordinary courage and capability. No Americans were harmed. They took care to avoid civilian casualties. After a firefight, they killed Osama bin Laden and took custody of his body. For over two decades, bin Laden has been al Qaeda's leader and symbol and has continued to plot attacks against our	direct attribution

country and our friends and allies. The death of bin Laden marks the most significant achievement to date in our nation's effort to defeat al Qaeda. Yet his death does notmark the end of our effort. There is no doubt that al Qaeda will continue to pursue attacks against us. We must and we will remain vigilant at home and abroad.'	–		–	consequences
The US has been trying to track him down since al Qaeda came to the fore in the late 1990s well before its September 11 attacks on the World Trade Centre and the Pentagon in 2001 in which around three thee-thousand people were killed.	background information	–		–
Hundreds of people have gathered outside the White House in Washington to celebrate the death of Osama bin Laden.	consequences	The announcement sparked scenes of jubilation outside the White House with people gathering to cheer and celebrate the death of America's most wanted terrorist.		
The attacks on 9/11 traumatized the American people and led to the so-called War on Terror.	background information	–		–

contextual information in news stories and an attempt here to conform to this practice/typical structure. News values may be another answer, as this background information includes a variety of linguistic devices that construe newsworthiness, such as Negativity (*its September 11 attacks on the World Trade Centre and the Pentagon in 2001 in which around three-thousand people were killed*; *The attacks on 9/11 traumatized the American people*), Superlativeness (*around three-thousand people were killed*) and Impact (of the 9/11 attacks). For this reason, we now turn to looking at news values in more depth.

3.4 News values

Looking at news values in general (cf. Chapter 3), the BBC report construes Superlativeness through intensification (*a dramatic late-night address*; *the world's most wanted man*) and quantification (*three thousand*; *hundreds of people*), references to strong emotions (*traumatized*) and metaphor (*war on terror*, albeit distanced through the use of *so-called*). It is also construed in the images of people celebrating: The gesturing and facial expressions display extreme emotional reactions, while the close-up angles ensure that the camera frame is bursting with revellers. Negativity is construed through references to negative emotions (*traumatized*) and negative vocabulary about 9/11 (*attacks*; *killed*), although we would not count the references to Osama's death (e.g. *killed*) as establishing Negativity here; compare our discussion of this in Chapter 3. Arguably, the sign 'Ding Dong Bin Laden is Dead' also construes Negativity in linking Osama intertextually with the 'wicked witch' in the *Wizard of Oz*, thereby also evaluating him negatively.

Images of the ruins of the World Trade Centre in New York construe both Negativity and Impact. In the verbal text, Impact is also established both through references to the consequences of 9/11 in terms of emotional and other impacts and effects (e.g. *traumatized*; *three-thousand people were killed*; *led to the so-called War on Terror*) and to the consequences of Osama's killing (e.g. *hundreds of people have gathered . . . to celebrate*).

The event is further construed as very timely, indeed, as breaking news, both through tense and aspect (e.g. *have been unfolding*, *has announced*, *have gathered*) and through references to time (*over the last hour*, *live*). References to *American*, *the US*, *the White House*, *the World Trade Centre*, *the Pentagon*, *Washington*, and so on construe Prominence, since the United States is arguably one of those 'elite' nations that is a global player.[3] Prominence is also construed through role labels (e.g. *President Obama*; *the founder and leader of al Qaeda Osama bin Laden*) and subsequent references to Obama and bin Laden, as well as in the visual depictions of bin Laden and Barack Obama. Novelty – although it is not emphasized as a news value – can also be seen in the report, mainly in the newsreader's evaluation of the events as *amazing* (in the news kernel) and perhaps in the explicit reference to the timing of the address (*late-night*), which may be regarded as out of the norm. Personalization is also rather weak, although we could perhaps argue that the references to and pictures of the emotional reactions of the 'ordinary' people outside the White House function to introduce a personal or human interest element to the story. Finally, we can see some evidence of Consonance in the use of expressions such as *War on Terror, track him down* and *most wanted* which link to a range of conventionalized metaphors and scripts associated with war, hunting and the Wild West. Overall, the BBC makes use of a range of resources throughout the news kernel, lead and lead development to emphasize news value.

The ABC report shows some similar features to the BBC summary as well as some areas of difference. Similarities range from a similar construal of news values to even the same/similar choice of words to construe a news value (*the world's most wanted man; a dramatic late-night address*). Differences concern individual news values as well as how they are construed. The ABC report construes Superlativeness through intensification and quantification (*a dramatic late-night address; the world's most wanted man; America's most wanted terrorist*), including that occurring in the Obama quote (e.g. *'extraordinary', 'the most significant', 'for over two decades'*).[4] A reference to a strong emotion also occurs (*jubilation*). Negativity, however, is only construed in the Obama quote (e.g. *'plot attacks', 'will continue to pursue attacks'*) and perhaps in the image of bin Laden firing a gun (a sign of aggression), and Impact concerns only the consequences of Osama's killing (e.g. *'the death of bin Laden marks the most significant achievement to date', sparked scenes of jubilation, people gathering to cheer and celebrate*). As present and present perfect make up almost half of all tense references in the story, the event is also clearly construed as very recent and ongoing (Timeliness). References to *US, the White House, America* including in Obama's speech and the use of role labels such as *US president Barack Obama, 'al Qaeda's leader and symbol'* again construe Prominence.[5] Novelty is not prominent (apart from the reference to the late-night address), neither is Personalization (again with exception of the references to and images of the celebrating Americans). Finally, Consonance only occurs in labelling Osama as *most wanted* (twice). Because 70 per cent of the ABC report is made up of direct speech, we can see that the quotes by Obama are quite significant in construing newsworthiness, through Obama's evaluations of bin Laden, al Qaeda and his death, for example, Superlativeness (e.g. *'the most significant achievement to date'*), Prominence (e.g. *'bin Laden has been al Qaeda's leader and symbol'*), Negativity (e.g. *'has continued to plot attacks against our country and our friends and allies'; 'will continue to pursue attacks against us'*).

What we can see from this discussion is that a different use of input material and structuring has an impact on the construal of news value – both in terms of which news values are construed and how/where (e.g. the differences between the two stories in terms of Negativity, Impact, Consonance). But we can also see that certain news values are clearly emphasized in both stories (Superlativeness, Timeliness, Prominence), while others remain less prominent in both (Novelty, Personalization). We could also argue that the way in which news values are construed through the direct quote from Obama (ABC) rather than the 'voice' of the institution can be compared to the way in which the BBC includes generally known background information to construe newsworthiness. Both of these are different in kind to the straightforward use of the newsreader (the 'voice' of the institution) to make a judgement of newsworthiness (*these amazing events*). Such considerations are related to issues of institutional voice and authority, which we will briefly discuss further below.

4 'Wherever you are, you're with the BBC': voice and authority in the two stories

While our discussion above has uncovered the use of similar devices in both the ABC and the BBC video summaries, one key difference has already become apparent throughout our discussion – the differing use of input material. We will now explore this and other devices for their impact on authority and voice (cf. Chapter 2: pp. 31–2, Chapter 4: p. 93).

Starting with the ABC, its authority and voice appear very much backgrounded, with 70 per cent of the report comprising direct speech from Obama and with the accompanying shots also showing Obama (an instance of overlap). Obama is thus given a clear voice, his authority is emphasized, and there is no blurring of the two voices (ABC/Obama). In fact, it shows how direct speech clearly differentiates between the voice of the news institution and that of the (frequently authoritative) source (Fairclough 1988: 127). Because of this, first-person pronouns (e.g. *my, our, us, we*) and a variety of evaluations (e.g. Emotivity – *extraordinary courage and capability, achievement*; Importance – *the most significant*; Reliability – *there is no doubt that*; Necessity – *We must . . . remain vigilant*) can be included in what is arguably a hard news story. As we have seen in Chapters 4 and 6, this is in fact common for many types of print and broadcast news programmes, as it allows for the appearance of objectivity, yet permits the inclusion of evaluations (in sources' speech) and other resources that construe newsworthiness. Briefly, it results in the representation of authentic speech which adds flavour and colour to the story, but crucially means that viewers mostly engage with Barack Obama's voice and authority rather than that of the news institution (ABC).

In contrast, the BBC newsreader's voice is used for the entire bulletin, even as Obama is seen on screen giving his *dramatic late-night* address to the nation. Thus, instead of letting the president speak for himself, we are given the female newsreader's paraphrase of his words, while the visual track shows the president speaking into a microphone (speech inaudible). With respect to text–image relations we can analyse this as displacement (cf. Chapter 5), as the paraphrase allows the newsreader to not only be more concise but also opens up the possibility of including additional information, such as evaluation (e.g. *the world's most wanted man*). This is a good example of indirect speech both incorporating actual words spoken by news sources and transforming words into the 'voice' of the news institution, thus resulting in a certain blurring of the two voices (Fairclough 1988: 127). We would argue that this inserts the BBC much more into the story than the ABC and foregrounds its authority as a news institution reporting on and interpreting events. As a result, viewers are treated very much to the BBC's version of events.

There are further devices in the BBC report that make the BBC, as an institution, appear a lot more visible, both in the words and the images selected. For example, the BBC summary begins in the studio (the ABC report goes straight to images of bin Laden) and the BBC logo appears consistently throughout the bulletin. Used as a wipe (segments of the BBC logo moving swiftly across the screen as a transition between shots) it connects the different shots through the institutional brand logo, whereas simple cuts are used in the ABC bulletin.[6] Further, in contrast to the ABC report's five camera shots (largely static, with only the shot of bin Laden walking – shot four – showing any camera movement), the BBC summary has more shots and more camera movement. Three shots use zooming in techniques and the final shot pans back and forth across the crowds of people: indeed it looks as if the cameraperson is being jostled by the crowd, thus enhancing the sense that they are right at the heart of the action (in comparison, the ABC report features footage that was taken with a long lens from across the street, emphasizing the distance between the cameras and the revellers). This 'busyness' of the BBC bulletin is further emphasized by the fact that it is approximately 20 seconds shorter than the ABC bulletin. Such techniques can have quite a significant effect, giving the impression of urgency and high drama. As a result, we are left with the impression that the BBC is truly 'breaking' a significant story and it is very much through the BBC's voice that we were getting this breaking news. Further research could investigate reasons behind this difference: Is it because the BBC is more of an internationally established authority than the ABC? Does it reflect general BBC/ABC style? Is it because of differences in funding or other factors in the production process?[7]

5 Covering 'special' news events

The aim of our analyses in this chapter was to provide insights into the reporting of a particular special/significant event (the death of Osama bin Laden), rather than into online video news summaries in general. The stories that we analysed are not necessarily representative of what the BBC *One-minute World News* or ABC *News in 90 Seconds* summaries usually look like. For instance, when no **one** event dominates the news as much, these summaries look more like broadcast headlines (cf. Chapter 4) and include the reporting of a variety of stories. Thus, on 21 June 2011 BBC *One-minute World News* reported on three different stories, which were introduced with 'the latest headlines from BBC World News', and the morning edition of ABC *News in 90 Seconds* on 22 June 2011, began with 'leading the news this morning', and covered a total of five news stories. In fact, the format for the ABC *News in 90 Seconds* bulletin is standardized to the extent that the bulletin usually begins and ends with a piece-to-camera by the journalist, while the rest of the bulletin should consist of back-to-back images with a wipe between each story. Each bulletin is intended to have an average of four stories, with some flexibility in relation to news flow (the number of stories on the ABC's news agenda on any given day) (Gaven Morris, 2009, personal communication). Given that this is the standard pattern for producing ABC *News in 90 Seconds* bulletins, we can immediately see how 'special' the bulletin analysed for this case study is. The journalists themselves did not appear in this particular ABC bulletin and the death of Osama bin Laden was the only story covered.

Thus, in order to analyse online video news summaries as a type of news discourse in general, we would need to collect more data on various events to see what these summaries normally look like, and we would need to collect more data on 'significant' events to see what the 'special' news summaries look like. This would tell us whether or not the findings in this chapter are specific to the reporting of Osama's death or whether they are typical of this kind of reporting.

To conclude, our analyses of the use of language and images in the reports have illustrated how some of the discourse in these stories reflects established news practice. At the same time, the reports clearly emphasize different voices/authorities. What our analysis has shown, then, is that while both stories covered the same event and made use of the same key source material (Obama's address), significant differences have emerged in the way in which these news organizations position themselves within the discourse.

6 Conclusion

In the nine chapters of this book our aim was both to offer readers an introduction to news discourse in general (e.g. Chapters 1, 2, 4, 5) and to introduce our own frameworks for analysing aspects of such discourse (news values, evaluation, composition: Chapters 3, 6, 7, 8, 9). We hope that we have demonstrated the insights such news analysis can offer researchers and furthermore, that we have enabled and encouraged readers to start their own investigations into news discourse. While we would welcome it very much if other researchers started applying the frameworks introduced in this book, we have also tried to include other perspectives and relevant readings to such perspectives. Because of space constraints, we have had to limit these alternative perspectives to key readings but these should be a useful starting point for further reading in the chosen area.

We see our own contribution particularly in the *discursive* approach that we apply, with a focus on how language and image contribute to the construction of news. This aligns us with other approaches in Linguistics/Semiotics/Journalism studies that focus on analysing news discourse as a product. We see this approach as complementary to studies that investigate the production of news as a process (e.g. through ethnographic research in the newsroom) and those that explore how readers/viewers/listeners interpret this product (e.g. through audience studies). More cross-disciplinary and interdisciplinary approaches to the analysis of news are required, particularly those that draw together insights from Journalism/Media Studies and Linguistics/Semiotics. We have tried to do this to a certain extent in this book, incorporating, in particular, notions such as newsworthiness and news values.

While our main focus in this book was on news discourse in the form of *newspaper* discourse, we have included as much as possible a discussion of other types of news discourse – whether news radio podcasts, online news or video news. We have also tried to include news data from around the English-speaking 'Western' world, discussing examples from Ireland, New Zealand, Australia, Canada, the United Kingdom and the United States. Clearly, given the wide range of news discourse from different countries (including other languages, cultures and regions), there is much room for future research projects, and this is certainly something that we hope this book has encouraged readers to do.

Another point that we have made throughout this book is that news discourse is much more than just words, and that words and press photographs/moving images work together to make meaning. This is a position that we feel has so far been neglected in both Linguistics and in Journalism and Media studies. On this note, we will end this book with a quote from Lacayo and Russell (1995), which aptly expresses some of the sentiments informing our approach to news discourse in this book:

> It has now been more than a century since photography first poked its head into the pages of the press. Soon pictures shouldered aside columns of print. And we can be sure that they will continue to press upon space that words alone once occupied, obliging us to weigh carefully the ways that each form operates upon the understanding. A picture is not worth

a thousand words. Pictures and words deal in separate coin that is not fully convertible. They reach in different directions, report to different faculties, create different impressions. In the practice of telling the news, pictures and words are like essential trading partners, two realms that deeply require each other. The form of their exchange will be the future of journalism itself. (1995: 171)

Notes

1 Talking about the BBC's *global* audience, the *One-minute World News* segment that we analyse in this chapter is only available to international audiences accessing the website outside the United Kingdom. Local audiences can access *BBC News Headlines* (www.bbc.co.uk/news/video_and_audio/) and this local bulletin may last up to 2 minutes.

2 Since we have already used these stories to exemplify intra- and intersemiotic relations in Chapter 5, we will only briefly comment on text–image relations (overlap, displacement, dichotomy) further below.

3 It could also be argued that these references construe Proximity, in as far as many viewers would be interested in happenings in the United States because of its special cultural and military relationship with Britain. In any case, it is interesting to note that the focus of the event is on the culturally more proximate and more prominent United States rather than, say, Pakistan.

4 Single quotation marks around expressions signify that the relevant expression occurs in the Obama quote.

5 And perhaps Proximity in as far as Australia, like Britain, has a special cultural and military relationship with the United States (and is in fact one of the *friends and allies* that Obama mentions in his speech). Compare also the use of inclusive first-person plural pronouns in Obama's speech (*we, our, us*, etc).

6 This is a common strategy in other BBC *One-minute World News* segments where the wipe normally separates different stories rather than shots within a story. ABC *News in 90 Seconds* also typically features a wipe (using the ABC News logo) between different stories, but this wipe is **not** used in the bulletin on Osama's death.

7 Simons notes that funding issues have resulted in the ABC featuring 'more "he says, she says" coverage, in which little is done other than reporting entirely predictable remarks by the usual suspects' (2011: 31).

Tables

Table A1.1 Potential resources for construing news values through language and image

News Value	Key Devices (L = Language; I = Image)
Negativity (the negative aspects of an event)	L: negative evaluative language, for example, *terrible news, a tragedy*
	L: references to negative emotions, for example, *distraught, worried, breaking our hearts*
	L: negative vocabulary, for example, *killed, deaths, bodies*
	I: images of negative events and their effects, for example, the aftermath of accidents, natural disasters, the injured/wounded, the wreckage/damage done to property
	I: images of people being arrested or with lawyers/barristers/police (as defendant)
	I: images showing people experiencing negative emotions
	I: high camera angle, putting viewer in dominant position (often used with photographs of offenders/prisoners of war)
	I: camera movement and blurring, combined with camera people moving around, running, ducking to avoid missiles, and so on
Timeliness (the relevance of the story in terms of time)	L: references to time, for example, *The Prime Minister today warned, yesterday's flash flooding*
	L: verb tense and aspect, for example, *rescuers have been trying to pluck survivors, it's a tragedy, it is testing our emergency resources, residents have described the horrific moments when they faced a brown wall of water*
	I: indications of time in the images, for example, the season may be implied in flora or environmental conditions, inclusion of cultural artefacts representative of event.

Contd.

Table A1.1 Contd.

News Value	Key Devices (L = Language; I = Image)
Proximity (the geographical and/or cultural nearness of the event)	L: references to place, for example, *Queensland, Brisbane, Canberra, Queensland's residents*
	L: references to the nation/community, for example, *it will test us as a community; The Prime Minister warned the nation it must brace for more deaths*
	L: first-person plural pronouns, for example, *It might be breaking our hearts at the moment, but it will not break our will*
	I: Images of well-known or iconic landmarks, natural features or cultural symbols
Superlativeness (the maximized or intensified aspects of an event)	L: intensification and quantification, for example: *thousands of Queensland residents* *a giant torrent, a tragedy of epic proportions* *the … storm … dumped 100 mm of rain in his gauge in just 30 minutes* *water was so strong that cars were stacked on top of each other* *houses that are completely collapsed* *the water levels today are … possibly going to become higher*
	L: references to strong emotions, for example, *they were petrified*
	L: comparison, for example, *this one has just maxed out every other flood*
	L: metaphor, for example, *an army of volunteers, a brown wall of water*
	L: simile, for example, *our Queens Park was like a raging river, it was like a World War II battle*
	I: repetition of key elements in the image frame, for example, not just one boat but an entire marina full of boats

	I: depiction of extreme emotions in participants
	I: placement of elements of different sizes next to each other (e.g. the tallest and the shortest member of a sports team)
	I: use of specific lens and angle settings to exaggerate or condense size differences
	I: camera movement and blurring, combined with camera people moving around, running, ducking to avoid missiles, and so on
Prominence (the high status of the individuals, organizations or nations in the event)	L: evaluative language indicating importance, for example, *pop star, celebrity bad boy*
	L: role labels, for example, *The Prime Minister, Queensland Premier Anna Bligh, Professor Roger Stone*
	I: images depicting easily recognizable key figures, people in uniform or with other regalia of officialdom
	I: showing elements like microphones/cameras, media scrum, being flanked by military, police or bodyguards
	I: showing context associated with an elite profession (e.g. books, lab, police station)
	I: low camera angle indicating power of participant in image
Impact (the effects or consequences of an event)	L: evaluative language relating to the impact of an event, for example, *a potentially momentous day*

Contd.

Table A1.1 Contd.

News Value	Key Devices (L = Language; I = Image)
	L: intensification and quantification referring specifically to the impact of an event, for example: *Power has been cut to thousands of Queensland's residents* *There have been massive landslides* *There are . . . homes a kilometre away from where they were* *Absolutely petrified* *the rushing waters savaged Toowoomba* *whole families are among the 72 people still unaccounted for*
	L: references to emotion caused by an event, for example: *They [two women washed away] were petrified.* *it was horrifying* *A terror that took their breath away*
	L: references to effects/impact on individuals, entities, and so on, for example: *overwhelming volumes of water . . . wrecking families and their fortunes* *flash flood deluged the town* *leaving scenes of destruction and people dead in their cars*
	I: images showing the after-effects (often negative) of events, for example, scenes of destruction or emotions caused by an event
	I: sequences of moving images that convey cause and effect relations
Novelty (the unexpected aspects of an event)	L: evaluative language indicating unexpectedness, for example, *a very different sort of disaster*
	L: comparison, for example, *I've lived in Toowoomba for 20 years and I've never seen anything like that*

	L: reference to the emotion of surprise/expectations, for example, *shocked residents; no one was expecting it; people just really can't believe it*
	I: depictions of people being shocked/surprised
	I: juxtaposition of elements in the frame that create stark contrast
Personalization (the personal or 'human interest' aspects of an event)	L: references to emotion, for example, *'It was pretty bloody scary'*
	L: quotes from 'ordinary' people, for example, *'Myself, I was almost pulled in by the torrent'*
	L: references to individuals, for example, *Panel-beater Colin McNamara*
	I: images of individuals, especially when using close-up and showing an emotional response and when individual is **not** acting in a professional role
Consonance (the stereotypical aspects of an event)	L: evaluative language indicating expectedness, for example, *legendary, notorious*
	L: repeated word combinations, for example, *Australia – sharks*
	L: conventionalized metaphors, for example, *a flood of immigrants*
	L: story structure
	L: comparison, for example, *yet another personal scandal*
	I: images that fit with the stereotypical imagery of an event/person/country, and so on
Aesthetics	I: images that are well composed and aesthetically pleasing
	L: aesthetic (e.g. 'poetic') uses of language – not usually found in hard news stories

Contd.

Table A1.2 Parameters of evaluation and examples

Parameter	Example Linguistic Resources	Examples in Use
Un/importance 'How important or how unimportant does this appear?'	*senior, top, leading, influential, prominent, supremo, star, crucial, vital, landmark, empire, made legal history, historic, crucial, key, momentous, of the century, high-rolling, celeb, famous, significant, urgent, emergency, keynote, major, minor, modest, substantial, . . .*	. . . I'm standing at one of the **major** checkpoints . . . . . . the rainfall is **unlikely to have a major impact** . . . . . . he's **one of the top ten executives** in the company
In/comprehensibility 'How comprehensible or easy, or how incomprehensible or difficult, does this appear?'	*easy, difficult, mystery, can't understand, clearly, no explanation for/why, am uncertain how to, be beyond human comprehension, there are simply no words to describe how, ambiguous, complex, less than definite, in plain language, vague, clarify, uncanny, unclear, begs the question why, raise questions about/why, clear, confused, . . .*	. . . that **didn't make it any easier** . . . . . . this really **unmistakeable** quality . . .
Im/possibility or In/ability 'How possible or how impossible does this appear?'	*(im)possible, can (not), could (not), able to, . . .*	. . . people who **haven't been able to** fly today . . . . . . you **can** minimize [risks] . . .
Un/necessity 'How necessary or how unnecessary does this appear?'	*need to, have to, it takes, to be, no choice but, should, . . .*	. . . new rules **are needed** . . . . . . if their presence is **not necessary** . . .
Emotivity 'How positive or how negative does this appear?'	*peaceful, beauty, welcome, aggressive, plain, sexual predator, wannabe, fiasco, racist, clanger, cash in on, worse, inappropriate, irresponsible, . . .*	. . . it's **worse than inappropriate**, it's **irresponsible** . . . The other aspect, and that's very **welcome** . . .
Un/genuineness or In/authenticity 'How real, true and authentic, or how fake, false and artificial, does this appear?'	*reality, genuine, fantasy, real, artificial, orchestrated, choreographed, stage-managed, fake, phoney, rigged, truth, . . .*	. . . a **genuine** love affair . . . . . . the Olympics are a **fake** smile . . .

Reliability 'How likely or how unlikely does it appear that this will happen?'	*put that in doubt, certainly, (unlikely), will, certain to, potential, could, may, undoubtedly, perhaps, doomed to, probably, ...*	. . . a huge sweep of the East Coast **will** see flakes . . . . . . it will **probably** take several flights . . .
Unexpectedness 'How expected or how unexpected does this appear?'	*amazing, astonishing, extraordinary, unexpected, unprecedented, normally, familiar, routine, little wonder that, inevitable, bombshell, sensation, ...* *but, although, as opposed to, despite, however, in contrast with, yet, ...* *seldom, rarely, only, scarcely, hardly, barely, little, few, without, no, not, none, nobody, no one, nothing, nowhere, never, neither, nor, ...*	a moment that **everyone had known would have to come** . . . In an **unexpected** development . . . . you'll **even** see seed down here for parrots . . . **nothing** has been taken away since the middle of last month . . . **Despite** its name it affects a variety of species . . .
Evidentiality 'How do we know? What is the basis of our knowledge? What kind of evidence do we have for this?'	*alleged, claims, reveal, confirm, advise, scream, sob, shout, whisper, mutter, threat, warn, promise, vow, pledge, accuse, attack, blame, praise, approve, make clear, hint, brag, boast, admit, believe, think, expect, predict, hope, fear, show, look, spotlight, voice, sound, display, sign, appear, apparently, seem, betray, on show, tests found/ confirmed, evidence/proof that, famously, notoriously, emerge, turn out, ...*	He **said** that they were wrong. He **thought** that they were wrong. He **expected** them to be wrong. He **hoped** that they were wrong. There are **signs** that they were wrong. **Evidently**, they were wrong. It's **well-known** that they were wrong. It **emerged** that they were wrong.
Mental State 'How do people feel (about this)?'	*believe, think, convinced, assume, accept, know, expect, fear, yearn, love, hope, anxiety, concerns for, appalled, furious, troubled, cheered, happy, pleasure, enraged, panic, frustration, force, willing to, intend to, want to, refuse to, ...*	. . . we all **believe in** the rights enshrined in our constitution . . . . People **know** of Maori . . . There's growing **frustration** along the Gulf Coast . . . . . . what they really **want** . . .

Table A1.3 lists all media outlets referred to in this book, including their name, country of origin and type of publication (see Chapter 1, n. 5 on the use of 'quality' and 'popular' here). We have included web addresses only for those outlets where we explicitly refer to online content.

Table A1.3 News media outlets

Media Form	Name	Country	Type
Newspapers	The *Age* www.theage.com.au	Australia	Quality metropolitan daily
	The *Sydney Morning Herald* www.smh.com.au	Australia	Quality metropolitan daily
	The *Sun-Herald*	Australia	Popular Sunday newspaper
	The *Australian* www.theaustralian.com.au	Australia	Quality national daily
	The *Daily Telegraph* www.dailytelegraph.com.au	Australia	Popular metropolitan daily
	mX	Australia	Daily afternoon freesheet
	www.crikey.com.au/	Australia	Online only national daily
	The *Dominion Post*	New Zealand	Quality metropolitan daily
	The *New Zealand Herald*	New Zealand	Quality national daily
	The *Press*	New Zealand	Quality metropolitan daily
	The *Daily Express*	UK	Popular national daily
	The *Daily Mail*	UK	Popular national daily
	The *Daily Mirror* www.mirror.co.uk	UK	Popular national daily
	The *Daily Star*	UK	Popular national daily
	Daily Telegraph	UK	Quality national daily
	The *Guardian* *Guardian Weekly* www.guardian.co.uk	UK	Quality national daily/ International weekly
	The *Independent*	UK	Quality national daily
	The *Sun*	UK	Popular national daily

Table A1.3 Contd.

Media Form	Name	Country	Type
Newspapers	*The Times* (of London) www.thetimes.co.uk	UK	Quality national daily
	Positive News www.positivenews.org.uk	UK	Not-for-profit positive newspaper, published four times per year through subscription
	Metro	UK	Daily morning freesheet
	Irish Independent	Ireland	Quality national daily
	The *Irish Times* www.irishtimes.com	Ireland	Quality national daily
	The *Ottawa Sun*	Canada	Popular metropolitan daily
	The *Globe and Mail*	Canada	Quality metropolitan daily
	The *Baltimore Sun*	US	Popular metropolitan daily
	The *Boston Herald*	US	Popular metropolitan daily
	Chicago Tribune	US	Quality metropolitan daily
	The *Daily Graphic*	US	Now defunct (1873–89) – first American newspaper to carry daily illustrations
	The *Daily* www.thedaily.com/	US	Tablet only national daily
	The *Los Angeles Times*	US	Quality metropolitan daily
	The *Miami Herald* (Int. edition)	US	Quality metropolitan daily, international edition
	The *New York Post*	US	Popular metropolitan daily
	The *New York Times* www.nytimes.com	US	Quality metropolitan daily
	The *Philadelphia Inquirer*	US	Quality metropolitan daily
	The *San Francisco Chronicle*	US	Quality metropolitan daily
	The *Seattle Times*	US	Quality metropolitan daily
	The *Wall Street Journal*	US	Quality metropolitan daily
	The *Washington Times*	US	Quality metropolitan daily

Contd.

Table A1.3 Contd.

Media Form	Name	Country	Type
Newspapers	The *Washington Post*	US	Quality metropolitan daily
	USA Today www.usatoday.com	US	Quality national daily
	China Daily	China	English-language national daily
	Jakarta Post	Indonesia	English-language national daily
Radio/ Television	ABC ABC News 24 www.abc.net.au/news/ abcnews24/ ABC News Radio	Australia	National public broadcaster
	Channel Seven	Australia	Commercial TV station
	Channel Ten	Australia	Commercial TV station
	Nine Network	Australia	Commercial TV station
	Radio New Zealand	New Zealand	National public broadcaster
	BBC www.bbc.co.uk/news/	UK	National public broadcaster
	RTÉ	Ireland	National public broadcaster
	CBS	Canada	National public broadcaster
	NPR	US	National public broadcaster
	CNN www.cnn.com	US	Commercial TV station

APPENDIX 2

Evaluation in the news – a model student assignment

Authors' comment

Below we have included a model student assignment on news discourse that uses aspects of the framework of evaluation that we introduced in Chapter 6 and illustrates how it can be applied by students. This assignment is written as a free-standing paper, and therefore treats the chapters in this book as any other reference to be incorporated into an assignment. In other words, it does not assume a reader who has just read these chapters. The model below is not a 'perfect' assignment – it is one possible model for how a student assignment can be structured and written and follows our own preferences. It assumes basic linguistic knowledge (e.g. a reader who is familiar with the terms *lemma, noun phrase, non-finite clause, reported speech*, etc.) and relates to the following hypothetical assessment task:

Using a parameter-based framework, identify evaluations of Emotivity, Evidentiality and Un/expectedness in the provided news story from the *Wall Street Journal* about Barack Obama's election to president and discuss their potential functions (focusing in particular on news values). Disregard any evaluations in reported speech and thought, and focus on discussing the main tendencies in the text. (3,500 words)

Our model is written for those unfamiliar with or less experienced in academic writing and is therefore annotated with comments on key academic writing conventions. This annotation draws on websites that provide academic writing support (such as the University of Sydney's *Clearer Writing* site at http://learningcentre.usyd.edu.au/clearer_writing, its *Write* site at writesite.elearn.usyd.edu.au/ and its *Wrise* site at http://learningcentre.usyd.edu.au/wrise/home-B.html) as well as our own experience as lecturers and researchers. We hope that lecturers reading this book may find this model and the annotations useful for working with their students; that junior researchers may find it helpful for thinking about how to structure journal articles or book chapters; and that students may find it of use in writing their own assignments. We recommend reading the model assignment twice – first without, then with comments. Following the assignment, we have listed a number of activities that can be undertaken by students in the classroom or in self-study.

Model student assignment

'Obama sweeps to historic victory' – a case study of evaluation in the news

Giving a specific title to your assignment (other than Assignment 1) provides a clear focus to your paper.

1. Introduction

This paper uses a parameter-based framework (Bednarek 2006, 2010) to analyse the expression of journalistic opinion (*evaluation*) in a news story from the *Wall Street Journal*. The analysed news story, 'Obama sweeps to historic victory' (5 November 2008) reports on the election of Barack Obama as the first African-American president of the United States (see Appendix for full text). It thus covers a historically significant event, making it particularly interesting to analyse from a linguistic point of view. This paper will explore the potential functions of evaluations in this news story, focusing on the main tendencies in the text. I will first introduce the analytical framework, before discussing the main findings. As will be seen, applying the parameter-based framework allows us to demonstrate the

The introduction to an assignment usually includes information on the WHAT/HOW/WHY and a preview of the STRUCTURE of your assignment. This includes your aim/object of research, your analytical/theoretical framework, and a brief description of the analysed texts. In some cases, an assignment will have a separate Data and Methodology section where you can elaborate on this.

The appendix to your assignment provides supplementary material. This should be mentioned, where relevant.

The use of *I* in certain contexts is appropriate, especially when talking about structure. Avoid using *we* unless there is more than one author.

multifunctionality of evaluations and gives an insight into how this historic event was reported in the Wall Street Journal, America's biggest-selling quality newspaper (Adams 2008).

> State why your research or aspects of it are important/interesting/significant (e.g. the reason for your analysis). Don't give away the results – the introduction is no abstract.

2. Background

> The Background section can include information of various kinds. For example, you could include a 'mini' review of relevant literature on your topic. Importantly, the background section needs to introduce any theories or frameworks that are referred to in the Analyses section so that the reader can understand and follow the discussion. Only include in this section what is **relevant** to your analyses. Incorporate information from relevant/appropriate academic publications (with in-text referencing).

Since this paper is concerned with analysing evaluation, the first step is to consider this linguistic concept in more detail. In other words, what is evaluation? *Evaluation* is a cover term for the way in which writer opinion can be expressed through language (Bednarek 2010). This opinion can relate to different meaning dimensions and has been theorized with the help of various analytical frameworks in Linguistics (Bednarek 2006: 19–39 gives an overview). In this paper I will follow Bednarek's (e.g. 2006, 2010) parameter-based framework. This framework assumes that when writers make evaluative acts through language, they 'can appeal to a number of evaluative standards, norms or dimensions, or . . . *evaluative parameters*' (Bednarek 2010: 18). The three dimensions or parameters that I will focus on in this paper are called Emotivity, Evidentiality and Un/expectedness.[1] According to Bednarek (2010: 21–2) the first parameter, Emotivity, is about the expression of approval (positive Emotivity) or disapproval (negative Emotivity), evaluating something positively (e.g. *brave comeback*) or negatively (e.g. *botched response*). This type of opinion can be present explicitly when evaluative language is used (as in the above examples in brackets), or it can be more indirectly implied (e.g. *Petrol prices were raised*). In the latter case, no explicitly evaluative language is present but positive or negative evaluation may nevertheless be implied 'depending on the reader's or writer's position, values, and background' (Bednarek 2010: 37). Both explicit and implicit examples will be discussed in Section 3.1.

> This is an example of in-text referencing, including author surname, year of publication and page numbers.

> This sentence could be improved by giving reasons for focusing on these three parameters in particular. Why these three? How are they important/interesting to analyse in this story?

> Footnotes or endnotes should be used only rarely and are sometimes discouraged altogether. If you use them, they should contain non-essential material or arguments that would otherwise interrupt the flow of the writing.

> Try using formal rather than informal vocabulary. For example, *positive/negative* are more appropriate for academic writing than *good/bad*.

> You can use references to sections within the paper to guide the reader and point to the relevance of introduced concepts.

[1] Only those evaluations that explicitly originate in the journalistic voice were analysed – in other words, evaluations in reported speech or thought were ignored.

The second parameter to analyse is Evidentiality. Evidentiality concerns evaluation of knowledge bases. It is about 'questions such as "how do we know? What is the basis of journalists' and others' knowledge? What kind of evidence do we have for this?"' (Bednarek 2010: 28). Subcategories of Evidentiality thus include speech/saying (*He said they were wrong*), thought/feeling (*He thought* . . .), expectation (*He expected* . . .), emotion (*He hoped* . . .), perception (*There are signs* . . .), proof (*Evidently* . . .), general knowledge (*it's well-known* . . .) or unspecified bases (*it emerged that.*). With Evidentiality: speech/saying, it is also important to consider who speaks as well as the kinds of reporting expressions that are used (Bednarek 2010: 31–3). Table 1 gives an overview of subcategories of reporting expressions.

Formatting conventions, for example, the use of italics, should be used to mark examples as such.

Evidentiality has also been investigated in news discourse from the run-up to the 2004 US presidential election (Garretson and Ädel 2008), which points to the significance attributed to this parameter.

You may find it useful to use a table to summarize aspects of the theoretical framework that you have applied or other aspects of relevant theory. Always introduce such tables using your own words.

The third parameter to analyse, Un/expectedness, concerns evaluations that express whether or not something was more or less un/expected. This can be realized in various ways,

Table 1 Categories of reporting expressions recognized in Bednarek (2010)

Subcategory	As Defined in Bednarek (2010)	Examples (from Bednarek 2010)
Neutral	'only refer to the act of saying' (31)	*said, according to*
Illocutionary	'mention the speaker's purpose or the function and force of the speech act' (32)	*instructed*
Declarative	'are dependent on a cultural-institutional setting' (32)	*acquit*
Discourse signalling	'mark the relation to the discourse' (32)	*asked, reply*
Paralinguistic	'comment on prosodic/paralinguistic aspects of the utterance' (32)	*whispers, said with a laugh*

including ways of indicating contrast through conjunctions (e.g. *but*), adverbs (e.g. *even*) and negation (e.g. *no*), but for reasons of scope such grammaticalized ways of expressing Un/expectedness were not included in the analysis. In addition to lexical means of evaluating Un/expectedness mentioned by Bednarek (2006, 2010), I also include certain comparisons (e.g. *the first time since . .*), as they clearly express Un/expectedness in the *Wall Street Journal* news story (see Section 3.3).

Evaluations in general fulfil many functions ranging from the reflection and construal of value systems and writer–reader relationships to organizing text (Thompson and Hunston 2000: 6). Evaluations in news discourse are also multifunctional. For instance, they can be used to 'create a system of shared values, a framework of a shared ideology' (Bednarek 2006: 203), but their functions can also be tied to news practice (Bednarek 2006). One important aspect of news practice that I will draw on in interpreting the function of evaluations in this paper is that of newsworthiness or news values. News values are 'the values by which events or facts are judged more newsworthy than others' (Bednarek 2006: 16). For example, Bednarek and Caple (2012: 43–4) mention that news stories are more newsworthy if they involve elite individuals, organizations or nations (news value of Prominence), if they can be framed in personal terms (news value of Personalization) and if they can be intensified/maximized (news value of Superlativeness). Language can construe newsworthiness discursively, and evaluations are one important way of doing so, as Bednarek and Caple (2012: 138–9) mention and the analyses below also demonstrate.

This section has introduced the concept of evaluation and some of its key functions in relation to news practice. I have also introduced the framework for analysing three evaluative parameters: Emotivity, Evidentiality and Un/expectedness. Section 3 will now report on

> As shown here, relevant readings can be introduced indirectly via paraphrase (summarizing Thompson and Hunston's 2000 points) or through using a direct quote (from Bednarek 2006).

> Do not use contractions in academic writing: for example, *I will* rather than *I'll* should be used.

> It can be useful to end sections with a brief summary and introduce the next section, especially if your assignment is longer.

instances of evaluations identified in the *Wall Street Journal* news story about Obama's election victory, and discuss their potential functions in terms of the main identified tendencies.

3. Analyses

3.1 Emotivity

Starting with evaluations of positive or negative Emotivity, it is noteworthy that there are not many instances in the news story where the journalist uses explicitly evaluative language to express approval or disapproval. This is in line with findings that news in contrast to commentary/opinion tends to background the subjective voice of the reporter (Feez et al. 2008: 200). There are however, many expressions that describe positive or negative events, especially in the context of the election (e.g. *victory*, *success*, *defeating*) but also in other contexts (e.g. *racial division*, *economic slump*, *Watergate scandal*, *crisis*, *best-selling book*), and we can also find examples where the journalist reports on evaluations by others, taking on another's point of view (e.g. *running as a promoter of the war in Iraq at a time when it was deeply* **unpopular**; *Florida and Ohio [. . .], two states that had* **bedeviled** *his party*; *he* **finally** *wrested Florida and Ohio from the GOP*). Such usage can (but need not) imply positive or negative evaluation. For example, describing McCain as promoting what is very unpopular among voters might imply that this was strategically a mistake on his part. Another interesting example is (1):

(1) What remains unclear, however, is whether Tuesday's results represent a vote for liberalism or against the failures of the Bush administration

If we look at the noun *failures* here, this seems to indicate negative evaluation of the Bush administration, but is somewhat backgrounded by tying it to the election results and hence the voters' wishes rather than the journalist's own

In your Analyses section you present the findings of your linguistic analysis and comment on (discuss, interpret) them. It is a good idea to first describe your results and then comment on them, focusing on the major tendencies and patterns. You can refer to the appendices for the complete analyses, as you will often be asked to provide these.

When you interpret the findings, it is a good idea to draw on relevant research and incorporate it with in-text referencing.

Omissions from examples and also from quotes should be signalled using three dot points, often enclosed in square brackets: [. . .]

Always make sure that you give examples to illustrate your findings, either separately numbered as here or incorporated in your writing as the examples in brackets above. Make sure that you introduce and comment upon examples that are separately listed.

opinion. Again, this shows how the journalistic voice is relatively backgrounded in this news story, yet implying evaluations of various kinds.

The usage of social labels also contributes to negative evaluation. An example is given in (2).

(2) A convicted felon, Tony Rezko, helped him [Obama] purchase a Chicago home

While *convicted felon* is technically speaking a descriptive label with origins in 'the institutionalised legal process' (White 1998: 131), associating Obama with a socially recognized 'criminal' has the potential to imply negative opinion of Obama, as someone accepting help from criminals. We are not told what crime Tony Rezko has committed or when he was convicted. In contrast, McCain is described with the labels *veteran lawmaker and Vietnam War hero* and members of the Republican party are referred to as *intellectual leaders*, both arguably implying approval.

Another way in which evaluation is implied in the news story is through references to struggle and inexperience, as seen in Examples (3) and (4):

> While you need to interpret and argue in your assignment, your opinion is backgrounded, de-emphasized. So rather than using expressions such as *I think, I believe, in my opinion* use expressions like *arguably, likely, it seems*, and make sure you argue well, drawing on examples and evidence.

(3) He [McCain] struggled to find a message that would resonate, running at various times as the experienced insider, a maverick who would shake up Washington, a bipartisan conciliator, a tax-cutting conservative and a tough-minded "Country First" war hero.

> Square brackets signal the author's intrusion, here clarifying who the *He* in the sentence refers to.

(4) . . . a candidate with less than four years of national political experience.

Here we could argue that describing McCain's struggle and contradictory messages and Obama's inexperience at a national level implicitly evaluates both negatively.

There are further examples of such implied evaluations throughout the news story (e.g. Obama's slogan is described as *optimistic, though vague*, an example where an evaluation of incomprehensibility seems to also imply negativity).

In contrast, there are only a few examples that are more explicitly evaluative, giving us insights into the evaluative position of the newspaper and into contexts where explicit evaluations are permitted. For example, McCain's concession speech is explicitly evaluated positively as *gracious*, indicating approval. In contrast, a reporting verb with negative connotations (*touted*) is used to attribute indirect speech to Democrats (*Democrats have touted*) and voting for Obama is evaluated as taking a risk (*to take a risk on a candidate with less than four years of national political experience*).[2] This indicates a pro-Republican stance.

Other explicit evaluations seem to relate to contexts that are perhaps seen as uncontested, for instance, evaluating the financial crisis negatively (*worst*), evaluating costs negatively (*a **looming** crisis in Social Security and Medicare spending; **looming** costs of Social Security and Medicare*), evaluating hurricane Katrina negatively (*the **calamity** of Hurricane Katrina*), evaluating the presidential campaign as very expensive (*the longest and **most expensive** presidential campaign*), in particular McCain's (*Sen. McCain's campaign was large and **expensive***). In such uncontested contexts, then, explicit evaluations seem to be sanctioned despite their subjective nature, possibly because they might be considered as almost 'objective' in the sense of being shared by the community.

Summing up the findings on Emotivity and focusing on political stance, both implicit and explicit evaluations in this story seem to give slight preference to Republicans over Democrats, despite certain negative evaluations of individual Republicans (e.g. McCain, Bush). This illustrates that evaluations in news stories enable news

> Expressions like *summing up, first, next, in contrast, further, to conclude* are useful devices for structuring your writing and at the same time for guiding readers, making it easier for them to follow your discussion.

---

[2] Even though this example does not feature reported speech or thought, its syntactic structure (*a Democratic tide, which spurred voters to take a risk on*) nevertheless seems to background the journalistic voice, as it implies voter intent and agentivity, almost implying that it is the voters rather than the journalist who think that voting for Obama means taking a risk.

organizations 'to express their own political stance' (Bednarek 2006: 201). In this context it is noteworthy that some commentators claim that the *Wall Street Journal* has become more politically conservative since it was purchased by Rupert Murdoch's News Corporation in 2007 (Carr 2009). This may be an example of stance being influenced by the news media as an institution, such as proprietors, managers, news executives (Bell 1991: 38–40). At the same time, explicitness or subjectivity is backgrounded in this story, in line with the news story genre.

3.2 *Evidentiality*

> Numbered headings are a good way of structuring your assignment and making that structure explicit to the reader.

Turning now to evaluations of Evidentiality, speech/saying and proof seem to be the most significant subcategories in this news story. In other words, where journalists give a basis for what they say (and they often do not), most frequently they make reference to speakers or some kind of proof. In fact, the high significance of Evidentiality: proof relates to the fact that this news story makes extensive use of polling data, as evidenced in Examples (5) and (6).

(5) National exit poll results found Sen. Obama increasing his vote percentages across the board, with particular success coming from the youth and black votes

(6) A Wall Street Journal/NBC News poll released Monday found that 81% of Obama supporters said their vote was for him, not against Sen. McCain.

This may turn out to be a typical feature for news coverage of election outcomes, as journalists have to work with data other than official election results to write up their stories.

> This is formulated as a hypothesis here and no references to relevant readings are incorporated. By drawing on readings on election coverage stronger claims could be made in this paper about how the findings for this story relate to election coverage in general.

In contrast, the high significance of Evidentiality: speech/saying is typical of news stories in general. In her study on British tabloid and broadsheet news stories, Bednarek found that Evidentiality/Style (in other words, Evidentiality: speech/saying as attributed via reporting expressions) was the most frequent of all parameter combinations, accounting for 32 per cent of all evaluations in her corpus (Bednarek 2006: 141). News has also been described as 'embedded talk' (Bell 1991: 52), with most information used being 'secondhand' (Bell 1991: 52). It is thus interesting to look at this parameter in more detail, considering what sources are used, what reporting expressions are employed and what functions the direct and indirect quotes may serve in this story. This is all the more important since '*Who says?* is one of the primary questions of news work' (Bell 1991: 190). Table 2 below gives an overview of the main sources cited in the news story.

First, as members of the elite, politicians belong to those sources that are very frequently cited in the news (Bell 1991: 191) making the

> It can be very useful to use tables for showing the main tendencies in the analysed texts. Make sure that you introduce the table, number it, caption it, and comment upon the information included in it.

Table 2 Sources quoted in the *Wall Street Journal* news story

Who Says	Examples from News Story
Elite politicians	*Joe Biden of Delaware as vice president, the veteran senator; Sen. McCain; The Arizona senator; President George W. Bush; Sen. Obama*
Unnamed group sources, including voters	*Democrats;* the [Republican] *party's intellectual leaders; Democratic leaders in Congress; aides; many in his campaign; 40%* [voters]; *six in 10 voters, 62% of voters; 81% of Obama supporters; two-thirds of voters in the Journal poll*
Individual (named) speakers	*Shelby Steele, a black writer and a fellow at Stanford's Hoover Institution, who voted for Sen. McCain; Eearl Simms, a 65-year-old former city safety manager; Willie Smiley, 65, a retired government worker from Detroit; Benjamin T. Jealous, president and CEO of the NAACP, the nation's oldest civil-rights group; Jennifer Cresent, a Macomb County, Mich., Republican who voted for . . . Sen. Obama*
Institutions	*the Center for Responsive Politics*
Unclear	*"Country First"* (It is unclear if the quotation marks are neutral or function as 'scare/snigger' quotes [Bednarek 2006: 182], indicating disapproval.)

reported event newsworthy by contributing to the news value of Prominence. Unnamed group sources are used in this article either because the identity of the speaker is considered by the journalist unimportant or perhaps because the source spoke on condition of anonymity (even though named sources are more valued, see Stenvall 2008). Individual speakers in this news story include African Americans, sometimes labelled as such or implied through what they say ('. . . *Lord, we're finally overcoming,*') and it is made clear to the reader who they voted for. The named speakers provide newsworthiness in terms of Prominence because some of them are attached to prestigious institutions such as *Stanford's Hoover Institution*, but also personalize the story (news value of Personalization). We can also see that several of the categories that Garretson and Ädel (2008) mention occur here, too, for example, mention of political affiliation or use of unnamed sources.

I now turn to the analysis of the kinds of reporting expressions used to attribute speech to the above sources. For the most part, these expressions are neutral (there are 17 occurrences of the lemma SAY [*said, saying, say*] and other neutral reporting expressions (*spoke of, told, according to*) with the majority of non-neutral reporting expressions falling into the subcategory of illocutionary, mainly referring to future intentions (e.g. *pledged, promised, vowed to*). The frequency of the latter may again turn out to be typical for news coverage of election outcomes, as election promises are seen as an important part of the process of the election campaign. Concerning the high frequency of neutral reporting expressions, this is again characteristic of news stories: Bednarek (2006) found that neutral reporting expressions are the most frequent in her corpus, noting that the newspapers' 'aim is to be or at least to appear objective' (Bednarek 2006: 141) and Garretson and Ädel (2008: 182) found that *say* and *tell* are most frequently used in US electoral reporting. Richardson (2007) also comments that 'objectivity

> When incorporating readings we have the choice of using neutral expressions (*comments, describes, states*, etc.) or using expressions that show that we agree (*point out, show, as X has demonstrated*) or disagree with/are less certain about what is said (*claim, suggest, propose*).

is a key defining value underwriting the practices of modern journalism' (Richardson 2007: 86), although this does not mean that news reporting is value free, having more to do with adherence to particular journalistic practices/strategies such as quotation (see Tuchman 1972, cited in Richardson 2007: 87).

Finally, considering the functions of the quotes, they can roughly be categorized as offering:

> If you haven't looked at a reading itself but have found a reference to it in another reading that you want to use, you must make this explicit, for example, using *cited in*. But it is in general better to access all readings directly and read them for yourself.

- emotional reactions and evaluations, including quotes from political winners and losers (quotes by McCain, Bush, Obama) and voices from the public (vox pop) giving emotional reactions and expressing evaluations (e.g. *"It's a feeling we feel all the way inside – Lord, we're finally overcoming,"*);

- voters' statements giving insight into voter behaviour (e.g. *six in 10 voters said she* [Sarah Palin] *is not qualified to be president*; *62% of voters said the economy was their top concern*);

- predictions about the future (e.g. *A shadow Treasury team could be in place by the end of the week, aides say*), including Obama's promises (manifold attributions using indirect speech and illocutionary reporting expressions to report his election promises);

- background information about the past (e.g. *The party's intellectual leaders spoke of a permanent Republican majority in Washington*).

Emotional reactions, especially in direct speech, may be associated with the news value of Personalization, 'promot[ing] straightforward feelings of identification, empathy or disapproval' (Fowler 1991: 15). Some of the evaluative content of the attributed statements may also have been included to increase other aspects of newsworthiness, for example, in terms of describing the event as a *historic moment*. Quotes from eyewitnesses (here: voters) also increase the facticity of the news story (Bednarek 2006: 126). Finally, many of the quotes can again be tied to the specifics of election coverage, providing the reader with insights into voter behaviour, background information and predictions about the future in terms of political transition.

Summing up the findings on Evidentiality, instances of Evidentiality: proof, illocutionary reporting expressions referring to future intention and the content of certain attributions seem to be related to the specific functions and features of election coverage, while instances of Evidentiality: speech and neutral reporting expressions are typical of news stories in general. Functions vary, but are often concerned with increasing newsworthiness.

3.3 Un/expectedness

This final section discusses evaluations of Un/expectedness. As in most news stories (cf. Bednarek 2006: 96), evaluations of Expectedness are rare (the only potential instance is . . . *as many in his campaign had predicted*) but evaluations of Unexpectedness are very frequent. It is not surprising that this aspect of newsworthiness is emphasized given the social and historical context of the United States, where the reported event is indeed the first of its kind and where racial issues are of high significance. In this news story, the most significant means of indicating Unexpectedness is through comparison. For instance, there are ten instances of comparison using *first*, with the following structural variants:

- *The* possessive *first* NOUN PHRASE (e.g. *the nation's first African-American president*)

  > Use technical terms. Define them unless they are basic linguistic knowledge (e.g. noun phrase) that you can take for granted.

- *The first* NOUN PHRASE (e.g. *the first black party nominee for president*)

- *The first* NOUN PHRASE with non-finite clause (*to*/past participle) (e.g. *the first woman – New York Sen. Hillary*

Clinton – to seriously contend for a party nomination)

● *The first time . . . since* (+ historical date) (e.g. *the first time a Democratic candidate has taken the state since Lyndon Johnson in 1964).*

There are also other comparisons in the news story that do not feature *first* but similarly compare the present to the past (*the worst financial crisis since the Great Depression; the longest and most expensive presidential campaign in U.S. history; the biggest voter turnout in the period since women got the vote in 1920; the most extensive use yet of the Internet; one of the lowest approval ratings on record*). Together with other instances of Unexpectedness in the news story (e.g. *record turnout; a startling turnaround*) such comparisons clearly construe newsworthiness in terms of Novelty. At the same time, these comparisons increase the Superlativeness of the event as well as locating it historically and ensuring that the reader understands its historic nature. The fact that such comparisons are multifunctional in terms of increasing news values might account for their frequency here.

> Linking devices are very useful for indicating logical relations of various kinds, e.g. addition (*furthermore, moreover*), contrast/ comparison (*however, on the other hand, similarly*), cause (*thus, hence, therefore*), exemplification (*for instance, e.g., for example*), restatement (*in other words, i.e.*), sequence (*first, secondly, finally*).

4. Conclusion

In conclusion, the above analyses have demonstrated how a linguistic analysis can give insights into the multifunctionality of evaluations in news discourse. The analysis of the *Wall Street Journal* news story on Obama's election has demonstrated that the political bias in the news story tends towards the conservative, and that the story adheres to general characteristics of news stories (e.g. backgrounding of journalistic subjectivity). It has also pointed to specific features that may be indicative of election news coverage, although further research on the coverage of election results in different newspapers and concerning

> The conclusion relates back to the introduction, 'closing the circle'. It summarizes the main findings, and does not add any new information. It should include a statement of significance: What is significant/ important about your results? What are the implications of your findings? In essence, this statement should answer the question *So what?*
>
> It is also possible to mention limitations (e.g. in terms of data or methodology), future research directions or any practical applications.

other elections needs to be undertaken to confirm this. The significance of these analyses lies in demonstrating how evaluation can be tied to the political stance of news institutions, to the specifics of election coverage and to the construal of newsworthiness. As has become apparent, analysing evaluation also increases our understanding of how a historically significant event is construed in news discourse.

> This statement of significance is rather 'weak' but at least it explicitly tries to indicate the significance of the analyses.

Appendix

Full text of analysed news story:

Obama Sweeps to Historic Victory
Nation Elects Its First African-American President Amid Record Turnout; Turmoil in Economy Dominates Voters' Concerns

By Jonathan Weisman and Laura Meckler

WASHINGTON – Sen. Barack Obama was elected the nation's first African-American president, defeating Sen. John McCain decisively Tuesday as citizens surged to the polls in a presidential race that climaxed amid the worst financial crisis since the Great Depression.

The culmination of the epic two-year campaign marks a historic moment in a nation that since its founding has struggled with racial divisions. It also ushers in a period of dominance for Democrats in Washington for the first time since the early years of President Bill Clinton's first term. With Tuesday's elections, Sen. Obama's party will control both houses of Congress as well as the White House, setting the scene for Democrats to push an ambitious agenda from health care to financial regulation to ending the war in Iraq.

In becoming the U.S.'s 44th president, Illinois Sen. Obama, 47 years old, defeated Arizona Sen. McCain, 72, a veteran lawmaker and Vietnam War hero. Despite a reputation for bucking his own party, Sen. McCain could not overcome a Democratic tide, which spurred voters to take a

> Appendices include details that are not necessary for understanding the main outcomes of your assignment. Readers should be able to follow your discussion without looking at the appendices, and you must make sure that you mention most important findings and incorporate examples in your Analyses section.
>
> Appendices can include the analysed texts and you will often be asked to also include your complete analysis of the texts in the appendix (e.g. in tables).
>
> Make sure that you refer to the appendices in your paper where relevant, for example, *The complete analysis is provided in Table A.1 in Appendix 1.*
>
> Appendices either precede or follow the References, and you will usually be advised where they should go. An advantage of having the References last is that it makes it easier for the reader to go directly to the References.

risk on a candidate with less than four years of national political experience. Sen. Obama is the first northern Democrat elected president since John F. Kennedy in 1960.

Also elected: Joe Biden of Delaware as vice president, the veteran senator who has promised to help Sen. Obama steer his agenda through Congress.

Sen. Obama's victory was built on record fund raising and a vast national campaign network. It remade the electoral map that had held fast for eight years. He overwhelmed reliable Democratic strongholds in the Northeast and West Coast. He won big in the industrial Midwest and contested fiercely in areas of traditional Republican strength. He won Virginia, the first time a Democratic candidate had taken the state since Lyndon Johnson in 1964. And he finally wrested Florida and Ohio from the GOP, two states that had bedeviled his party in the last two elections.

The president-elect will enter office with a long policy wish list that includes ending the war in Iraq, implementing a near-universal health-insurance plan and finding alternatives to Middle Eastern oil. All this will have to be carried out amid record budget deficits, a looming crisis in Social Security and Medicare spending as the baby-boom generation retires and fears that the nation is on the edge of a deep recession.

Democrats have touted the prospect of a big sweep not just as a partisan conquest but as an ideological turning point, one that could reverse the last great shift in 1980, when Ronald Reagan ushered in a period dominated by tax-cutting conservatism and muscular foreign policy.

It's a startling turnaround from just four years ago, when Republicans controlled Congress and the White House, and benefited from a conservative majority on the Supreme Court. The party's intellectual leaders spoke of a permanent Republican majority in Washington.

What remains unclear, however, is whether Tuesday's results represent a vote for liberalism or against the failures of the Bush administration, including the early war years in Iraq, the calamity of Hurricane Katrina and the current economic slump.

The transition to an Obama administration could begin almost immediately. A shadow Treasury team could be in place by the end of the week, aides say. In many ways, the transition has already started. John Podesta, a former White House chief of staff under President Clinton, has been leading quiet conversations about key positions, especially those relating to the economy.

Late in the evening, Sen. Obama hit 338 electoral-college votes – far exceeding the threshold of 270 needed to win – with victories in the battleground states of Florida, Ohio and Virginia. National exit poll results found Sen. Obama increasing his vote percentages across the board, with particular success coming from the youth and black votes, as many in his campaign had predicted. Although a preliminary figure, his 51% of the popular vote marks the first time since Mr. Johnson that a Democrat had clearly won more than half the nation's vote.

Sen. Obama took 96% of black voters, who increased their share of the electorate to 13% from 11%. Sen. John Kerry of Massachusetts won 88% of the black vote in 2004. Sen. Obama won two-thirds of Hispanics and more than two-thirds of voters aged 18 to 29.

One important swing was the Roman Catholic vote, which went 47% to Sen. Kerry in 2004, compared with 53% for Sen. Obama.

Sen. Obama won among independents but divided the suburban vote. And among voters in families earning over $200,000 a year, Sen. Obama improved over Sen. Kerry by 17 points.

Helping Sen. Obama: Democrats made up a larger share of the electorate this year than they did four years ago, when equal numbers of voters identified as Democrats and as Republicans. This time, 40% said they were Democrats and just 32% said they were Republicans.

Sen. Obama's campaign organization reached corners of the country largely untouched by previous Democratic candidates, from Boise, Idaho, to Biloxi, Miss. It didn't work out everywhere – he lost North Dakota and Georgia. But he put long-standing Republican territory into play, a tactic that put Sen. McCain on the defensive.

Democrats also bolstered their majorities on Capitol Hill. The party secured a number of Senate victories, bringing it teasingly close to a filibuster-proof margin. Party leaders will likely be able to make up the one or two additional votes with moderate Republicans. The party picked up at least 10 House seats, a number expected to grow significantly.

In Arizona, Sen. McCain offered congratulations to his opponent and spoke of the historic moment and the importance of the day to African-Americans. A century ago, he recalled, there was outrage in many quarters when President Theodore Roosevelt invited Booker T. Washington to visit the White House.

"America today is a world away from the cruel and prideful bigotry of that time," Sen. McCain said during a gracious concession speech. "There is no better evidence of this than the election of an African-American to the presidency of the United States."

The Arizona senator also pledged to put the bitterness of the campaign aside and to work with the new president through the difficult times facing the nation.

Sen. McCain phoned Sen. Obama to concede the race and both men pledged to work together. President George W. Bush also phoned the victor and promised a smooth transition. "You are about to go on one of the great journeys of life. Congratulations and go enjoy yourself," the president told his successor.

Sen. Obama declared victory in Chicago's Grant Park in front of an audience of 125,000 people, saying, "If there is anyone out there who still doubts America is a place where all things are possible, who still wonders if the dream of our founders are alive in our time, who still questions the power of our democracy, tonight is your answer."

The 2008 election, the longest and most expensive presidential campaign in U.S. history, was a watershed in many ways. It featured the first woman – New York Sen. Hillary Clinton – to seriously contend for a party nomination. Gov. Sarah Palin of Alaska became the first woman to appear on the Republican ticket. And Sen. Obama broke ground as the first black party nominee for president.

"Obama is documentation of America's moral progress, the moral evolution we have gone through in the past 40 years," said Shelby Steele, a black writer and a fellow at Stanford's Hoover Institution, who voted for Sen. McCain. "Whites don't get credit for it. But having grown up myself in segregation – America has changed enormously."

The candidates spent about $1.6 billion on the election, double the 2004 presidential race, according to the Center for Responsive Politics. When all is tallied, Sen. Obama is expected to have raised around $700 million, a sum made possible when he opted to forgo public financing, the first candidate to do so since the system was implemented in the wake of the Watergate scandal. That decision, and the resulting bonanza, is likely to change how future campaigns are funded.

Indications from early voting and lengthy lines at the polls point to the biggest voter turnout in the period since women got the vote in 1920. In total, voter registration numbers were up 7.3% compared with the last presidential election, for a total of 153 million eligible voters.

The race also featured the most extensive use yet of the Internet. Online social networks spread the campaign to corners of the country that had never before experienced such intense electioneering.

"I wanted to be part of this historic day in our country and watch people in this community exercise their God-given right," said Earl Simms, a 65-year-old former city safety manager standing at the head of the line at his Jacksonville, Fla., precinct.

By tradition, the first ballots were cast just after midnight in tiny Dixville Notch, N.H. Sen. Obama got 15 votes and Sen. McCain six.

Many African-Americans were celebrating how far a black man had come.

"It's a feeling we feel all the way inside – Lord, we're finally overcoming," said Willie Smiley, 65, a retired government worker from Detroit.

Benjamin T. Jealous, president and CEO of the NAACP, the nation's oldest civil-rights group, said his 92-year-old grandmother, whose grandfather was a slave, is "giddy" at the prospect of seeing young black girls holding pajama parties at the White House.

"At this moment, it feels as if anything is possible, and that is the way it needs to be in this country," he said in an interview Tuesday.

Sen. Obama launched his candidacy on the statehouse steps of Springfield, Ill., nearly two years ago. He was a freshman senator, largely unknown, noted mostly for a keynote speech at the 2004 Democratic Convention and a best-selling book. The son of a white woman from Kansas and a Kenyan immigrant who once herded goats, the relative newcomer came with a foreign-sounding name and associations that would prove to be liabilities.

His spiritual adviser, the Rev, Jeremiah Wright, had issued incendiary sermons from the pulpit of Sen. Obama's church. A convicted felon, Tony Rezko, helped him purchase a Chicago home. And Republicans tried to tie Sen. Obama to an associate and neighbor, William Ayers, a member of a domestic terrorist organization in the 1960s.

With that baggage, he took on one of the most powerful names in Democratic politics, Sen. Hillary Rodham Clinton, defeating her after an epic primary fight. Sen. Obama's campaign beat the formidable Clinton machine by going where she was not, racking up victories in states such as Idaho, Kansas and Wyoming.

In the general election campaign, Sen. Obama held the lead for most of the summer. Following back-to-back conventions, Sen. McCain briefly pulled ahead after he energized his party by choosing Gov. Palin as his running mate. When the financial crisis hit, causing stocks to plummet and the government to embark on a series of unprecedented interventions in markets, voters were reminded of their economic concerns and Sen. Obama pulled ahead again. He never lost the lead.

"I've been in denial for too long," said Jennifer Cresent, a Macomb County, Mich., Republican who voted for President Bush four years ago and Sen. Obama Tuesday. "I thought we were really fine and people complained too much. Then every other house on my street became vacant. And so many people are out of work. Now I really worry about crime."

During the primaries, Sen. McCain's campaign was large and expensive and nearly collapsed. He began again with a bare-bones operation, running as a promoter of the war in Iraq at a time when it was deeply unpopular. He pushed for and then backed the early 2007 surge in troops that turned out to be an important factor in the country's turnaround.

After winning the nomination, Sen. McCain still had work to do with the conservative base of his party. Many in the base were angered by his push to change the nation's immigration laws and campaign-finance rules, his support for embryonic stem cell research and his opposition to the Bush tax cuts.

He struggled to find a message that would resonate, running at various times as the experienced insider, a maverick who would shake up Washington, a bipartisan conciliator, a tax-cutting conservative and a tough-minded "Country First" war hero.

The choice of Gov. Palin thrilled conservatives but turned off other voters, especially independents. Early exit polls Tuesday found that six in 10 voters said she is not qualified to be president. Those voters overwhelmingly favored Sen. Obama.

Sen. McCain's campaign received a jolt in October when taxes became a hot issue, but it was never enough to overcome Sen. Obama's optimistic, though vague slogan of hope, which appealed to an electorate angry over war, the economy and President Bush, who has one of the lowest approval ratings on record.

According to early exit poll data, 62% of voters said the economy was their top concern. All other issues, including terrorism and the war in Iraq, were far behind. In 2004, terrorism and the economy were tied at about 20%.

Sen. Obama's promises will be a challenge to keep in the face of a likely recession, two wars and record budget deficits.

He has promised to end the war in Iraq and reduce troop levels quickly. He has also vowed to redouble efforts to stabilize Afghanistan, beef up the U.S. military presence there and to reinvigorate efforts against al Qaeda, both in Afghanistan and Pakistan.

He promised to create a new government-organized health care marketplace and cut taxes for every family earning less than $200,000 and raise them for families over $250,000.

He has vowed to wean the country of Middle Eastern oil over 10 years, dedicating $150 billion to alternative and renewable energy research and development, likening the challenge to that of putting a man on the moon. He has said he will cap greenhouse-gas emissions and force polluters to begin paying for emission permits in order to tackle global warming.

He has also promised billions of federal dollars for education, teacher training and recruitment. College applicants would be given tax incentives to offset tuition in exchange for national service.

In the short run, Sen. Obama has promised to prime the flagging economy with billions of dollars for infrastructure, unemployment insurance and Medicaid. Banks would have to temporarily halt home foreclosures in exchange for government assistance.

The incoming president will have some advantages, including the apparent enthusiastic backing of voters. A Wall Street Journal/NBC News poll released Monday found that 81% of Obama supporters said their vote was for him, not against Sen. McCain. Exit polls found 56% of voters were either optimistic or excited about what Sen. Obama would do as president.

And two-thirds of voters in the Journal poll said they understand Sen. Obama's message and know what he will do as president, just shy of the 72% who said that about President Bush when he stood for re-election in 2004.

With strong majorities in Congress, President-elect Obama is likely to start fast, with a large economic-stimulus package, legislation to fund embryonic stem-cell research and an expansion of the State Children's Health Insurance Program, a government insurance program, which will be financed with a rise in the tobacco tax.

After that, Democrats are divided over how to proceed. Old-guard liberals want to move as fast as possible while they have solid majorities and an electoral mandate. Conservative Democrats want more attention paid to a federal budget deficit that could approach $1 trillion this fiscal year.

Democratic leaders in Congress, mindful of Bill Clinton's health-care debacle of 1993 and the Republican resurgence that swept them from power the next year, counsel a cautious approach that builds bipartisan and voter support before moving on the president-elect's big-ticket items.

The president-elect will not have much time to decide. By early February, he will have to produce a budget that lays out his spending and tax priorities at least over the next five years and hints at what he will do to confront the looming costs of Social Security and Medicare.

(Weisman, J. and Meckler, L. (2008), 'Obama sweeps to historic victory,' *Wall Street Journal*, November 5, 2008, p. 1.)

References

Adams, R. (2008), 'Circulation falls faster at big U.S. newspapers,' *Wall Street Journal*, available at http://online.wsj.com/article/SB122511935114372069.html – accessed 17 January 2011.

Bednarek, M. (2006), *Evaluation in Media Discourse: Analysis of a Newspaper Corpus*. London/New York: Continuum.

Bednarek, M. (2010), 'Evaluation in the news: a methodological framework for analysing evaluative language in journalism', *Australian Journal of Communication*, 37 (2), 15–50.

Bednarek, M. and Caple, H. (2012), *News Discourse*. London/New York: Continuum.

Bell, A. (1991), *The Language of News Media*. Oxford: Blackwell.

Carr, D. (2009), 'Under Murdoch, tilting rightwards at *The Journal*,' *The New York Times*, available at http://www.nytimes.com/2009/12/14/business/media/14carr.html?_r=3 – accessed 27 January 2011.

Feez, S., Iedema, R. and White, P. R. R. (2008), *Media Literacy*. Surry Hills, NSW: NSW Adult Migrant Education Service.

Fowler, R. (1991), *Language in the News: Discourse and Ideology in the Press*. London/New York: Routledge.

The reference list allows your reader to see what publications you have used. It must be accurate and complete, that is, include details of any readings referred to in the paper, so that your reader can locate the reading and check your argumentation or evidence.

Do not list references that you may have read but didn't mention (but, be careful not to commit plagiarism: you must acknowledge any passages or ideas that are taken from readings and that are not your own – unless they are obvious truths.)

The formatting of the reference list must follow specific conventions, for example, the Harvard or APA style. Imagine readers of your assignment want to look at the listed publications themselves. A reference list formatted according to recognized conventions gives them all of the necessary information to find the publications and know what kinds of publications they are (book, chapter, journal article). In this reference list we have used the Continuum house style and we have treated this book itself as if it was an external reading.

This is a non-academic reference (a newspaper article), which should never be used to back up linguistic claims but may occasionally be used for background information. Avoid non-academic references (including Wikipedia and non-educational websites) wherever you can.

Garretson, G. and Ädel, A. (2008), 'Who's speaking? Evidentiality in US newspapers during the 2004 presidential campaign', in A. Ädel and R. Reppen (eds), *Corpora and Discourse: The Challenges of Different Settings*. Amsterdam: John Benjamins, pp. 157–88.

Richardson, J. E. (2007), *Analysing Newspapers: An Approach from Critical Discourse Analysis*. Houndmills/New York: Palgrave Macmillan.

Stenvall, M. (2008), 'Unnamed sources as rhetorical constructs in news agency reports', *Journalism Studies*, 9, (2), 229–43.

Thompson, G. and Hunston, S. (2000), 'Evaluation: an introduction', in S. Hunston and G. Thompson (eds), *Evaluation in Text: Authorial Stance and the Construction of Discourse*. Oxford: Oxford University Press, pp. 1–27.

Tuchman, G. (1972), *Making News. A Study in the Construction of Reality*. New York: Free Press.

White, P. R. R. (1998). 'Telling media tales: the news story as rhetoric', Unpublished Ph.D. dissertation, University of Sydney, Sydney.

* * *

Activities for students

- Discussing rather than simply describing findings is difficult but very important. The discussion can focus on commenting on the effect or purpose of linguistic choices that you have identified or on comparing your findings with those of other researchers. Look closely at the Analyses section in the above paper to identify how the findings are discussed. Note that the focus of the discussion is also dependent on the research/assignment question and may be on confirming/rejecting a specific hypothesis.

- Use a bibliographical database such as the MLA International Bibliography, Linguistic and Language Behaviour Abstracts or Communication and Mass Media Complete in order to find out whether there is any research on election coverage that confirms the hypotheses made in this paper.

- The conclusion to the above paper is rather weak (see annotation). Try rewriting it to improve it, for example, by strengthening the claims about the significance of the analyses.

- Find out what the preferred referencing conventions (e.g. APA, Harvard) for your subject are and where you can access a style guide.

- Write an abstract or annotated bibliographical entry for this paper.

- Write your own annotations to the model assignment.

REFERENCES

ABC Annual Report (2010), *Public Broadcasting, Public Benefit*. Australian Broadcasting Corporation, available at www.abc.net.au/corp/annual_reports/ ar10/ – accessed 15 September 2011.

Aitchison, J. (2007), *The Word Weavers: Newshounds and Wordsmiths*. Cambridge: Cambridge University Press.

Almeida, E. (1992), 'A category system for the analysis of factuality in newspaper discourse', *Text*, 12, 233–62.

Altengarten, J. (2004), 'Creativity and the Rule of Thirds', *Photo Composition Articles*, available at http://photoinf.com/Golden_Mean/Jim_Altengarten/ Creativity_and_the_ Rule_of_Thirds.htm – accessed 20 February 2006.

Arnheim, R. (1954), *Art and Visual Perception: A Psychology of the Creative Eye*. Berkeley: University of California Press.

— (1982), *The Power of the Centre: A Study of Composition in the Visual Arts*. Berkeley: University of California Press.

Baker, P. (2006), *Using Corpora in Discourse Analysis*. London/New York: Continuum.

Baker, P. and McEnery, A. (2005), 'A corpus-based approach to discourses of refugees and asylum seekers in UN and newspaper texts', *Language and Politics*, 4 (2), 197–226.

Baker, P., Gabrielatos, C., Khosravinik, M., Krzyzanowski, M., McEnery, T. and Wodak, R. (2008), 'A useful methodological synergy? Combining critical discourse analysis and corpus linguistics to examine discourses of refugees and asylum seekers in the UK press', *Discourse and Society*, 19 (3), 273–306.

Barkho, L. (2008), 'The BBC's discursive strategy and practices vis-a-vis the Palestinian-Israeli conflict', *Journalism Studies*, 9 (2), 278–94.

Barnhurst, K. G. and Nerone, J. (2001), *The Form of News: A History*. New York: Guilford.

Barthes, R. (1977), *Image, Music, Text*. London: Fontana.

Bateman, J. (2008), *Multimodality and Genre: A Foundation for the Systemic Analysis of Multimodal Documents*. Basingstoke: Palgrave Macmillan.

Becker, K. E. (1992/2003), 'Photojournalism and the tabloid press', in L. Wells (ed.), *The Photography Reader*. London: Routledge, pp. 291–308.

Bednarek, M. (2006a), 'Epistemological positioning and evidentiality in English news discourse: a text-driven approach', *Text and Talk*, 26 (6), 635–60.

— (2006b), 'Evaluating Europe: parameters of evaluation in the British press', in C. Leung and J. Jenkins (eds), *Reconfiguring Europe – the Contribution of Applied Linguistics* (British Studies in Applied Linguistics 20). London: BAAL/Equinox, pp. 137–56.

— (2006c), *Evaluation in Media Discourse: Analysis of a Newspaper Corpus.* London/New York: Continuum.

— (2006d), 'Subjectivity and cognition: Inscribing, evoking and provoking opinion', in H. Pishwa (ed.), *Language and Memory.* Berlin: Mouton de Gruyter, pp. 187–221.

— (2008a), *Emotion Talk Across Corpora.* Houndmills/New York: Palgrave Macmillan.

— (2008b), '"An increasingly familiar tragedy": evaluative collocation and conflation', *Functions of Language*, 15 (1), 7–34.

— (2009), 'Polyphony in Appraisal: typological and topological perspectives', *Linguistics and the Human Sciences*, 3 (2), 107–36.

— (2010a), 'Evaluation in the news: a methodological framework for analysing evaluative language in journalism', *Australian Journal of Communication*, 37 (2), 15–50.

— (2010b), *The Language of Fictional Television: Drama and Identity.* London/ New York: Continuum.

Bednarek, M. and Caple, H. (2010), 'Playing with environmental stories in the news: good or bad practice?', *Discourse & Communication*, 4 (1), 5–31.

Bell, A. (1984), 'Good copy, bad news', in P. Trudgill (ed.), *Applied Sociolinguistics.* London/Orlando: Academic Press, pp. 73–116.

— (1991), *The Language of News Media.* Oxford: Blackwell.

— (1994), 'Telling stories', in D. Graddol and O. Boyd-Barrett (eds), *Media Texts: Authors and Readers.* Clevedon: Multilingual Matters, pp. 119–36.

Bell, P. and van Leeuwen, T. (1994), *The Media Interview: Confessions, Contest, Conversation.* Sydney: University of New South Wales.

Ben-Aaron, D. (2005), 'Given and news: evaluation in newspaper stories about national anniversaries', *Text*, 25 (5), 691–718.

Berdan, R. (2004), 'Composition and the elements of visual design', *Photo Composition Articles*, available at http://photoinf.com/General/Robert_Berdan/Composition_and_ the_Element s_of_Visual_Design.htm – accessed 18 January 2009.

Biber, D. and Conrad, S. (2009), *Register, Genre and Style.* Cambridge: Cambridge University Press.

Biber, D., Johansson, S., Leech, G., Conrad, S. and Finegan, E. (1999), *Longman Grammar of Spoken and Written English.* London: Longman.

Bignell, J. (2002), *Media Semiotics: An Introduction* (2nd edition). Manchester: Manchester University Press.

Bordwell, D. and Thompson, K. (2008), *Film Art: An Introduction* (8th edition). New York: McGraw Hill.

Brenton, H. and Hare, D. (1985), *Pravda. A Fleet Street Comedy.* London/New York: Methuen.

Brighton, P. and Foy, D. (2007), *News Values.* London: Sage.

Brone, G. and Coulson, S. (2010), 'Processing deliberate ambiguity in newspaper headlines: double grounding', *Discourse Processes*, 47 (3), 212–36.

Brownlees, N. (ed.) (2006), *News Discourse in Early Modern Britain: Selected Papers of CHINED 2004.* Bern: Peter Lang.

The Brumby Dump (2010), Swinburne University of Technology, Australia, available at www.swinburne.edu.au/chancellery/mediacentre/staff/news/2010/10/the-brumby-dump – accessed 30 August 2011.

Buyouts and layoffs in the newspaper industry (2011), *Paper Cuts*, available at http://newspaperlayoffs.com/ – accessed 23 September 2011.

Caldas-Coulthard, C. R. (1994), 'On reporting reporting: the representation of speech in factual and factional narratives', in M. Coulthard (ed.), *Advances in Written Text Analysis*. London: Routledge, pp. 295–308.

— (1997), *News as Social Practice*. Florianopolis: ARES.

Canadians love their newspapers! (2010), *NADbank Newspaper Audience Databank Inc.*, available at www.nadbank.com/en/system/files/Canadians%20Love%20their%20Newspapers.pdf – accessed 22 November 2010.

Caple, H. (2006), 'Nuclearity in the news story: the genesis of image-nuclear news stories', in C. Anyanwu (ed.), *Empowerment, Creativity and Innovation: Challenging Media and Communication in the 21st Century*. Adelaide: Australia and New Zealand Communication Association and the University of Adelaide, pp. 1–12.

— (2008a), 'Intermodal relations in image-nuclear news stories', in L. Unsworth (ed.), *Multimodal Semiotics: Functional Analysis in Contexts of Education*. London: Continuum, pp. 125–38.

— (2008b), 'Reconciling the co-articulation of meaning between words and pictures: exploring instantiation and commitment in image-nuclear news stories', in A. Mahboob and N. Knight (eds), *Questioning Linguistics*. Newcastle: Cambridge Scholars Press, pp. 77–94.

— (2009a), 'Multisemiotic communication in an Australian broadsheet: a new news story genre', in C. Bazerman, A. Bonini and D. Figueiredo (eds), *Genre in a Changing World: Perspectives on Writing*. Fort Collins, Colorado: The WAC Clearinghouse and Parlor Press, pp. 243–54. Available for download at wac.colostate.edu/books/genre/

— (2009b), 'Playing with words and pictures: intersemiosis in a new genre of news reportage', Ph.D. Thesis, Department of Linguistics, University of Sydney. Available for download at http://ses.library.usyd.edu.au/handle/2123/7024

— (2010a), 'Doubling-up: allusion and bonding in multi-semiotic news stories', in M. Bednarek and J. R. Martin (eds), *New Discourse on Language: Functional Perspectives on Multimodality, Identity, and Affiliation*. London/New York: Continuum, pp. 111–33.

— (2010b), 'What you see and what you get: the evolving role of news photographs in an Australian broadsheet', in V. Rupar (ed.), *Journalism and Meaning-making: Reading the Newspaper*. Cresskill, NJ: Hampton Press, pp. 199–220.

— (in press), *Photojournalism: A Multisemiotic Approach*. Basingstoke: Palgrave Macmillan.

Caple, H. and Knox, J. (in press), 'Online news galleries, photojournalism and the photo essay', *Visual Communication*.

Carter, R. (1988), 'Front pages: lexis, style and newspaper reporting', in M. Ghadessy (ed.), *Registers of Written English*. London: Pinter Publishers, pp. 8–16.

Carvalho, A. (2008), 'Media(ted) discourse and society', *Journalism Studies*, 9 (2), 161–77.

Chalaby, J. K. (1998), *The Invention of Journalism*. Basingstoke: Macmillan.

Clark, K. (1992), 'The linguistics of blame: representation of women in *The Sun's* reporting of crimes of sexual violence', in M. Toolan (ed.), *Language, Text and Context: Essays in Stylistics*. London/New York: Routledge, pp. 208–24.

Clayman, S. and Heritage, J. (2002), *The News Interview: Journalists and Public Figures on the Air*. Cambridge: Cambridge University Press.

CNN Hologram TV First (2008), online video, available at www.youtube.com/watch?v=thOxW19vsTg – accessed 3 January 2011.

Conboy, M. (2002), *The Press and Popular Culture*. London/Thousand Oaks/New Delhi: Sage.

— (2006), *Tabloid Britain: Constructing a Community through Language*. Abingdon/New York: Routledge.

— (2007), *The Language of the News*. London/New York: Routledge.

— (2010), *The Language of Newspapers: Socio-Historical Perspectives*. London/New York: Continuum.

Conley, D. (1997), *The Daily Miracle: An Introduction to Journalism*. Melbourne: Oxford University Press.

Conrad, S. and Biber, D. (2000), 'Adverbial marking of stance in speech and writing', in S. Hunston and G. Thompson (eds), *Evaluation in Text: Authorial Stance and the Construction of Discourse*. Oxford: Oxford University Press, pp. 56–73.

Cortina-Borja, M. and Chappas, C. (2006), 'A stylometric analysis of newspapers, periodicals and news scripts', *Journal of Quantitative Linguistics*, 13 (2–3), 285–312.

Cotter, C. (2003), 'Prescriptions and practice: motivations behind change in news discourse', *Journal of Historical Pragmatics*, 4 (1), 45–74.

— (2010), *News Talk: Investigating the Language of Journalism*. Cambridge: CUP.

Cowan, J. (2011), 'Obama won't release bin Laden photo', *ABC News*, available at www.abc.net.au/news/stories/2011/05/05/3208049.htm? section=world – accessed 5 May 2011.

Craig, D. A. (2011), *Excellence in Online Journalism*. London: Sage.

Craig, G. (1994), 'Press photographs and news values', *Australian Studies in Journalism*, 3, 182–200.

Crolley, L. and Teso, E. (2007), 'Gendered narratives in Spain: the representation of female athletes in *Marca* and *El País*', *International Review for the Sociology of Sport*, 42 (2), 149–66.

Crystal, D. and Davy, D. (1969), *Investigating English Style*. London: Longman.

Dondis, D. A. (1973), *A Primer of Visual Literacy*. London: MIT Press.

Durant, A. and Lambrou, M. (2009), *Language and Media: A Resource Book for Students*. London/New York: Routledge.

Economou, D. (2006), 'The big picture: the role of the lead image in print feature stories', in I. Lassen, J. Strunck and T. Vestergaard (eds), *Mediating Ideology in Text and Image: Ten Critical Studies*. Amsterdam: John Benjamins, pp. 211–33.

— (2008), 'Pulling readers in: news photos in Greek and Australian broadsheets', in P. R. R. White and E. A. Thomson (eds), *Communicating Conflict:*

Multilingual Case Studies of the News Media. London: Continuum, pp. 253–80.

— (2010), 'Having it both ways? Images and text face off in the broadsheet feature story', in V. Rupar (ed.), *Journalism & Meaning-Making: Reading the Newspaper*. Cresskill, NJ: Hampton Press, pp. 175–98.

Fairclough, N. (1988), 'Discourse representation in media discourse', *Sociolinguistics*, 17, 125–39.

— (1995), *Media Discourse*. London: Edward Arnold.

Feez, S., Iedema, R. and White, P. R. R. (2008), *Media Literacy*. Surry Hills, NSW: NSW Adult Migrant Education Service.

Ferguson, C. A. (1983), 'Sports announcer talk: syntactic aspects of register variation', *Language in Society*, 12, 153–72.

Fowler, R. (1991), *Language in the News: Discourse and Ideology in the Press*. London/New York: Routledge.

Fries, U. and Schneider, P. (2000), 'ZEN: preparing the Zurich English Newspaper corpus', in F. Ungerer (ed.), *English Media Texts Past and Present: Language and Textual Structure*. Amsterdam/Philadelphia: John Benjamins, pp. 3–24.

Fulton, H. (2005), 'Introduction: the power of narrative', in H. Fulton, R. Huisman, J. Murphet and A. Dunn, *Narrative and Media*. Cambridge: Cambridge University Press, pp. 1–7.

Galtung, J. and Ruge, M. (1965), 'The structure of foreign news', *Journal of Peace Research*, 1, 64–90.

Garretson, G. and Ädel, A. (2008), 'Who's speaking? Evidentiality in US newspapers during the 2004 presidential campaign', in A. Ädel and R. Reppen (eds), *Corpora and Discourse: The Challenges of Different Settings*. Amsterdam: John Benjamins, pp. 157–88.

Gernsheim, H. (1955), *The History of Photography*. London: Oxford University Press.

Ghadessy, M. (1988), 'Front pages: lexis, style and newspaper reports', in M. Ghadessy (ed.), *Registers of Written English: Situational Factors and Linguistic Features*. London: Pinter, pp. 8–16.

Goffman, E. (1981), *Forms of Talk*. Oxford: Blackwell.

Gonzalez Rodriguez, M. J. (2006), 'Noun phrase complexity in the description and differentiation of language varieties: a study of stylistics', *RLA, Revista de Linguistica Teorica y Aplicada*, 44 (2), 23–46.

Greatbatch, D. (1998), 'Conversation analysis: neutralism in British news interviews', in A. Bell and P. Garrett (eds), *Approaches to Media Discourse*. Oxford/Malden, MA: Blackwell, pp. 163–85.

Greenbaum, S. (1969), *Studies in English Adverbial Usage*. London: Longman.

Haarman, L. (2004), '"John, what's going on?" Some features of live exchanges on television news', in A. Partington, J. Morley and L. Haarman (eds), *Corpora and Discourse*. Bern: Peter Lang, pp. 71–87.

Haarman, L. and Lombardo, L. (eds) (2009), *Evaluation and Stance in War News: A Linguistic Analysis of American, British and Italian Television News Reporting of the 2003 Iraqi War*. London: Continuum.

Hall, S. (1981), 'The determinations of news photographs', in S. Cohen and J. Young (eds), *The Manufacture of News: Deviance, Social Problems and the Mass Media*. London: Sage, pp. 226–43.

Halliday, M. A. K. (1985), *An Introduction to Functional Grammar*. London: Edward Arnold.

Halliday, M. A. K. and Hasan, R. (1985), *Language, Context and Text: Aspects of Language in a Social-Semiotic Perspective*. Geelong: Deakin University Press.

Halliday, M. A. K. and Matthiessen, C. M. I. M. (2004), *An Introduction to Functional Grammar* (3rd edition). London: Arnold.

Harcup, T. and O'Neill, D. (2001), 'What is news? Galtung and Ruge revisited', *Journalism Studies*, 2 (2), 261–80.

Hart, A. (2011), 'Amy Winehouse. How Twitter broke the news. The social network as news source', *Stylist*, available at www.stylist.co.uk/life/amy-winehouse-how-twitter-broke-the-news#image-rotator-2 – accessed 30 August 2011

Hartley, J. (1982), *Understanding News*. London: Methuen.

— (2007), 'Documenting Kate Moss: fashion photography and the persistence of photojournalism', *Journalism Studies*, 8 (4), 555–65.

Hartley, J. and Rennie, E. (2004), '"About a girl": fashion photography as photojournalism', *Journalism*, 5 (4), 458–79.

Ho, J. (2009), 'A corpus approach to figurative expressions of fear in business reports', *Cognitive Science Research Papers*, 1, 93–102.

Hood, S. and Martin, J. R. (2007), 'Invoking attitude: the play of graduation in appraising discourse', in R. Hasan, C. M. I. M. Matthiessen and J. Webster (eds), *Continuing Discourse on Language: A Functional Perspective* (Volume 2). London: Equinox, pp. 739–64.

Hoye, L. (1997), *Adverbs and Modality in English*. London/New York: Longman.

Hunston, S. (2011), *Corpus Approaches to Evaluation. Phraseology and Evaluative Language*. London/New York: Routledge.

Hunston, S. and Thompson, G. (eds) (2000), *Evaluation in Text: Authorial Stance and the Construction of Discourse*. Oxford: Oxford University Press.

Ifantidou, E. (2009), 'Newspaper headlines and relevance: ad hoc concepts in ad hoc contexts', *Journal of Pragmatics*, 41 (4), 699–720.

Jaworski, A., Fitzgerald, R., Morris, D. and Galasiński, D. (2003), 'Beyond recency: the discourse of the future in BBC radio news', *BELL*, 1, 61–72.

Jucker, A. H. (1986), *News Interviews: A Pragmalinguistic Analysis*. Amsterdam/Philadelphia: John Benjamins.

— (1992), *Social Stylistics: Syntactic Variation in British Newspapers*. Berlin/New York: Mouton de Gruyter.

— (ed.) (2009), *Early Modern English News Discourse. Newspapers, Pamphlets and Scientific News Discourse* (Pragmatics & Beyond New Series 187). Amsterdam/Philadelphia: John Benjamins.

Kniffka, H. (1980), *Soziolinguistik und empirische Textanalyse: Schlagzeilen- und Leadformulierung in amerikanischen Tageszeitungen*. Tübingen: Niemeyer.

Knox, J. S. (2007), 'Visual/verbal communication on online newspaper home pages', *Visual Communication*, 6 (1), 19–53.

— (2009), 'Punctuating the home page: image as language in an online newspaper', *Discourse and Communication*, 3 (2), 145–72.

— (2010), 'Online newspapers: evolving genres and evolving theory', in C. Coffin, T. Lillis and K. O'Halloran (eds), *Applied Linguistics Methods: A Reader*. London/New York: Routledge, pp. 33–51.

Koteyko, N., Nerlich, B., Crawford, P. and Wright, N. (2008), '"Not rocket science" or "No silver bullet"? Media and government discourses about MRSA and cleanliness', *Applied Linguistics*, 29 (2), 223–43.

Kress, G. and van Leeuwen, T. (1990/1996), *Reading Images: The Grammar of Visual Design*. London: Routledge.

— (1998), 'Front pages: (the critical) analysis of newspaper layout', in A. Bell and P. Garrett (eds), *Approaches to Media Discourse*. Oxford: Blackwell, pp. 186–219.

— (2006), *Reading Images: The Grammar of Visual Design* (2nd edition). London: Routledge.

Kwek, G., Tatnell, P., Hunter, T. and wires (2011), 'A terror that took their breath away . . . and it's coming again', *Sydney Morning Herald*, available at www. smh.com.au/environment/weather/a-terror-that--took-their-breath-away--and-its-coming-again-20110111-19lur.html – accessed 9 June 2011.

Lacayo, R. and Russell, G. (1995), *Eyewitness: 150 Years of Photojournalism* (2nd edition). New York: Time.

Lamble, S. (2011), *News As It Happens*. Melbourne: Oxford University Press.

Lauerbach, G. E. (2007), 'Presenting television election nights in Britain, the United States and Germany: cross-cultural analyses', in A. Fetzer and G. E. Lauerbach (eds), *Political Discourse in the Media: Cross-Cultural Perspectives*. Amsterdam/Philadelphia: John Benjamins, pp. 315–75.

Layton, R. (2011), *Editing and News Design: How to Shape the News in Print and Online Journalism*. Melbourne: Palgrave Macmillan.

Leitner, G. (1986), 'Reporting the "events of the day": uses and functions of reported speech', *Studia Anglica Posnaniensia*, 18, 189–204.

Lennon, P. (2004), *Allusions in the Press*. Berlin: Walter de Gruyter.

Lin, E. (2010), 'SFN report: More than 166 U.S. newspapers have closed or stopped printing since '08', *Shaping the Future of the Newspaper*, available at www.sfnblog.com/industry_trends/2010/07/sfn_report_more_than_166_us_newspapers_h.php – accessed 23 September 2011.

Ljung, M. (2000), 'Newspaper genres and newspaper English', in F. Ungerer (ed.), *English Media Texts Past and Present: Language and Textual Structure*. Amsterdam/Philadelphia: John Benjamins, pp. 131–50.

Lombardo, L. (2004), 'That-clauses and reporting verbs as evaluation in TV news', in A. Partington, J. Morley and L. Haarman (eds), *Corpora and Discourse*. Bern: Peter Lang, pp. 221–38.

Lukin, A., Butt, D. and Matthiessen, C. M. I. M. (2004), 'Reporting war: grammar as covert operation', *Pacific Journalism Review*, 10 (1), 58–74.

Macken-Horarik, M. (2003), 'A telling symbiosis in the discourse of hatred: multimodal news texts about the "children overboard" affair', *Australian Review of Applied Linguistics*, 26 (2), 1–16.

McQuail, D. (1969), *Towards a Sociology of Mass Communication*. London: Collier-Macmillan.

Malaria control 'best in decades': WHO (2010), *CBC News*, available at www.cbc.ca/world/story/2010/12/14/malaria-who-africa.html – accessed 21 December 2010.

Mardth, I. (1980), *Headlinese: On the Grammar of English Front Page Headlines*. Lund: CWK Gleerup.

Martin, J. R. (1992), 'Macro-proposals: meaning by degree', in W. C. Mann and S. Thompson (eds), *Discourse Description: Diverse Analyses of a Fund Raising Text*. Amsterdam: Benjamins, pp. 359–95.

Martin, J. R. and Rose, D. (2007), *Working with Discourse: Meaning beyond the Clause*. London/New York: Continuum.

Martin, J. R. and White, P. R. R. (2005), *The Language of Evaluation: Appraisal in English*. Basingstoke/New York: Palgrave Macmillan.

Martinec, R. and Salway, A. (2005), 'A system for image-text relations in new (and old) media', *Visual Communication*, 4 (3), 337–71.

Mautner, G. (2000), *Der britische Europa-Diskurs. Methodenreflexion und Fallstudien zur Berichterstattung in der Tagespresse*. Wien: Passagen Verlag.

Meinhof, U. H. (1994), 'Double talk in news broadcasts: a cross-cultural comparison of pictures and texts in television news', in D. Graddol and O. Boyd-Barrett (eds), *Media Texts: Authors and Readers*. Clevedon: Open University Press, pp. 212–23.

Montgomery, M. (2007), *The Discourse of Broadcast News: A Linguistic Approach*. Abingdon/New York: Routledge.

— (2008), 'The discourse of the broadcast news interview: a typology', *Journalism Studies*, 9 (2), 260–77.

Montgomery, M., Tolson, A. and Garton, G. (1989), 'Media discourse in the 1987 general election: ideology, scripts and metaphors', *English Language Research*, 3, 173–204.

Moos, J. (2011), 'Newspaper front pages capture elation, relief that Osama bin Laden was killed', *Poynter*, available at www.poynter.org/latest-news/top-stories/130349/newspaper-front-pages-capture-elation-relief-that-osama-bin-laden-was-captured-killed/ – accessed 21 September 2011.

Morley, J. and Bayley, P. (eds) (2009), *Corpus-Assisted Discourse Studies on the Iraq Conflict: Wording the War*. London/New York: Routledge.

Murata, K. (2007), 'Pro- and anti-whaling discourses in British and Japanese newspaper reports in comparison: a cross-cultural perspective', *Discourse & Society*, 18 (6), 741–64.

Napoli, P. M. (1999), 'Deconstructing the diversity principle', *Journal of Communication*, 49 (4), 7–34.

Neighbour, S. (2011), 'The United States of Chris Mitchell: the power of a Murdoch man', *Monthly*, August 2011, 18–28.

Newspaper crib sheets (2010), *Facts & Figures*, *Newspaper Marketing Agency*, available at www.nmauk.co.uk – accessed 22 November 2010.

O'Connell, D. C., Kowal, S. and Dill, E. J. (2004), 'Dialogicality in TV news interviews', *Journal of Pragmatics*, 36 (2), 185–205.

O'Halloran, K. A. (2010), 'How to use corpus linguistics in the study of media discourse', in A. O'Keeffe and M. McCarthy (eds), *The Routledge Handbook of Corpus Linguistics* (Routledge Handbooks in Applied Linguistics). Abingdon: Routledge, pp. 563–76.

O'Halloran, K. L. (2008), 'Multimodality around the world: past, present, and future directions for research', Plenary paper presented at the 35th International Systemic Functional Congress (ISFC), Sydney, 21–25 July 2008.

O'Keeffe, A. (2006), *Investigating Media Discourse*. London/New York: Routledge.

O'Shaughnessy, M. and Stadler, J. (2008), *Media & Society*. Oxford: Oxford University Press.

Over half your news is spin (2010), available at www.crikey.com.au/2010/03/15/over-half-your-news-is-spin/ – accessed 19 November 2010.

Overview of results (2010), *2010 NADbank Study*, *NADbank Newspaper Audience Databank Inc.*, available at www.nadbank.com/en/study/readership – accessed 1 September 2011.

Paganoni, M. C. (2008), 'Local and global identity on news sites: Al Jazeera's English-language website', in M. Solly, M. Conoscenti and S. Campagna (eds), *Verbal/Visual Narrative Texts in Higher Education*. Bern: Peter Lang, pp. 331–49.

Painter, C., Martin, J. R. and Unsworth, L. (2011), 'Organising visual meaning: FRAMING and BALANCE in picture book images', in S. Dreyfus, S. Hood and M. Stenglin (eds), *Semiotic Margins: Meaning in Modalities*. London/New York: Continuum, pp. 125–43.

Palmer, F. R. (1995), *Modality and the English Modals*. London: Longman.

Perkins, M. R. (1983), *Modal Expression in English*. Norwood, NJ: Ablex.

Piakova, T. (2007), 'Grammatical analysis of American newspaper headlines', *Casopis pro Moderni Filologii*, 89 (1), 20–8.

Piazza, R. and Haarman, L. (2011), 'Towards a definition and classification of human interest narratives in television war reporting', *Journal of Pragmatics*, 43, 1540–9.

Polar Texas oil spill (2006), 'Fact Sheet 06-08-032', *Washington State Department of Ecology*, available at www.ecy.wa.gov/pubs/0608032.pdf – accessed 15 September 2011.

Pounds, G. (2010), 'Attitude and subjectivity in Italian and British hard-news reporting: the construction of a culture-specific "reporter" voice', *Discourse Studies*, 12 (1), 106–37.

Präkel, D. (2006), *Composition*. London: AVA.

Quinn, S. and Stark Adam, P. (2008), *Eye-Tracking the News: A Study of Print and Online Reading*. St Petersburg, FL: Poynter Institute, Eyetrack07. Available at http://eyetrack.poynter.org/index.html#contact – accessed 2 May 2011.

Rau, C. (2010), *Dealing with the Media*. Sydney: University of New South Wales Press.

Reah, D. (1998), *The Language of Newspapers*. London/New York: Routledge.

Richardson, J. E. (2007), *Analysing Newspapers: An Approach from Critical Discourse Analysis*. Houndmills/New York: Palgrave Macmillan.

— (ed.) (2008a), *Journalism Studies*, 9 (2), special issue on language and journalism.

— (2008b), 'Language and journalism: an expanding research agenda', *Journalism Studies*, 9 (2), 152–60.

Rose, G. (2007), *Visual Methodologies: An Introduction to the Interpretation of Visual Materials* (2nd edition). London: Sage.

Rosenblum, N. (2007), 'History of photography', *Encyclopædia Britannica Online*, available at www.britannica.com/eb/article-252873 – accessed 15 March 2007.

Royce, T. (2002), 'Multimodality in the TESOL classroom: exploring visual–verbal synergy', *TESOL Quarterly*, 36 (2), 191–205.

Sands, N. (2011), 'NZ quake leaves 65 dead, 100 missing', *Age*, available at http://news.theage.com.au/breaking-news-world/nz-quake-leaves-65-dead-100-missing-20110222-1b36m.html – accessed 9 June 2011.

Schaffer, D. (1995), 'Shocking secrets revealed! The Language of tabloid headlines', *ETC: A Review of General Semantics*, 52 (1), 27–46.

Schirato, T. and Webb, J. (2004), *Reading the Visual*. Crows Nest, NSW: Allen & Unwin.

Schudson, M. (1978), *Discovering the News: A Social History of American Newspapers*. New York: Basic Books.

Schultz, J. (ed.) (1994), *Not Just Another Business*. Leichhardt: Pluto Press.

Scott, C. (2008), 'Reporting armistice: authorial and non-authorial voices in the *Sydney Morning Herald* 1902–2003', in C. Wu, C. M. I. M. Matthiessen and M. Herke (eds), *Proceedings of the 35th International Systemic Functional Congress* (Volume 1). Macquarie University, Sydney: The 35th ISFC Organising Committee, pp. 131–6.

Scott, M. and Tribble, C. (2006), *Textual Patterns: Key Words and Corpus Analysis in Language Education*. Amsterdam/Philadelphia: Benjamins.

Semino, E. (2002), 'A sturdy baby or a derailing train? Metaphorical representations of the euro in British and Italian newspapers', *Text*, 22 (1), 107–39.

Semino, E. and Short, M. (2004), *Corpus Stylistics: Speech, Writing and Thought Presentation in a Corpus of English Writing*. London/New York: Routledge.

Sidnell, J. (2010), *Conversation Analysis: An Introduction*. Malden/Oxford: Wiley-Blackwell.

Simons, M. (2011), 'Second life: Mark Scott embarks on another five-year term', *Monthly*, July, 26–31.

Sontag, S. (2003), *Regarding the Pain of Others*. London: Hamish Hamilton.

Stenvall, M. (2008), 'Unnamed sources as rhetorical constructs in news agency reports', *Journalism Studies*, 9 (2), 229–43.

Stroebel, L. D., Todd, H. N. and Zakia, R. D. (1980), *Visual Concepts for Photographers*. Boston: Focal Press.

Sturken, M. and Cartwright, L. (2009), *Practices of Looking: An Introduction to Visual Culture* (2nd edition). New York/London: Oxford University Press.

Taboada, M. and Trnavac, R. (2011), 'Nonveridicality, evaluation and coherence relations', Panel paper presented at the 12th International Pragmatics Conference (IPRA), Manchester, 3–8 July 2011.

Thetela, P. (1997), 'Evaluated entities and parameters of value in academic research articles', *English for Specific Purposes*, 16, 101–18.

Thompson, G. and Hunston, S. (2000), 'Evaluation: an introduction', in S. Hunston and G. Thompson (eds), *Evaluation in Text: Authorial Stance and the Construction of Discourse*. Oxford: Oxford University Press, pp. 1–27.

Thomson, E. A. and White, P. R. R. (eds) (2008), *Communicating Conflict: Multilingual Case Studies of the News Media*. London/New York: Continuum.

Thornborrow, J. and Montgomery, M. (eds) (2010), *Discourse & Communication*, 4 (2), special issue on personalization in the broadcast.

Tickle, S. and Keshvani, N. (2000), 'Electronic news futures', *Australian Journalism Review*, 22 (1), 68–80.

Tolson, A. (2006), *Media Talk: Spoken Discourse on TV and Radio*. Edinburgh: Edinburgh University Press.

Tuchman, G. (1973/1997), 'Making news by doing work: routinizing the unexpected', in D. Berkowitz (ed.), *Social Meanings of News: A Text-Reader*. London: Sage, pp. 173–92.

Tunstall, J. (1996), *Newspaper Power: The New National Press in Britain*. Oxford: Oxford University Press.

Ungerer, F. (1997), 'Emotions and emotional language in English and German news stories', in S. Niemeier and R. Dirven (eds), *The Language of Emotions*. Amsterdam/Philadelphia: John Benjamins, pp. 307–28.

— (ed.) (2000), *English Media Texts Past and Present*. Amsterdam: John Benjamins.

— (2002), 'When news stories are no longer stories: the emergence of the top-down structure in news reports in English newspapers', in A. Fischer, G. Tottie and H. M. Lehmann (eds), *Text Types and Corpora: Studies in Honour of Udo Fries*. Tübingen: Gunter Narr Verlag, pp. 91–104.

— (2004), 'Ads as news stories, news stories as ads: the interaction of advertisements and editorial texts', *Text*, 24 (3), 307–28.

van Dijk, T. (1988a), *News Analysis: Case Studies of International and National News in the Press*. Hillsdale, NJ: Erlbaum.

— (1988b), *News as Discourse*. Hillsdale, NJ: Erlbaum.

van Hout, T. and Macgilchrist, F. (2010), 'Framing the news: an ethnographic view of business newswriting', *Text and Talk*, 30 (2), 169–91.

van Leeuwen, T. (1991), 'Conjunctive structure in documentary film and television', *Continuum*, 5 (1), 76–114.

— (2005), *Introducing Social Semiotics*. London/New York: Routledge.

— (2008), *Discourse and Practice: New Tools for Critical Discourse Analysis*. Oxford: Oxford University Press.

Verschueren, J. (1985), *International News Reporting*. Amsterdam: Benjamins.

Wallace, W. (1977), 'How registers register: a study in the language of news and sports', *Studies in Linguistic Sciences*, 7 (1), 46–78.

Walsh, P. (2004), 'Throwing light on prediction: insights from a corpus of financial news articles', in A. Partington, J. Morley and L. Haarman (eds), *Corpora and Discourse*. Bern: Peter Lang, pp. 335–48.

Watson, J. (2008), *Media Communication: An Introduction to Theory and Process* (3rd edition). Basingstoke: Palgrave Macmillan.

Weerakkody, N. (2009), *Research Methods for Media and Communications*. Melbourne: Oxford University Press.

Weisman, J. and Meckler, L. (2008), 'Obama sweeps to historic victory,' *Wall Street Journal*, November 5, 2008, p. 1.

Welling, W. (1987), *Photography in America: The Formative Years, 1839–1900*. Albuquerque: University of New Mexico Press.

Westin, I. (2002), *Language Change in English Newspaper Editorials*. Amsterdam/New York: Rodopi.

Wheeler, M. (1997), *Politics and the Mass Media*. Oxford: Blackwell.

White, P. R. R. (1997), 'Death, disruption and the moral order: the narrative impulse in mass media "hard news" reporting', in F. Christie and J. R. Martin (eds), *Genres and Institutions: Social Processes in the Workplace and School.* London: Cassell, pp. 101–33.

— (1998). 'Telling media tales: the news story as rhetoric', unpublished Ph.D. dissertation, University of Sydney, Sydney. Available for download at www. grammatics.com/appraisal/whiteprr_phd.html

— (2000), 'Media objectivity and the rhetoric of news story structure', in E. Ventola (ed.), *Discourse and Community: Doing Functional Linguistics* (Language Performance 21). Tübingen: Gunter Narr Verlag, pp. 379–97.

— (2002), 'Appraisal', in J. Verschueren, J.-O. Östman, J. Blommaert and C. Bulcaen (eds), *Handbook of Pragmatics.* Amsterdam/Philadelphia: John Benjamins, pp. 1–27.

— (2003a), 'Beyond modality and hedging: a dialogic view of the language of intersubjective stance', *Text*, 23, 259–84.

— (2003b), 'News as history: your daily gossip', in J. R. Martin and R. Wodak (eds), *Re/reading the Past: Critical and Functional Perspectives on Time and Value.* Amsterdam: John Benjamins, pp. 61–89.

— (2004), 'Subjectivity, evaluation and point of view in media discourse', in C. Coffin (ed.), *Applying English Grammar: Functional and Corpus Approaches.* London: Arnold, pp. 229–46.

— (2006), 'Evaluative semantics and ideological positioning in journalistic discourse: a new framework for analysis', in I. Lassen, J. Strunck and T. Vestergaard (eds), *Mediating Ideology in Text and Image: Ten Critical Studies.* Amsterdam: John Benjamins, pp. 37–67.

Wilkinson, J. S., Grant, A. E. and Fisher, D. J. (2009), *Principles of Convergent Journalism.* New York/Oxford: Oxford University Press.

Wynne, M. (ed.) (2005), *Developing Linguistic Corpora: A Guide to Good Practice.* Oxford: Oxbow Books/Arts and Humanities Data Service.

Zakia, R. D. (1997), *Perception and Imaging.* Boston: Focal Press.

Zelizer, B. (2004), 'When war is reduced to a photograph', in S. Allan and B. Zelizer (eds), *Reporting War: Journalism in Wartime.* London/New York: Routledge, pp. 115–35.

— (2005), 'Journalism through the camera's eye', in S. Allan (ed.), *Journalism: Critical Issues.* Maidenhead: Open University Press, pp. 167–76.

INDEX

Made in the USA
Lexington, KY
15 April 2013